The Politics of Prov

Wolfgang Mieder

The Politics of Proverbs

*From Traditional Wisdom
to Proverbial Stereotypes*

The University of Wisconsin Press

The University of Wisconsin Press
114 North Murray Street
Madison, Wisconsin 53715

3 Henrietta Street
London WC2E 8LU, England

5   4   3   2   1

Printed in the United States of America

Library of Congress Cataloging-in-Publication Data
Mieder, Wolfgang.
    The politics of proverbs: from traditional wisdom to proverbial
stereotypes / Wolfgang Mieder.
    272 pp.   cm.
    Includes bibliographical references and indexes.
    ISBN 0–299–15450–5 (cloth: alk. paper)
    ISBN 0–299–15454–8 (paper: alk. paper)
    1. Proverbs—History and criticism.   2. Proverbs—Political
aspects.   I. Title.
PN6401.M485   1997
398.9—dc20   96–41944

Dedicated to
THOMAS P. SALMON
Former Governor of the State of Vermont
and now
President of the University of Vermont

Contents

Acknowledgments

It is my pleasant task to express my appreciation to a number of friends and colleagues for their help and support during the research and writing of the various chapters that make up this book. I owe much thanks to the efforts of Patricia E. Mardeusz, Barbara Lambert, and Daryl Purvee of the Interlibrary Loan Department of the Bailey-Howe Library at the University of Vermont for providing elusive secondary literature. My secretary Janet Sobieski was as helpful as always with the preparation of this manuscript, and I appreciate her constant support of my research efforts. The invaluable help of Professors Shirley L. Arora, George B. Bryan, and Alan Dundes also should be acknowledged. It is good to know that these three friends continue to show so much interest in my work. Their friendship and support over so many years have meant so much to me and have provided me with the strength to carry on with my proverb studies. Thanks are due as well to the journal editors for granting me permission to include four previously published chapters in this book, and to Lydia Howarth for her excellent job copy-editing the manuscript.

Finally, I would like to dedicate this book to Thomas P. Salmon, former Governor of the State of Vermont and current President of the University of Vermont. As a politician he made ample use of proverbial metaphors, sometimes getting them mixed up in humorous twists. He still does so in a charming way in his role as university president. But he also takes care that proverbial stereotypes are not part of the political discourse at this university. His commitment to academic freedom and increased diversity at the University of Vermont is exemplary and a model for us all. He certainly is an impressive example of how a political and intellectual leader can make positive use of proverbial language.

The Politics of Proverbs

Introduction

The fascination with proverbs can be traced back to the earliest written records. The ancient Sumerian people included small proverb collections on their cuneiform tablets, and rich Greek and Latin proverb collections illustrate the high regard for this formulaic wisdom in classical antiquity. Proverbs have been collected throughout the world to the present day, and literally thousands of collections attest to the ubiquity of this wisdom literature couched in short metaphorical sentences. Paremiographers have studied the history of the numerous collections which range from small, popular books for the mass market to serious historical, comparative, and annotated compendia. Yet as valuable as this scholarly preoccupation with proverb collections is, other paremiological concerns also continue to occupy proverb scholars.

Paremiologists have long recognized that these traditional bits of wisdom play a major role in everyday oral and written communication. Small and massive proverb collections indicate very little about the actual use and function of proverbs in speech acts. In order to explain their rhetorical value, scholars have investigated the appearance of proverbs in literary works dating from classical texts and the Bible to their frequent employment in medieval literature. Much has been made of the preoccupation with proverbs by such important authors as Geoffrey Chaucer, François Rabelais, William Shakespeare, Miguel de Cervantes Saavedra, Johann Wolfgang von Goethe, Benjamin Franklin, Mark Twain, Agatha Christie, and many others. In the belief that regional authors might be especially prone to employing proverbs for didactic purposes or for the sake of adding local color to their literary works, scholars to this day have not tired of excerpting and commenting on their proverbial language. The result is many literary proverb investigations for the various national and regional literatures. They serve both paremiographical and paremiological purposes if they integrate the two tasks of identification and interpretation of the proverbial texts. The lexicographically oriented paremiographers excerpt proverbs primarily for the sake of creating new and better proverb collections based on historical principles, while paremiologists interpret the function and meaning of these texts within the literary works. Literary proverb studies have thus served linguists and folklorists as well as cultural historians, in addition to providing much insight into the literary craftsmanship of the particular author under investigation.

In the past two decades scholars have also made impressive advances in analyzing proverbs in the mass media, ranging from their appearance in newspapers and magazines to their inclusion in cartoons, comic strips, and advertisements. One realm, however, that has received regrettably little attention is proverbs in the political arena. Cicero, one of the greatest Roman orators, used proverbs, and humanists and reformers like Erasmus of Rotterdam and Martin Luther practiced the shrewd and manipulative use of proverbs to fight their intellectual and theological battles. The politics of the nineteenth century saw Abraham Lincoln and Otto von Bismarck making rhetorical use of proverbial language, and in the early part of the twentieth century, Theodore Roosevelt and Vladimir I. Lenin appreciated the proverb as a ready-made tool to effect political change. In more modern times Winston S. Churchill, Nikita Khrushchev, and Ross Perot serve as examples of politicians who flavored their utterances with didactic wisdom. But save for a book-length study of the proverbial rhetorician Churchill and a few isolated small studies, very little is known about the effective use of proverbs in the political fray. As can be imagined, proverbs as a powerful verbal tool in the hands of politicians become a two-edged sword, employed both as a positive and negative device to influence, if not manipulate, citizens.

The purpose of this book is to show how proverbs and to a lesser extent also proverbial expressions have played a significant role in the political life of the twentieth century. Rather than looking at the use of proverbial language in the politics of a single country—for example in the presidential campaigns of the United States since World War II—this book offers three representative chapters dealing with three major figures of twentieth-century politics, namely Adolf Hitler, Winston S. Churchill, and Harry S. Truman. Each of these chapters shows how one political figure has used proverbs to push through a definite political agenda, be it that of the horrors of Nazi Germany, the very fight against this menace, or the struggles of a modern American president. Following these studies of the proverbial language of individual political leaders, I examine how the political issues of the Cold War were depicted in cartoons and caricatures based on proverbial metaphors. For close to five decades, similar proverbial messages dominated the international mass media commenting on the ills of the Cold War period. I have devoted the two concluding chapters to the origin, history, meaning, and danger of two proverbial slurs, one against Native Americans and the other against

Asian Americans. These chapters are, of course, mere examples of the much larger and dangerous phenomenon of verbal stereotypes that threaten minorities everywhere. Collectively, these six chapters are representative statements on the use and misuse of proverbial wisdom in world and personal politics. These six case studies amply prove that proverbs are not merely quaint expressions but that they can take on powerful expressive characteristics when hurled as verbal weapons against other people. As a whole, the book argues that, in politics, proverbs are anything but harmless, and pleads for careful attention to them as dangerously ambiguous modes of expression.

Chapter 1 on "Proverbial Manipulation in Adolf Hitler's *Mein Kampf*" shows that Hitler was aware of the propagandistic value of proverbial language in his infamous *Mein Kampf* (1925–26). He repeatedly used proverbs and proverbial expressions in *Mein Kampf* to outline the political and social goals of National Socialism and especially employed them in his invectives against Jews and Communists. There is hardly a page in this hateful book that does not contain a proverbial phrase from the Bible or oral tradition. By making use of this authoritative language, Hitler hoped to convince his readers that his nationalistic and racial ideas were sanctioned by established wisdom. He cited proverbs and proverbial slurs to discredit all enemies of National Socialism, launching literal proverbial tirades in *Mein Kampf* that were repeated in his aggressive speeches. The result is political rhetoric filled with verbal slander that was a precursor to the actual physical violation of people's right to live. In the hands of Adolf Hitler, proverbs became ready-made tools of manipulation and stereotyping and dangerous weapons in justifying the destructive aims of National Socialism. There is no doubt that proverbial speech helped Hitler to communicate his evil plans and thus played its part in leading Germany on its path toward the mass killings of millions of innocent people. Hitler misused and manipulated proverbs as he did the German language in general to establish his Third Reich. While their metaphorical language was at first understood only figuratively, their actual meaning was taken more and more literally as time went on, until proverbs like "An eye for an eye, a tooth for a tooth" were eventually carried out through murder and destruction.

Fortunately Winston S. Churchill, who actually had read *Mein Kampf,* not only understood Hitler's evil designs relatively early, but as a master of the English language, he also knew only too well that proverbs add a great amount of authority and metaphorical expressiveness to political communication. He put his mastery of proverbs to work in the battle against Nazi Germany, using proverbial language to arouse his compatriots to fight against the menace that threatened the political structure of

Europe. In many of his famous speeches, Churchill introduced a proverb at exactly the right moment to convince his audience of the correctness of his idea or plan of action. After World War II when Churchill wrote his six-volume study *The Second World War* (1948–54), he made use of vast materials from his own archive: memoranda, telegrams, letters, and speeches. All of them contain much proverbial language, and Churchill added numerous other metaphors to his historical account. As the second chapter on "Proverbial Rhetoric in Winston Churchill's *The Second World War*" shows, the result is a style filled with traditional wisdom and wit. But Churchill was by no means a slave to this formulaic language. Whenever he saw fit, he altered a traditional proverb to make it suit his political purpose. At times Churchill also used proverbs to manipulate people and to win an argument through their inherent claim of authority, but in general he relied both on the traditional and innovative use of proverbial speech to lead Britain and the rest of the free world in their struggle against Nazi Germany.

The third chapter on "Harry S. Truman's Proverbial Plain English" investigates how this American president intentionally used plain English in his long career as a public servant in order to reach as many people as possible with his speeches and books. Proverbs and proverbial expressions, many of which Truman had learned while growing up in a rural American farm community, abound in all of his oral and written communications, save perhaps for some of the major speeches he made during his presidency. Even then he would add a proverb or two to texts which for the most part had been prepared by his team of professional speechwriters. In addition to his speeches, his letters to his wife Bess and daughter Margaret show Truman's fondness for proverbial language, and at times even offer Truman's explanations of the origin and meaning of a particular proverbial text. Later in his presidential years, he steadily improved his prepared speeches by adding traditional folkloristic material to otherwise factual statements. But he is especially remembered for the off-the-cuff speeches which he gave from the back platform of his train during the 1948 presidential campaign and which were repeated when he campaigned for Adlai Stevenson in 1952. These short impromptu speeches showed Truman as a masterful "proverbialist," who knew exactly how to reach the voters' minds and hearts by speaking a proverbial language that everybody could understand. Truman was a natural and honest communicator who did not mince words in his speeches, press conferences, and writings. He was not afraid to speak his mind, and to some degree, at least, his proverbial speech patterns endeared him to the American people.

During Truman's presidency the nations of the world separated into two camps with the Soviet Union and the United States being the major players in what is called the "Cold War." The fourth chapter analyzes how "Proverbs and Political Cartoons of the Cold War" mirror this time of political tension, the arms race, and the threat of nuclear war. It may seem questionable that the ancient wisdom expressed in proverbs would have any value whatsoever regarding the modern politics symbolized by the image of the "Iron Curtain." But a fascinating aspect of proverbs is how they always adapt to new environments and situations. Their formulaic metaphors, expressing in vivid imagery repetitive patterns of human behavior, are applicable to a multitude of contexts. Not surprisingly, therefore, proverbs like "Hear no evil, see no evil, speak no evil" and "Big fish eat little fish" frequently appeared in cartoons and caricatures during the almost five decades of the Cold War. Modern mass media helped to disseminate internationally these two proverbs in particular. They appeared in the mass media of the former Soviet Union, Europe, and the United States, a fact which underscores how universal and ubiquitous this metaphorical language is. Other proverbs and proverbial expressions, such as the powerful images of the "Trojan horse" and "Damocles' sword," which have been used as symbols for deceit and peril since classical times, were reinterpreted during this time as satirical commentaries on the Cold War. Since proverbs can be interpreted as verbal images, artists almost inevitably depicted some of them in the mass media as powerful and telling images of the precarious political scene.

Much stereotyping took place during the Cold War years, with Ronald Reagan, for example, calling the Soviet Union the "evil empire." Regrettably, a large group of proverbs and proverbial expressions contain some sort of stereotype or slur. People have always couched their fears and anxieties about others in proverbial utterances, and some can be traced back to the very beginning of recorded history. Minorities are seen as bothersome outsiders, citizens from other countries are interpreted as inferior, members of another religious orientation are demonized, Jews and Gypsies are branded as undesirable and exterminated, and African Americans are kept from enjoying the same rights as the rest of society. Such sociopolitical, racial, and ethnic matters find their verbal reflection in linguistic formulas that are repeated often enough to become standard proverbs and proverbial expressions. The last two chapters of this book look in considerable detail at two American stereotypes that were coined in the nineteenth century and are current still to this day. Chapter 5 treats the origin, history, and meaning of the terrible invective "The only good Indian is a dead Indian," which has long become the structural formula "The only good X is a dead X." The variable has been replaced by such terms as "Jew," "Nigger," "German," or "Serb," and an alarming internationalization of this proverbial pattern has taken place in recent years.

At the same time, the original proverbial stereotype against Native Americans continues to survive together with other slurs. The same is true for another popular American proverbial slur that ridicules Asian Americans. The sixth and last chapter traces the origin and background of the proverb "No tickee, no washee" and shows how this ill-spirited slur is still used today to set a minority apart from mainstream American society. These two case studies of proverbial stereotypes show that proverbs are neither sacrosanct nor infallible and that some should not be repeated. They point as well to a perennial human tendency to develop new proverbial slurs and argue that responsible and humane citizens must keep watch against such dangerous stereotypes.

Seen as a whole, the six chapters of this book illustrate that traditional proverbs are a living part of modern political discourse. They play a significant role in the speeches and writings of major politicians, who employ them both positively and negatively to reach their political goals. Proverbs and proverbial phrases also frequently appear in the political reporting of the mass media, in headlines of lead articles, in captions, and in satirical caricatures. They normally fulfill a useful communicative role, but when employed in a manipulative or discriminatory fashion, these expressions and images can become aggressive and harmful tools strengthened by the claim of proverbial authority behind them. Proverbs in the political arena are thus speech patterns that should be understood with care and caution. While they are often nothing more than harmless metaphorical additions to otherwise tedious political rhetoric, they can take on serious stereotypical and manipulative roles. In the hands of demagogues, bigots, and racists, proverbs can be shaped into dangerous verbal weapons. Proverbs are at best ambivalent bits of wisdom, and since they will remain a vital part of political rhetoric, they deserve to be watched carefully as both positive and negative elements of communication.

1

"As If I Were the Master of the Situation"

Proverbial Manipulation in Adolf Hitler's
Mein Kampf

While there is no dearth of scholarly studies on language use in Nazi Germany,[1] recent investigators have pointed out that such analyses should look not only at the language of National Socialism but also at the German language as it was used throughout the country during the years of the Nazi regime.[2] Two early documents from that time clearly illustrate the latter desideratum. In his satirical work *Die dritte Walpurgisnacht* (1933), the Austrian cultural critic Karl Kraus exposes and attacks the rising National Socialism by way of its slogans, phrases, and proverbial expressions. He points out that right from the start, this "politische Phrasenvernebelung" (political smoke screen of phrases) had a marked influence on the general German population which, however, for the most part did not become aware of "what reality lies hidden behind such expressions."[3] Varying the German proverb "Die Sonne bringt es an den Tag" (The sun will bring it to light), Kraus writes that "Die Sprache [language] bringt es an den Tag."[4] This altered proverb is also cited several times in the autobiographical yet scholarly book entitled *L[ingua] T[ertii] I[mperii]: Notizbuch eines Philologen* (1947) by the Holocaust survivor Victor Klemperer[5] in order to point to the thoughtless and immoral language used during the Third Reich. And there is also the courageous essay "An ihrer Sprache sollt Ihr sie erkennen: Die Gleichschaltung [political coordination] der deutschen Sprache" (1938), in which Hans Jacob talks about the spreading "Vergewaltigung des Sprachgeistes" (rape of the spirit of the language) in Nazi Germany.[6] The title is a parody of the biblical proverb "An ihren Früchten sollt ihr sie erkennen" (Matt. 7:16; Ye shall know them by their fruits), and the article itself explains that German citizens should pay attention to the language of Hitler and his followers in order to comprehend their evil designs. Hitler used this same proverb on 23 March 1933, in a sarcastic speech against the Social Democrats. There he adds that "the fruits testify against them"[7] to the prophetic proverb, but little did Hitler know that in due time the fruits of his words and deeds would incriminate himself and his loyal Nazis.

Obviously the National Socialists had their special vocabulary which underpinned their political program with a pronounced rhetorical and propagandistic style. Studies by Cornelia Berning, Werner Betz, Siegfried Bork, Rolf Glunk, Heinz Paechter, Wolfgang Sauer, and Eugen Seidel and Ingeborg Seidel-Slotty, among others, have detailed the special Nazi vocabulary,[8] but it must not be forgotten that the Nazis also made considerable use of all aspects of folk speech. At a party convention in 1934 Joseph Goebbels called directly for the use of such language: "We must speak the language which the folk understands. Whoever wants to speak to the folk must, as Luther says, pay heed to folk speech."[9] Hitler actually had already said something quite similar in *Mein Kampf* (1925–26): "*I must not measure the speech of a statesman to his people by the impression which it leaves in a university professor, but by the effect it exerts on the people*" (477).[10] What Hitler claims to be of specific importance to a speaker addressing the common folk is of equal significance for the language of propaganda, which he analyzes in various sections of his book: "All propaganda must be popular and its intellectual level must be adjusted to the most limited intelligence among those it is addressed to. Consequently, the greater the mass it is intended to reach, the lower its purely intellectual level will have to be" (180).[11] Little wonder then that elements of folk speech appear with considerable frequency in Hitler's "Kampfbuch" (book of struggle), in the official party newspaper *Völkischer Beobachter,* and in all the Nazis' other publications, leaflets, and posters. In this regard Hitler's *Mein Kampf* is not so much an autobiographical account but in large parts rather "the typical life experience and the current ideological clichés . . . of the collective social experience."[12] These language clichés reach from stereotypes to vulgar expressions in the form of slogans and curses,[13] which attain their grotesque and aggressive climax in the anti-Marxist and anti-Semitic tirades. The cultural historian George Steiner describes the role and the "guilt" of the German language in the atrocities of the Nazis in this way: "Hitler sensed in German another music than that of Goethe, Heine, and Mann; a rasping cadence, half nebulous jargon, half obscenity. And instead of turning away in nauseated disbelief, the German people gave massive echo to the man's bellowing."[14]

This linguistic crudity is apparent particularly in the Nazis' generous employment of metaphors and formulaic structures.[15] The inclination of the Nazis toward the slogan, the headline, the quotation, the Bible verse—

in short the almost mechanical use of formulaic phrases in oral speech and written texts—has been shown repeatedly by a number of scholars.[16] Detlev Grieswelle even speaks of a "Hammerschlagtaktik"[17] (hammer-blow tactic) to describe the way in which these formulaic structures are again and again integrated into speeches and written texts. Hitler was quite conscious of the effectiveness of this approach, as can be seen from the following quotation concerning "The Importance of the Spoken Word" (107; running head) in *Mein Kampf:* "But the power which has always started the greatest religious and political avalanches in history rolling has from time immemorial been the magic power of the spoken word. . . . Only a storm of hot passion can turn the destinies of peoples, and he alone can arouse passion who bears it within himself. It alone gives its chosen one the words which like hammer blows can open the gates to the hearts of a people" (106–7). The problem with the use of these ready-made formulas was, of course, that they were not intended to enlighten people but were cited to legitimize National Socialist ideology. This legitimization was pursued so seriously that already by 1937 new slogans created by the Nazi propaganda machine were included in the Nazified standard collection of quotations, Georg Büchmann's *Geflügelte Worte,* the German equivalent to the *Oxford Dictionary of Quotations* or John Bartlett's *Familiar Quotations.* Gunther Haupt and Werner Rust, as editors of the Nazified collection, incorporated ten pages of quotations and slogans of National Socialism in their "Nazi-Büchmann," among them "Blutzeuge" (blood witness); "Mit den Juden gibt es kein Paktieren, sondern nur das harte Entweder-Oder" (out of *Mein Kampf* [206]: "There is no making pacts with Jews; there can only be the hard either-or"); "der Trommler" (the drummer); "Wahrer Sozialismus heißt nicht: allen das Gleiche, sondern: jedem das Seine" (True socialism does not mean: to everybody the same, but rather: each to his own); "Nur wer gehorchen kann, kann später auch befehlen!" (Only he who can obey, can later also command); "Gemeinnutz [geht] vor Eigennutz" (The common good takes precedence over self-interest); "Gleichschaltung" (political coordination); "Ein Führer, ein Volk, ein Staat" (One leader, one folk, one state); "Kraft durch Freude" (strength through joy); and at the end even the first stanza of Horst Wessel's Nazi anthem "Die Fahne hoch!" (Raise high the banner!).[18]

This short list also includes two proverbs, but they too were misused and manipulated by the National Socialists in due time, as Theodor Heuß, Bertolt Brecht, and Ernst Bloch have clearly shown in the case of "Gemeinnutz geht vor Eigennutz."[19] The proverbial concept of solidarity was quickly reinterpreted in order to justify the military and racist plans of the Nazis. And also the seemingly harmless proverb "Jedem das Seine" took on an inhuman quality as a grotesque slogan at the main gate of the Buchenwald concentration camp.[20] The same is true, of course, of the revolting use of the proverb "Arbeit macht frei" (Work makes free) at the main gate at Auschwitz. Ruth Klüger includes an unnerving account of the Nazi use of this and other proverbs in her autobiography *weiter leben* (1992), wherein she describes her life and survival at Auschwitz as a young Jewish girl:

> Everybody knows the proverb "Arbeit macht frei" (Work makes free) as the slogan with a murderous irony. There were other such proverbs at the crossbeams of our barracks [at Auschwitz]. REDEN IST SILBER, SCHWEIGEN IST GOLD (Speech is silver, silence is gold) was one of them. Even better was LEBEN UND LEBEN LASSEN (Live and let live). An earlier transport which did not exist any longer had had to affix these proverbs. I stared at them every day, disgusted by their absolute claim of truth, which this reality exposed as a total lie. German proverbs are an abomination for me since then, I can't hear a single one without imagining the crossbeams of a concentration camp barrack, and immediately weakening it by a devaluing remark. I have irritated many a pious soul who did not get acquainted with such life-supporting wisdom in the extermination camp with such apparent cynicism.[21]

This sobering statement is reminiscent of the motto which Friedrich Wolf places at the beginning of his poem "Der Sprichwort-Song" (1932) in which the three German proverbs "Armut schändet nicht" (Poverty is no disgrace), "Trocken Brot macht Wangen rot" (Dry bread makes red cheeks), and "Hunger ist der beste Koch" (Hunger is the best cook) are critically analyzed from a social point of view: "Selbst die Sprichwörter entlarven die Ideologie der jeweils herrschenden Klasse" (Even proverbs unmask the ideology of the ruling class at any given time).[22]

In an article on "Proverbs in Nazi Germany" (1982),[23] I have shown what important but dangerous role proverbs played in the Third Reich. This study discusses primarily anti-Semitic proverb collections and the use of anti-Semitic proverbs and proverbial expressions during that time, showing in particular the cruel and inhuman functions this proverbial wisdom assumed during the persecution and extermination of the Jews. Proverbial stereotypes were turned into life-threatening weapons against innocent victims of the Nazi regime. What originally were hateful verbal slurs grew into murderous action against millions of people. How correct Karl Kraus was to observe in 1933, at the time when Hitler came to power, that his rise meant an "Aufbruch der Phrase zur Tat"[24] (a change from the cliché to action). What once were metaphorical proverbs or proverbial expressions turned into aggressive action. This phenomenon is well explained by Hitler himself in his speech of 30 January 1942, in which the biblical proverb "Auge um Auge, Zahn um Zahn" (Exod. 21:24; Matt. 5:38; An eye for an eye, a tooth for a tooth) is perverted into a folkloric justification of the actual extermination of the European Jews:

> We recognize clearly that the war can end only with the extermination of the Aryan peoples or with the disappearance of the Jews from Europe. I have stated it already on September 1, 1939 (actually already on January 30, 1939) in the German Reichstag—and I am careful when it comes to premature prophecies—that this war will not end in the way that the Jews imagine it, namely that the European-Aryan peoples will be exterminated, but rather that the result of this war will be the destruction of Jewry. For the first time the authentic old Jewish law will be employed: "An eye for an eye, a tooth for a tooth!"
>
> And the further these fights are extended, the more anti-Semitism will spread—this the world jewry better understand. . . . And the hour will come when *this most evil world enemy of all times* will have ceased playing *its* role for at least *a thousand years.*[25]

The question arises whether Hitler only made such "devilish" statements in the middle of the Second World War, or whether this transformation of the cliché (among them proverbs and proverbial expressions) into dreadful deeds can be noticed already much earlier. The autobiographical *Mein Kampf* is particularly suited to answer this question. After all, it is only partially a report of Hitler's early life to about 1925 and much more a propagandistic declaration of the ideology of and the "Kampf" (struggle) for National Socialism in Germany. A few scholars have mentioned Hitler's use of proverbial phrases in *Mein Kampf,* but there has never been a systematic and complete identification of all proverbial texts as well as a detailed interpretation of their rhetorical function. Sigrid Frind quotes sixteen examples in order to show that Hitler "integrated colloquial speech rather liberally into the text."[26] Seven examples are noted by Siegfried Bork, who refers to Hitler's "linguistic carelessness" while stating, however, that Hitler "consciously integrated primitive jargon" because "he wanted to rule the masses, and since the masses were not 'educated,' they had to be spoken to in such a fashion that they could identify with that which was being said."[27] He comes a bit closer to the crux of the matter in another section of his *Mißbrauch der Sprache* (1970) (*The Misuse of Language* [by the Nazis]) when he refers to Hitler's and the Nazis' use of "'hammering' phraseology." Such slogans as "Deutschland erwache!" (Germany awaken!), "Kraft durch Freude" (Strength through joy), or "Wo der Führer ist, ist der Sieg" (Where the "Führer" is, there is victory) were used as ideological *leitmotifs* to manipulate people's opinions and to feign legitimation of all aspects of National Socialism, especially its racial doctrines.[28] A third study, by Kirsten Gomard, on linguistic usage during the Third Reich argues that Hitler used metaphorical expressions merely in order "to make his text more understandable, partially through illustrations and partially through simplifications."[29] These scholarly observations are not incorrect, but in their brevity and superficiality they do not do justice to Hitler's consciously crafted rhetorical style and his programmatic intentions.

It is generally known, after all, that *Mein Kampf* was intended to be a kind of "Bible of National Socialism" in which Hitler intentionally used the style of the "charlatan agitator" as well as the propagandistic "language of mass fanaticism."[30] The American critic of culture and language Kenneth Burke noticed in his significant early essay on "The Rhetoric of Hitler's 'Battle'" (1939) that *Mein Kampf* suffers on account of its constant repetitions. But this endless reiteration of arguments and phrases was in Hitler's way of thinking absolutely effective, for "by means of it Hitler provided a 'world view' for people who had previously seen the world but piecemeal."[31] It must be stressed, however, that *Mein Kampf* was available only in two rather large volumes until 1930 when it was printed in a more appealing one-volume "Volksausgabe" (folk edition). Until 30 January 1933, the total sales of the book in Germany amounted to just 287,000 copies, which to a certain degree justifies the claim that there was a "Nichtbeachtung" (ignoring) or "Nichtvertrautheit" (unfamiliarity) with the book before Hitler's actual rise to power in 1933.[32] After that, the sale numbers rose dramatically, reaching 5,450,000 copies by 1939 and 9,840,000 by 1943, that is, almost ten million books sold.[33] The reasons for this "success" are known—Hitler's book was expected to be on the bookshelf. Civil servants received it as a present for special accomplishments, justices of the peace gave it to newlyweds as a state gift, and so on. But the book was not necessarily read. This is unfortunate indeed, for it contains in black and white what Hitler was planning for Germany and Europe and in what brutal manner he intended to construct his Thousand Year Reich. But while people might not have read this book, thousands of them certainly listened voluntarily, or were obliged to listen, to his many inflammatory and hateful speeches. They often contained verbatim sections out of *Mein Kampf* so that people were confronted with its absurd goals whether they liked it or not. Hitler's book was also frequently quoted by teachers in schools which quickly became Nazified. His slogans from this book appeared on posters, in headlines, and on the radio, and they even wound up as sententious remarks in the Büchmann book of German quotations. There is no way to deny the effectiveness of *Mein Kampf.* It found its readers one way or the other, just as Hitler lured people in droves to listen to his speeches. The book together with his oral rhetoric helped Hitler to gain ultimate power,[34] and his manipulative and shrewd (mis)use of folk speech with its proverbs and proverbial expressions played a considerable role in this process.

Hitler's rhetorical "art" as author and speaker consisted from the start, at least in part, in the way he employed pithy metaphorical expressions from colloquial speech in order to clarify or augment more abstract arguments or ideas. Quite often he used so-called twin formulas whose alliteration, rhyme, formulaic structure, and metaphors add expressive color and emotion to his otherwise tedious and lengthy sentences or paragraphs. The following contextualized examples show clearly how effectively such twin formulas as "mit Ach und Krach" (with fits and starts), "Zeter und Mordio jammern" (to raise the hue and cry), "außer Rand und Band geraten" (to go hog wild and pig crazy), "in Fleisch und Blut übergehen" (to enter one's flesh and blood), "hinter Schloß und Riegel" (under lock and key), "auf Biegen und Brechen" (through thick and thin), "sang- und klanglos" (unheralded and unsung), and "Mord und Totschlag" (mayhem and murder) were integrated into the prose text, adding much expressive power through the formulaic nature of folk speech:

Morally poisoned, physically undernourished, his poor little head full of lice, the young "citizen" goes off to public school. After many fits and starts he may learn to read and write, but that is about all. (32)

In this case, to be sure, the party [the Social Democrats] will raise the hue and cry; though it has long despised all state authority, it will set up a howling cry for that same authority and in most cases will actually attain its goal amid the general confusion. (44)

I [Hitler] was even more indignant that the same Viennese press which made the most obsequious bows to every rickety horse in the Court, and went hog wild and pig crazy if he accidentally swished his tail, should, with supposed concern, yet, as it seemed to me, ill-concealed malice, express its criticisms of the German Kaiser. (54)

When these principles enter the flesh and blood of our supporters, the movement will become unshakable and invincible. (352)[35]

And so if National Socialists wanted to hold meetings in certain places and the unions declared that this would lead to resistance on the part of their members, the police, you may rest assured, did not put these blackmailing scoundrels under lock and key, but forbade our meeting. (487)

I made it clear to the lads [the SA] that today probably for the first time they would have to show themselves loyal to the movement through thick and thin, and that not a man of us must leave the hall unless we were carried out dead. (504)

> Everywhere these organizations sprang up out of the ground, only to vanish unheralded and unsung. (218)

> Unfortunately, it was raining in the morning, and the fear seemed founded that under such circumstances many people would prefer to stay home, instead of hurrying through the rain and snow to a meeting at which there might possibly be mayhem and murder. (499)

These examples illustrate Hitler's aggressive style based on folk speech, and it becomes clear that he uses the twin formulas in particular to characterize or embarrass his political enemies. He does the same with such expressions which declare enemies of the movement to be "Neunmalkluge" (smart alecks), "Angsthasen" (chicken-hearted), "Faulpelze" (lazybones), "Einfaltspinsel" (blockheads), and "Strohköpfe" (thickheads). In *Mein Kampf* Hitler already knows everything better than anybody else. Whoever attempts to argue against him is quickly brushed aside as being incapable, stupid, or timid:

> The art of propaganda lies in understanding the emotional ideas of the great masses. . . . The fact that our smart alecks do not understand this merely shows how mentally lazy and conceited they are. (180)

> For the cursing and "beefing" you could hear at the front [during World War I] were never an incitement to shirk duty or a glorification of the chicken-hearted. No! The coward still passed as a coward and as nothing else. (192)

> To them also belongs the type of lazybones who could perfectly well think, but from sheer mental laziness seizes gratefully on everything that someone else has thought, with the modest assumption that the someone else has exerted himself considerably. (241)

> Only a bourgeois blockhead is capable of imagining that Bolshevism has been exorcised. (661)

> We were treated to the spectacle (as we still are today!) of the greatest parliamentary thickheads [straw heads] . . . suddenly setting themselves on the pedestal of statesmen, from which they could lecture down at plain ordinary mortals. (671)

Hitler was a real virtuoso in declaring other people to be stupid. This is also evident from his repetitive employment of the proverbial expression "keine blasse Ahnung haben" (not to have the faintest [foggiest] idea) which appears five times as a *leitmotif* in this book. The frequent use of this phrase indicates Hitler's arrogance and presumptuousness and shows how he already considered himself at this early stage of his career as the all-knowing prophet:

We no longer had the faintest idea concerning the essence of the force which can lead men to their death of their own free will and decision. (153)

People didn't have the foggiest idea that enthusiasm once scotched cannot be reawakened at need. (167)

Independent thinking sometimes seems to these circles a true sin against holy advancement, so that we may not be surprised if even today a Bavarian state ministry, for example, still has not the faintest idea that the Jews are members of a *people*[36] and not of a *"religion."*(306)

Anyone who believes today that a folkish National Socialist state must distinguish itself from other states only in a purely mechanical sense, by a superior construction of its economic life, . . . , has not gone beyond the most superficial aspect of the matter and has not the faintest idea of what we call a philosophy. (443)

Millions of German blockheads babbled this nonsense [about an apolitical existence] after him [the Jew in general], without having even the faintest idea that in this way they were for practical purposes disarming themselves and exposing themselves defenseless to the Jew. (533)

It is interesting to note in these examples how Hitler's repeated use of a rather "faint" expression—one that packs little metaphorical punch—can turn it into a powerful rhetorical weapon against the Germans themselves or the Jewish population. By often insisting that those he criticizes haven't the faintest idea what they are doing or talking about, Hitler adopts a superior pose that insists on his own authority, and this sense of his superiority is further strengthened linguistically and emotionally by his use of phrases from folk speech.

Hitler also delights in citing the proverbial expression "jdm. das Handwerk legen" (to put an end to someone's wheeling and dealing) in order to state belligerently how he will stop the activities of people whom he dislikes. The phrase is not necessarily threatening in normal language usage, but Hitler's use of it in *Mein Kampf* expresses his obsession for power, his anti-Semitism, and his hate for Marxism at this early stage of his political development:

By it [absolute authority of leadership] alone can an end be put to the wheeling and dealing of such ruinous elements [Hitler means the Jews]. (362)

On the whole, the bourgeois press, as usual, was partly pitiful and partly contemptible, and only a few honest newspapers greeted the fact that in one place at least someone has dared to put a halt to the wheeling and dealing of the Marxist highwayman. (551)[37]

> We would have to pay most catastrophically if in the spring of 1923 we did not avail ourselves of the opportunity to halt the wheeling and dealing of the Marxist traitors and murderers of the nation for good. (678–79)

Another proverbial expression, "mit einem Schlage" (with one blow [stroke]), appears seven times in *Mein Kampf.* Hitler uses it to insist on his own spontaneity and forceful engagement when it comes to "hammering" out the program of his National Socialist movement. This cliché reappears like the forceful blows of a "Schlaghammer" (sledgehammer) throughout *Mein Kampf,* signaling perhaps also Hitler's growing explosiveness and fits of temper in later years:

> I was captivated with one blow [by Wagner's opera "Lohengrin"]. (17)[38]

> In the last hour . . . a means was chosen which seemed suited to stifle the German spring attack in the germ with one blow, to make victory impossible. (195)

> At one stroke the means was found to restore the sinking confidence of the Allied soldiers . . . (197)

> No more than Nature desires the mating of weaker with stronger individuals, even less does she desire the blending of a higher with a lower race, since, if she did, her whole work of higher breeding, over perhaps hundreds of thousands of years, might be ruined with one blow. (286)

> The banner-bearers of the Red International would then, . . . , emit a fiery call to the proletarian masses, and their struggle at one stroke would be removed from the stuffy air of our parliamentary meeting halls to the factories and the streets. (377)

> *The further result would be that at one stroke Germany would be freed from her unfavorable strategic position.* (665)

It should not be surprising that Hitler makes frequent use of other formulaic phrases which, like "mit einem Schlage," date from the warfare of the Middle Ages or the military in general. After all, he called the book *My Battle,* and such proverbial phrases as "gegen jdn. Sturm laufen" (to be up in arms against), "Spiegelfechterei" (shadowboxing), "auf Leben und Tod" (for life and death), "bei der Stange halten" (to stick to one's guns), "jdn. aus dem Felde schlagen" (to drive someone from the field [of battle]), "eine Bresche schlagen" (to make a breach), and "die Lunte ans Pulverfaß legen" (to place the fuse under the powder-barrel) vividly suggest the power struggle between the National Socialists and their enemies:

> Since the Social Democrats best know the value of force from their own experience, they are most up in arms against those in whose nature they detect any of this substance which is so rare. (43)

No! This is shadow-boxing and must be regarded as an attempt to divert attention. (47)

For me [Hitler], to be sure, these incidents had the virtue that the squad of my loyal followers came to feel really attached to me, and was soon sworn for life and death by my side. (558)

The enormous propaganda which had made the British people persevere and stick to their guns in this war, which recklessly incited them and stirred up all their deepest instincts and passions, now inevitably weighed like lead on the decisions of British statesmen. (616)

And so he [the Jew] inevitably drives every competitor in this sphere from the field in a short time. (322)

This, above all, is the fighting factor which makes a breach and opens the way for the recognition of basic religious views. (380)

They [the meetings of the National Socialists] were like a powder barrel that could blow up at any moment, with a burning fuse placed already under it. (484)

The rather philosophical quotation from *Hamlet,* "Sein oder Nichtsein (to be or not to be)," is also interpreted militaristically by Hitler. This sententious remark turned proverb appears six times in *Mein Kampf,* and Hitler also used it repeatedly in his speeches, especially in his proclamations of the "Endkampf" (final battle) during 1944 and 1945. At the end of the Thousand Year Reich, Hitler was indeed concerned only with the struggle over the life or death of the German people:

It is our duty to inform all weaklings that this [the struggle against Social Democracy] is a question of to be or not to be. (44)

A fight for freedom had begun, . . . and this time not the fate of Serbia or Austria was involved, but whether the German nation was to be or not to be. (161)

For me it was not that Austria was fighting for some Serbian satisfaction, but that Germany was fighting for her existence, the German nation for to be or not to be, for freedom and future. (162)

Just as the Republic today can dissolve parties, this method should have been used at that time, with more reason. For to be or not to be of a whole nation was at stake! (169–70)

When the nations of this planet fight for existence—when the question of destiny, "to be or not to be," cries out for a solution—then all considerations of humanitarianism or aesthetics crumble into nothingness. (177)

> ... the whole attention of a people must be focused and concentrated on this
> one question [the sin against blood and race], as though to be or not to be
> depended on its solution. (249)

In a speech on 5 March 1932 at Bad Blankenburg in Thuringia Hitler declared rather sarcastically and provokingly: "They are quite right, our enemies, when they say: It is a matter of to be or not to be. Very true! 'To be or not to be, that is the motto for Germany.'"[39] Twelve years later, on 12 November 1944, the still prophetic "Führer" was speaking of the determination that "in the vast battle of our people for to be or not to be the final victory will belong to it, the fighting front, and the not less heroically fighting homeland."[40] The quotation is repeated two more times in this speech with Hitler referring to the "common battle of all for to be or not to be" and to the "times of the battle of fate of all for to be or not to be."[41] Finally, Hitler uses the *Hamlet* quotation in his 1 January 1945 New Year's message to the German soldiers. Given the hopelessness of the German war effort by that time, Hitler's coupling of the phrase with the twin formula "um Leben oder Tod" (for life or death) seems to signal a growing desperation on his part:

> Soldiers!
> The world decisive meaning of the war in which we are engaged is today very
> clear to the German people: a merciless battle for to be or not to be, that is,
> for life or death! Because the goal of our opposing Jewish-international
> world conspiracy is the extermination of our people.[42]

What incredible twisting of the actual situation! After all, Hitler knew only too well who was being "exterminated" in Germany at that time. This proverbial statement by Hitler is once again a clear indication of how he used his powerful rhetoric to the very end in order to convince the Germans to engage themselves in the senseless final battle.

It is a known fact that Hitler's speeches usually included some sections of wild roaring and incomprehensible screaming. It is not surprising then that in *Mein Kampf* Hitler characterized the grotesque rhetorical style of his early political speeches with such proverbial statements as "in my little circle I talked my tongue sore and my throat hoarse" (62) and "at that time I often talked my throat hoarse" (680). Generally Hitler prefers proverbial expressions which refer to the body. Such folk metaphors underscore his aggressive tirades and they mirror the violence of his thoughts. There are literally dozens of proverbial expressions which refer to such body parts as the eyes, feet, hair, head, backbone, finger, mouth, hands, body, ears, and shoulders. The following examples from *Mein Kampf* are a representative sample of this effective somatic rhetoric based on folk speech:

When I [Hitler] recognized the Jew as the leader of the Social Democracy, the scales dropped from my eyes. (60)

I, too, was determined to leap into this new world, with both feet, and fight my way through. (25)

The corrosive insolence of his [a young despiser of authority] behavior, combined with an immorality, even at this age, which would make your hair stand on end. (33)

Only the board fences around the brains of all so-called "experts" were preserved for posterity. (214)

You felt like dashing your head against the wall in despair over such people! (464)

With the *occupation of the Ruhr,* the French hoped not only to break the moral backbone of Germany once and for all, but to put us into an embarrassing economic situation. (675)

It [the state] must keep a sharp eye on the fingers of the press. (242)

At that time . . . I saw no enlightenment in this direction [about the peace treaties] from the parties which today have their mouths so full of words and act as if *they* had brought about the change in public opinion. (468)

It is as plain as one's hand that combating Jewry on such a [religious] basis could provide the Jews with small cause for concern. (120)[43]

For to come to grips with the body of that plague [syphilis], tremendous sacrifices and equally great labors are necessary. (251)

Only when a nation is healthy in all its members, in body and soul, can every man's joy in belonging to it rightfully be magnified to that high sentiment which we designate as national pride. (427)

Again and again, I begged them [certain politicians] to give free rein to fate, and to give our movement an opportunity for a reckoning with Marxism; but I preached to deaf ears. (681)

They [the petty bourgeois] will laugh at it [at racial purity] or shrug their crooked shoulders and moan forth their eternal excuse: "That would be very nice in itself, but it can't be done!" (405–6)

Let anyone who is inclined to shrug his shoulders at this ["prostitution of the people's soul"] just study the basic statistical facts on the dissemination of this plague. (257)

In two of the preceding examples the somatic expressions are used in statements dealing with Hitler's despising of prostitution and syphilis. They both appear in the chapter on "Causes of the Collapse [in the First

World War]" in which Hitler in a special section (246–66) also describes the "terrible poisoning of the health of the national body" (246) in drastic metaphors. He adopts the thundering tone of a preacher condemning his flock for its sins, and scorns especially those people who do not battle the syphilitic plague energetically enough:

> They wrap themselves in a saint's cloak of prudishness as absurd as it is hypocritical; they speak of this whole field [syphilis] as if it were a great sin, and above all express their profound indignation against every sinner caught in the act, then close their eyes in pious horror to this godless plague and pray God to let sulphur and brimstone—preferably after their own death—rain down on this whole Sodom and Gomorrah, thus once again making an instructive example of this shameless humanity. (248)

His use of two twin formulas in this passage, both drawn from the Bible, helps create an image of Germany as a hellhole on the verge of destruction.

One might even argue that Hitler has a kind of language power here and elsewhere which is reminiscent of Martin Luther, who integrated many proverbs and proverbial expressions into his folk sermons.[44] But the following paragraph from *Mein Kampf* makes it obvious that Hitler's reliance on biblical language has nothing to do with a concept of religious sin. Syphilis operates here as nothing more than a symbol of the sinful impurity of the German-Aryan race through the Jews. He underscores this absurd claim with a shrewdly misused biblical proverb (Exod. 20:5) whose claim of authority strengthens the psychological and propagandistic manipulation of the German citizenry:

> But then more than ever the question becomes: Which people will be the first and only one to master this plague by its own strength, and which nations will perish from it? And this is the crux of the whole matter. Here again we have a touchstone of a race's value—the race which cannot stand the test will simply die out, making place for healthier or tougher and more resistant races. For since this question primarily regards the offspring, it is one of those about which it is said with such terrible justice that the sins of the fathers are visited down to the tenth generation. But this truth applies only to profanation of the blood and the race. *Blood sin and desecration of the race are the original sin in this world and the end of humanity which surrenders to it.* (248–49)

At the end of this section on syphilis Hitler adds the threatening exclamation: "Woe to the peoples who can no longer be the master of this disease!" (259). The simple expression "Herr der Lage sein" (to be the master of the situation) refers without doubt to Hitler's ideal of the Aryan "superman." No one will be surprised to learn that Hitler used this phrase a total of seven times as a guiding *leitmotif* throughout *Mein*

Kampf.[45] Its first occurrence indicates the "master" Hitler in his anti-Semitic confrontation with the Jews, a relationship which reappears in many places throughout the book: "Who, in view of the diabolical craftiness of these seducers [the Jews], could damn the luckless victims [the Germans]? How hard it was, even for me, to become the master of this race of dialectical liars!" (63). About one hundred pages later, Hitler cites the expression for the second time, but in this instance he refers to his other archenemy, the deeply hated Marxism: "Now for the first time I turned my attention to the attempts to become the master of this world plague" (154). His own rhetorical question, "What should now be done?" (169) in order to get rid of the Marxists, is answered with the despicable use of the word "Ausrottung" (extermination), whose naked force is immediately underscored by confrontational proverbial expressions: "The leaders of the whole movement should at once have been put under lock and key, brought to trial, and thus removed from the nation's neck. All the implements of military power should have been ruthlessly used for the extermination of this pestilence" (169). Hitler's predilection for the adjective "rücksichtslos" (ruthless) is well known, and in connection with the noun "Ausrottung" (extermination), it later came to mean the thousandfold murder of Marxists, Jews, and other people.

Hitler was not only interested in ridding his Aryan race of all sexual diseases. He also wanted to achieve something like a health program for all the people, whose famous slogan of "Kraft durch Freude" (Strength through Joy) achieved proverbial status after being coined in 1933.[46] Hitler went so far as to speak of people with "indomitable energy and will . . . in whom spirit and body had acquired those military virtues which can perhaps best be described as follows: swift as greyhounds, tough as leather, and hard as Krupp steel" (356). This then is Hitler's ideal of a healthy human being, and its slogan "Flink wie Jagdhunde, zäh wie Leder und hart wie Kruppstahl" also became proverbial during the Nazi regime. Hitler made it particularly popular during a speech to 54,000 members of the Hitler Youth, where he declared it to be the official slogan of the youth program:

> Today we don't see the ideal of the German people in the former beer drinking bourgeois any more but in men and girls, who are very healthy and solid of body. What we wish of our German youth is something different from what the past has wished. In our eyes the German boy of the future must be slender and slim, swift as greyhounds, tough as leather, and hard as Krupp steel. We have to educate a new human being so that our people will not be destroyed by the degenerative symptoms of the time.[47]

It will not be surprising to learn that, with such an interest in a healthy body, Hitler had a special liking for the classical proverb "Mens sana in corpore sano," which appears in *Mein Kampf* three times in its German loan translation of "Ein gesunder Geist in einem gesunden Körper" (A healthy mind in a healthy body). As the following examples show, even this proverb proved vulnerable to the perverse service of Hitler's racist plans. In the first part of *Mein Kampf* one finds the following program-matic statement:

> Above all, in our present education a balance must be created between mental instruction and physical training. The institution that is called a *Gymnasium* today is a mockery of the Greek model. In our educational sys-tem it has been utterly forgotten that in the long run a healthy mind can dwell only in a healthy body. Especially if we bear in mind the mass of the people, aside from a few exceptions, this statement becomes absolutely valid. (253)

Some two hundred pages later, Hitler returns to this proverb and manip-ulates it in an even more obvious manner. Hitler speaks no longer of a balance between the mind and the body, but he clearly prefers the "kör-perliche Ertüchtigung" (physical training) or "körperliche Gesundheit" (physical health) over the mind or intellect. The Greek ideal is lost, as the proverb is used to help justify Hitler's powerful racial politics:

> And as in general the precondition for spiritual achievement lies in the racial quality of the human material at hand, education in particular must first of all consider and promote physical health; for taken in the mass, a healthy, forceful spirit will be found only in a healthy and forceful body. The fact that geniuses are sometimes physically not very fit, or actually sick, is no argu-ment against this. Here we have to do with exceptions which—as every-where—only confirm the rule. (407–8)

It is interesting to note how the genius is interpreted proverbially to be the exception that justifies the rule. Hitler thus argues his point with the persuasive power and authority of two proverbs, a rhetorical method which he repeats one page later in this section of his book on the "Edu-cational Principles of the Folkish State" (407–12). Here he combines General Helmuth Moltke's sententious remark "Glück hat auf die Dauer doch nur der Tüchtige" (In the long run only the able man has luck) that has attained proverbial character with the paraphrased classical proverb in order to call once again for strong physical fitness, which is more im-portant than the development of the mind:

> If Moltke's saying, "In the long run only the able man has luck," is anywhere applicable, it is surely to the relation between body and mind; the mind, too, if it is healthy, will as a rule and in the long run dwell only in the healthy body. (408)

Hitler's anti-intellectualism is apparent here, as it is in his resolute rejection of elected representatives in *Mein Kampf*. But the following quotation is also indicative of Hitler's disrespect of people in general (even his own Germans) which is apparent in other sections of this book:

> It is to be hoped that no one will suppose that the ballots of an electorate which is anything else than brilliant will give rise to statesmen by the hundreds. Altogether we cannot be too sharp in condemning the absurd notion that geniuses can be born from general elections. In the first place, a nation only produces a real statesman once in a blue moon and not a hundred or more at once; and in the second place, the revulsion of the masses from every outstanding genius is positively instinctive. Sooner will a camel pass through a needle's eye than a great man be "discovered" by an election. (88)

One cannot help notice the revealing irony in this statement when read with Hitler's later rise to power in mind. According to his own definition, Hitler was no genius, even though he always considered himself to be quite an extraordinary person. When he was finally elected, this decision had nothing to do with his genius but rather with mass manipulation and mass hysteria. Hitler's reference to the Biblical proverb "It is easier for a camel to go through the eye of a needle, than for a rich man to enter into the kingdom of God" (Matt. 19:24) proved to be a correct prophecy in his own case, for his "election" did indeed not discover a great man, and instead of winding up in the kingdom of God he landed in the hell of the devil. This grotesque and prophetic element in *Mein Kampf* can also be seen in Hitler's use of the biblical proverb "Whatsoever a man soweth, that shall he also reap" (Gal. 6:7), if one thinks about the devastation that awaited Germany by the year 1945:

> This, too, is a sign of our declining culture and our general collapse. . . . And we have no call for surprise if under such a deity [substitute "Hitler"] little sense of heroism remains. The present time is only reaping what the immediate past has sown. (266)

Hitler includes the asseverative formula "Gott sei Lob und Dank" (Let God be praised and thanked) in his narrative prose from time to time (see 403, 479, 481, 494), but even this somewhat religious phrase in Hitler's mouth appears today as blasphemy. When he refers to the early National Socialists as "arme Teufel" (poor devils; see 353 and 355), this also has a grotesque significance in hindsight when one thinks of the truly devilish murderers among them. The biblical dichotomy of God and Satan thus also plays a role in *Mein Kampf*, and proverbs and proverbial expressions out of the Bible[48] give this book with its pseudo-religious passages a macabre character.

Hitler's disdain of all his compatriots alluded to earlier can indeed be found on many pages in *Mein Kampf.* No one escapes criticism, and here proverbial expressions help him attack his enemies in a more indirect than direct fashion. He thus refers to the "dummen Schafsgeduld" (stupid sheeplike patience; 48) of the German people or to the "großen stupiden Hammelherde unseres schafsgeduldigen Volkes" (great stupid sheep's herd of patient lamblike people; 608). Hitler's rhetorical supply included an unlimited association of human beings with animals. The following examples are drawn from a large number of similar metaphors in *Mein Kampf:*

The parliamentary rats leave the party ship. (104)

The sly fox knows perfectly well that this has nothing to do with religion. (115)

By entrusting the fate of his war on the Marxists to the well-wishing of bourgeois democracy, the Iron Chancellor set the wolf to mind the sheep. (172–73)

With the result that the previous speaker, even before I [Hitler] was finished, left the hall like a wet poodle. (219)

It [the defeat during World War I] is only the greatest outward symptom of decay amidst a whole series of inner symptoms, which perhaps had remained hidden and invisible to the eyes of most people, or which like ostriches people did not want to see. (229–30)[49]

For after all the biggest so-called bourgeois mass meeting would scatter at the sight of a dozen Communists like hares running from a hound. (357)

In those days I saw them [the petty bourgeois] nowhere, all the great folkish apostles of today. Perhaps they spoke in little clubs, at teatables, or in circles of like-minded people, but where they should have been, among the wolves, they did not venture; except if there was a chance to howl with the pack. (464)

Whenever Hitler does not use animal metaphors to dehumanize his opponents, he ridicules them by means of such proverbial expressions as "Hans Dampf in allen Gassen" (Jack-of-all-trades), once again shrewdly cloaking his often ridiculous arguments in the persuasively wise garment of folk speech:

Nothing is more dangerous for a political party than to be led by those jacks-of-all-trades who want everything but can never really achieve anything. (118)

Even then I had an instinctive revulsion from men who start everything and never carry anything out. These jacks-of-all-trades were loathsome to me. I regarded the activity of such people as worse than doing nothing. (223)

Especially dangerous in this regard is Hitler's integration of the proverbial expression "aus demselben Holz geschnitzt sein" (to be carved of the
same wood) into his perverted interpretation of Darwin's theory of the
survival of the fittest:

> It is different [than in the case of nature], however, when man undertakes the
> limitation of his number. He is not carved of the same wood, he is "hu-
> mane." He knows better than the cruel queen of wisdom [nature]. He limits
> not the conservation of the individual, but procreation itself. This seems to
> him, who always sees himself and never the race, more human and more jus-
> tified than the opposite way. (132)

Here Hitler attacks humaneness itself since it apparently stands in his way
of "breeding" a perfect Aryan race. Later this belief led to the gruesome
program of euthanasia which was carried out against innocent and helpless victims. Hitler wanted only healthy and strong Aryans in his German
folk, and every form of human weakness was ridiculed in public. An edu-
cational program which did not aim at producing "strong men" was also
scorned in *Mein Kampf:*

> Even less emphasis was laid . . . on the training of will and force of decision.
> Its results, you may be sure, were not strong men, but compliant "walking
> encyclopedias," as we Germans were generally looked upon and accordingly
> estimated before the War. People liked the German because he was easy to
> make use of, but respected him little, precisely because of his weakness of
> will. It was not for nothing that more than almost any other people he was
> prone to lose his nationality and fatherland. The lovely proverb, "with hat in
> hand, he travels all about the land," tells the whole story. (237)

With the proverb "Mit dem Hute in der Hand kommt man durch das
ganze Land" (With one's hat in hand, one travels all about the land),
Hitler alludes to the stereotypical submissiveness or even servility of the
Germans which prevents them from standing up for their own rights. It
is interesting to note that the cultural critic Herbert Jhering cited this very
proverb in his satirical essay on "Die kleinen Redensarten" (1932; "The
Harmless Proverbs") in order to activate these passive Germans against
Hitler and his National Socialists: "'With one's hat in hand, one travels
all about the land': One lets oneself be kicked, one lets oneself be thrown
out, but one remains servile with the hat in hand. There is no other
proverb which demands so much submissiveness as this one."[50] Here one
can see the variable function of one and the same proverb, which can act
as a most effective tool for the argumentation and manipulation of contradictory goals.

Hitler used this proverb again in his so-called *Zweites Buch,* which
was not published until 1961 and which remains to this day relatively un-

known. The manuscript was written in 1928, but Hitler decided against its publication at the time. Much in this book is a repetition of Hitler's thoughts on foreign affairs already expressed in *Mein Kampf.* The proverb appears with three additional proverbs in a section (136–39) in which Hitler scolds the German population for its political disinterest and its lack of commitment to the political issues of the time:

> Yes, there are to be sure not a few people who believe today that one should not do anything. They summarize their opinion in the claim that Germany should smartly stand back, that it should not get involved anywhere, and that one should keep an eye on the development of matters without oneself taking part in it. This will enable the German people to play the role of the laughing third party who will gain success while the two others are fighting.
>
> Yes, yes, so smart and wise are our present-day bourgeois politicians. This is a political stance that is not bothered by any knowledge of history. There are not a few proverbs which have become a true curse for our people. For example, "Der Gescheitere gibt nach" [The smarter person gives in] or "Kleider machen Leute" [Clothes make the man] or "Mit dem Hute in der Hand kommt man durchs ganze Land" [With one's hat in hand, one travels all about the land] or "Wenn zwei sich streiten, freut sich der Dritte" [If two quarrel the third one will gain the upper hand].[51]

Hitler did not want his Thousand Year Reich to occupy this apparently advantageous position of the third party, for "the belief that a careful re-strained neutrality toward the unfolding struggles in Europe and else-where will one day lead to the enjoyment as a [proverbial] laughing third party is wrong and stupid."[52] He had entirely different plans for Germany and its active military. According to Hitler there could only be the ag-gressive battle by National Socialists for power and dominance in order *"to secure for the German people the land and soil to which they are en-titled on this earth"* (652; for the twin formula "land and soil," see also 309, 612–13, 643). In order to secure this expanded living space for its people, Germany has to grow into an expansionist superpower; and do so violently: "All the intelligence that used to believe that one could pull peoples out of the dangers of a general disinterest has up till now always proven to be a timid and stupid mistake. He who does not want to be a hammer will be an anvil in history."[53] This last sentence is a slightly changed version of the proverb "Man muß entweder Hammer oder Amboß sein" (One has to be either hammer or anvil), a saying which also was, of course, transformed into dreadful action when Hitler and his ac-complices, as roaring hammers, reduced Europe to a beaten anvil.

It was primarily the Jewish population that was to feel the harsh hammer blows of Hitler's Third Reich, but in his tirades against the Jews,

Hitler often attacks Marxists as well. Separate or combined in one person, Judaism and Marxism are made responsible for all ills in Germany and Europe. Hitler also equates the German Social Democracy with "Jewish" Marxism, and in *Mein Kampf* he presents the most invalid generalizations in order to foster Germany's already growing anti-Semitism:

> . . . *Only a knowledge of the Jews provides the key with which to comprehend the inner, and consequently real, aims of Social Democracy.*
>
> The erroneous conceptions of the aim and meaning of this party fall from our eyes like veils, once we come to know this people, and from the fog and mist of social phrases rises the leering grimace of Marxism. (51)

The actual facts are once again twisted in a typical fashion by Hitler. The fog and mist that he mentions are a much more appropriate description of the slogans and phrases of National Socialism which prevented the veils from falling from people's eyes. National Socialism was certainly guilty of preventing people from gaining a fair and objective understanding of Jewish Social Democrats or even Marxists. But with such over-generalizations, Hitler begins the "wisdom" of his long book, and when he arrives more or less at the end, he closes with a dehumanizing statement that brands Jews and Marxists as proverbial devils: "*The fight against Jewish world Bolshevization requires a clear attitude toward Soviet Russia. You cannot drive out the Devil with Beelzebub*" (662).

There is, however, a third and perhaps very revealing passage in Hitler's "Kampfbuch" which once again equates Jews and Communists. This time Hitler accuses Jewish Marxists for having brought about Germany's defeat at the end of the First World War:

> But in exact proportion as, in the course of the War, the German worker and the German soldier fell back into the hands of the Marxist leaders, in exactly that proportion he was lost to the fatherland. If at the beginning of the War and during the War twelve or fifteen thousand of these Hebrew corrupters of the people had been held under poison gas, as happened to hundreds of thousands of our very best German workers in the field, the sacrifice of millions at the front would not have been in vain. On the contrary: twelve thousand scoundrels eliminated in time might have saved the lives of a million real Germans, valuable for the future. But it just happened to be in the line of bourgeois "statesmanship" to subject millions to a bloody end on the battlefield without batting an eyelash, but to regard ten or twelve thousand traitors, profiteers, usurers, and swindlers as a sacred national treasure and openly proclaim inviolability. We never know which is greater in this bourgeois world, the imbecility, weakness, and cowardice, or their deep-dyed corruption. It is truly a class doomed by Fate, but unfortunately, however, it is dragging a whole nation with it into the abyss. (679–80)

This long statement is quoted here for the reason that it might be an early (the first?) and perhaps still subconscious claim by Hitler that "these Hebrew corrupters of the people [must be] held under poison gas." Was Hitler not at this early stage considering the use of gas as a tool of genocide? This interpretation also lends even more meaning to the proverbial expression "ohne mit der Wimper zu zucken" (without batting an eyelash) that is part of this statement. What eventually took place in the gas chambers of the concentration camps was executed by the murderers "without batting an eyelash."[54] Without a human sign of compassion these orderlies of mass destruction performed their evil deeds on their victims with a rigid sense of duty and order.

The "devilization" of the Jewish population goes so far that Hitler even transfers Mephistopheles' infamous self-characterization "[Ich bin] ein Teil von jener Kraft, die stets das Böse will und stets das Gute schafft" ([I am] a part of that force which, always willing evil, always produces good) out of Goethe's *Faust* onto the Jews. In his absurd chapter on "Nation and Race" (284–329) Hitler certainly makes no secret of his blatant anti-Semitism:

> No, the Jew possesses no culture-creating force of any sort, since the idealism, without which there is no true higher development of man, is not present in him and never was present. Hence his intellect will never have a constructive effect, but will be destructive, and in very rare cases perhaps will at most be stimulating, but then as a prototype of the "force which, always willing evil, always produces good." Not through him does any progress of mankind occur, but in spite of him. (303)

Here the Jew is reduced in almost all cases to the archetype of evil, and a well-known Goethean quotation is cited out of context to supply "classical" proof of the assertion.[55]

Hitler also insisted that his anti-Semitic program was based on "racial knowledge instead of religious ideas" (119) since otherwise "in the worst case a splash of baptismal water could still save the business [of the Jews] and Jewry at the same time" (120). Whoever thought that conversion to Christianity or worldly assimilation might solve the "Judenproblem" (Jewish problem) was, according to Hitler, definitely on the wrong path since Jews are not Aryan but rather "rassenfremd" (alien to the race).[56] In this regard Hitler speaks in *Mein Kampf* of "a sham anti-Semitism which was almost worse than none at all; for it lulled people into security; they thought they had the foe by the ears, while in reality they themselves were being led by the nose" (121). Again, Hitler uses a proverbial statement to express very clearly his intention of acting against the Jewish population. Proverbial language, in the form of a rhymed twin formula, expresses

Hitler's inexhaustible hatred of the Jews in a section against the "Jewish Press" (351–52), whose journalists are called blatant liars:

> It must, over and over again, be pointed out to adherents of the movement and in a broader sense to the whole people that the Jew and his newspapers always lie and that even an occasional truth is only intended to cover a bigger falsification and is therefore itself in turn a deliberate untruth. The Jew is the great master in lying,[57] and "Lug und Trug" (lies and perfidy) are his weapons in struggle.
>
> Every Jewish slander and every Jewish lie are a scar of honor on the body of our warriors.
>
> The man they have most reviled stands closest to us and the man they hate worst is our best friend. (351–52)

Such defamations, strengthened by twin formulas like "Lug und Trug" (lies and perfidy), should have exposed this book at its first publication as unworthy of being printed or read, but instead it became a best-seller! There were even philologists and Germanists who, as convinced National Socialists, had nothing but praise for the brutal style of Hitler and his followers. Manfred Pechau, for example, includes a disgusting chapter on "Linguistic Structures out of the Battle against Jewry"[58] in his 1934 dissertation on the language of National Socialism. In 1935 Karl Müller glorified Hitler's rhetoric in *Mein Kampf* as showing his supposedly masterful command of the German language.[59]

I want to turn now to those proverbial statements in *Mein Kampf* in which Hitler employs these formulaic elements of folk speech in order to elevate himself into the position of omniscient and prophetic "Führer." In the long chapter on "General Political Considerations Based on My Vienna Period" (66–125), Hitler already observes prophetically "how easy it is for a tyranny to cover itself with the cloak of so-called 'legality'" (97). What is expressed here metaphorically by the German proverbial expression "einer Sache ein Mäntelchen umhängen" (to cover something with a cloak) becomes later exactly what Hitler in fact does. He uses every means to make his tyrannical power appear to be legitimate. In addition Hitler varies the old legal proverb "Bedingt Recht bricht Landrecht"[60] (Specific law cancels provincial law) to the seemingly emancipated slogan "Menschenrecht bricht Staatsrecht" (Human law cancels state law; 96). But Hitler refers here, of course, only to the human rights of the German (Aryan) people and not to those of his enemies. This proverb variation is nothing but an emotional manipulation of his readers to make them believe that he is adhering to old legal wisdom. About a page later Hitler demands very clearly "that in all questions regarding Germanism one should show one's colors without reserve, and never descend to compromises" (98).[61] The proverbial "Farbe bekennen" (to show one's colors) is used to insist that the German people adopt all aspects of National Socialism, and here Hitler even uses the adjective "rücksichtslos" (without reserve or ruthless). Ruthlessness will later become a defining characteristic of National Socialists as they take on power and lead Germany to war and mass murder.

In addition to generating such pseudo-proverbs based on folk proverbs, Hitler also made use of traditional proverbs to underscore his program of National Socialism and his planned leadership of it. In turning to common proverbs to strengthen his message, he is no different than other twentieth-century politicians, for example, Vladimir Ilyich Lenin, Winston S. Churchill, Franklin D. Roosevelt, Willy Brandt, and Ronald Reagan.[62] Hitler's use of proverbs serves the important role of convincing the readers of *Mein Kampf* and above all the listeners to his speeches of the absolute and final wisdom of National Socialism. Their use for the purpose of propaganda is blatantly clear from a speech that Hitler delivered on 16 March 1936: "German people . . . I am waiting for your decision, and I know, it will prove me to be right! I will accept your decision as the voice of the people which is the voice of God."[63] Here Hitler interprets the classical proverb "Vox populi, vox Dei" (The voice of the people is the voice of God) the only way that he sees fit; "the voice of the people" refers only to the National Socialist German people and excludes all other and different voices. Victor Klemperer mentions in this regard the many outrageous lies which were disseminated during the Nazi regime as "the voice of the people" and makes the following telling observation in his *LTI:* "But there is not such a thing as *vox populi,* but rather only *voces populi,* and which of these differentiated voices might be the correct one, I mean the one that determines the path of events, that can be determined always only afterwards."[64] The Jewish scholar Klemperer, who actually survived Nazi Germany in that country, knew only too well that Hitler's voice alone counted in the long run. And Hitler in his absurd drive toward absolute power was also more than willing to interpret the entire proverb "vox populi, vox Dei" for himself as the "Führergott" (Godlike leader) against the heterogeneous voices of the people.

It is generally known that proverbs often take on a didactic function,[65] and this obvious didacticism also plays a significant role in Hitler's shrewd integration of proverbial wisdom. Proverbs contain the knowledge, experience, and observation of generations of people, and this distilled wisdom gives them their generally valid character and claim of authority. This does not mean, however, that Hitler was always satisfied with the traditional wording of folk proverbs. He thus lengthens the proverb "Was der Mensch wünscht, das hofft er" (What people wish they hope for)[66] to "Was der Mensch will, das hofft und glaubt er" (What people want they hope for and believe; 162). The verb "wünschen" (wish) is replaced by the stronger modal verb "wollen" (want) and the added verb "glauben" (believe) signifies Hitler's insistence on blind adherence and obedience. According to this expanded proverb, Hitler needs only to explain to the people what they should want, and then they will believe with much hope in its mission. Such "small" alterations of traditional proverbs thus prove to be subtle propagandistic manipulations of the people.

Even though Hitler is very much aware of the basic truth of the proverb that "der Prophet im eigenen Lande selten etwas zu gelten pflegt" (the prophet seldom has any honor in his own country; 293), he nevertheless again and again moves down the deceptive path of the prophet. He thus sets up the "Grundsatz" (principle) that committed and disciplined people can create a National Socialist movement, for "Unmöglich ist gar nichts, und es geht alles, wenn man will" (Nothing at all is impossible, and everything can be done if you only want to; 356). With his typical rhetorical craftiness, Hitler has combined the two proverbs "Es ist nichts unmöglich" (Nothing is impossible) and "Es geht alles, wenn man's nur am rechten Zipfel anpackt"[67] (Everything can be done if you only grasp it at the right lappet) into a prophetic statement which will instill courage and confidence in his fellow fighters through its linguistic simplicity. Here too Hitler stresses the unconditional "wollen" (wanting) and underlines his own will to gain power more directly than through the metaphor of grasping a lappet, or loose fold of cloth.

Such unquestioning "wollen" (wanting) is, of course, also part of the belief in the National Socialist program and its indisputable "Führer." Little wonder that Hitler makes use of the biblical expression "Der Glaube versetzt Berge" (Faith can remove mountains) in his description of the early political meetings of the National Socialist movement:

> There were violent arguments in which I upheld the view . . . that we must not let ourselves be misled by failures, that the road we had taken was the right one, and that sooner or later, with steady perseverance, success was bound to come. All in all, this whole period of winter 1919–20 was a single struggle to strengthen confidence in the victorious might of the young movement and raise it to that fanaticism of faith which can remove mountains. (358)

The "believable" proverb of a faith so strong that it can remove mountains is employed as a supportive slogan in the struggle and fanaticism which are to lead to the final grasp of power.[68] Hitler is, of course, not talking of a religious faith in God any more and does not have any use for the full biblical statement from which this proverb is drawn: "Though I have all faith, so that I could remove mountains, and have not charity, I am nothing" (1 Cor. 13:2). There was no room for charity in pursuing the ends of National Socialism, which indicates how empty of meaning, and how purely manipulative, Hitler's use of this metaphor was.

Hitler's book is not only entitled *Mein Kampf*, it really is a true "Kampfbuch" (book of struggle) where the noun "Kampf" (struggle) appears (sometimes several times) as an omnipresent *leitmotif* on literally every page. Even the integration of usually didactic proverbs is subordinated to this very struggle. In the following two examples, Hitler's struggle and will to power are joined with the authoritative claim of the quoted proverbs in order effectively to communicate assertions, explanations, and above all political instruction:

> A condition which is fundamentally one of paralysis is replaced by a period of struggle, but as everywhere and always in this world, here, too, the saying remains valid that "wer rastet—rostet" ("he who rests—rusts"), and, furthermore, that victory lies eternally and exclusively in attack. The greater the goal we have in mind in our struggle, . . . , all the more gigantic . . . will be the success, . . . , if the struggle is carried through with unswerving perseverance. (398)

> The greatest danger that can threaten a movement is a membership which has grown abnormally as a result of too rapid successes. . . . In consequence of their first victory, so many inferior, unworthy, and worst of all cowardly, elements have entered their organization that these inferior people finally achieve predominance over the militants . . . and do nothing to complete the victory of the original idea. The fanatical zeal has been blurred, the fighting force paralyzed, or, as the bourgeois world correctly puts it in such cases: "In den Wein ist nun auch Wasser gekommen." Und dann können allerdings die Bäume nicht mehr in den Himmel wachsen. ("Water has been mixed with the wine." And when that happens, the trees can no longer grow skyward). (584–85)

It is obvious why Hitler would find "watered-down wine" an apt description for the nonmilitant National Socialists he scorned. More interesting is his use of the proverb "Es ist dafür gesorgt, daß die Bäume nicht in den Himmel wachsen"[69] (It is ordained that trees do not grow skyward). Hitler has dropped out the part of "It is ordained" since he is implying indirectly that under National Socialism the trees will indeed grow skyward. The rather humble folk proverb is thus changed into an expression of struggle toward a better life under Hitler's party. It is interesting to note that Hitler uses the proverb in its complete wording in another section of *Mein Kampf* where he describes the unsuccessful disruption in 1921 of a meeting of the National Socialists by the Social Democrats (see 502–7). According to Hitler, the latter took great advantage of this incident in order "to agitate against the movement in the most unrestrained fashion, and among other things to hint with their customary loose tongue at what must soon follow. They hinted that it is ordained that our trees would not grow skyward, but rather that proletarian fists would intervene before it was too late" (502). It is, however, important to note that the proverb is cited in the subjunctive form of indirect discourse since Hitler places it into the mouths of his enemies in this instance. The implication is that the Social Democrats relate the proverb to the Nazis, and that implies that they want to argue away their possible political success. Hitler's quotation of this proverbial statement, on the other hand, is intended to argue that the "trees" (National Socialists) will nevertheless grow "skyward" (into success).

This political success can come about only through the forceful engagement of all members of the National Socialist party. Despite all the small successes of the movement, people must not forget "the first principle which is the premise for every success, namely: *Was du tust, tue ganz (Whatever you do, do it completely)*" (635). The actual proverb is worded "Was du tust, das tue mit Fleiß"[70] (Whatever you do, do it with diligence), but Hitler has radicalized it in his typical fashion. Now it is no longer simply diligence that will lead to the goal but rather *complete* (later in his life Hitler preferred the adjective "total") submission and self-sacrifice to the National Socialist movement. The variation "Was du tust, das tue ganz" appears today as a metaphor for the total "Endkampf" (final struggle) and the infamous "Endlösung" (final solution) which were executed ruthlessly and totally at the end of Nazi regime.

Having seen the way Hitler manipulates proverbs, it will perhaps not be surprising to learn that he even makes use of the motto "Das Recht geht mit der Macht" (Justice goes with power; 542). He uses it to characterize the Weimar Republic, but obviously he himself had no difficulty in agreeing with this dangerous premise. But once again this is a malicious variation of the old legal proverb "Recht geht vor Macht"[71] (Justice goes before power), a social principle that should be adhered to by any government or politician. The mere exchange of a preposition suffices to turn an honorable legal proverb into a proverbial motto that appears to justify the undemocratic power of a dictator. It should be mentioned here, however, that the contradictory proverb "Macht geht vor Recht"[72] (Power goes before justice) also exists in the German language to reflect earlier misapplied power politics. One might characterize it as an "Antisprichwort" (anti-proverb) which unfortunately fits the political situation of certain times. Such contrasting proverb pairs are rather common in folk speech, and they indicate once and for all that proverbs have no claim at being universal truths.[73] On the contrary, proverbs reflect the partiality and contradiction of life itself, but the appropriate proverb used at the right time and in the fitting context will hit the proverbial nail on the head. In *Mein Kampf* Hitler still speaks at least of justice that goes *with* the power—later in Nazi Germany only the much more drastic proverb of "Macht geht *vor* Recht" (Power goes *before* justice) remained applicable.

Finally, of special interest in *Mein Kampf* is the title of a short chapter (see 508–17) in which Hitler cites a "geflügeltes Wort" (winged word or sententious remark) from Friedrich Schiller's drama *Wilhelm Tell,* namely "Der Starke ist am mächtigsten allein"[74] (The Strong Man Is Mightiest Alone; 508). One might assume that this chapter would cover Hitler's own early rise to the leadership of the National Socialists, but this is not the case. Instead, in this chapter, Hitler wants to show how the National Socialist party was able to bring what he calls the "folkish splintering" (see 512–14) under control in Germany. And yet, Kenneth Burke is absolutely correct when in his analysis of *Mein Kampf* he observes that throughout this chapter one senses "a spontaneous identification between leader and people."[75] In his speech of 20 March 1936, Hitler explained this identity of "Führer" and National Socialists in the following manner: "From the people I have grown, among the people I have stayed, to the people I return!"[76] A second "proverbial" quotation from Schiller's *Wilhelm Tell*—one that has become quite popular in recent years because of its use as a slogan during the process of German reunification—also appears in *Mein Kampf* as "Wir sind ein einig Volk von Brüdern"[77] (We are a united people of brothers; 482). But Hitler warns his readers and later his listeners that in his German utopia only the Aryan race can be counted among these privileged people and that he as the only "Führer" will brutally exclude (later exterminate) all outsiders:

> It must never be forgotten that nothing that is really great in this world has ever been achieved by coalitions. . . . Great, truly world-shaking revolutions of a spiritual nature are not even conceivable and realizable except as the titanic struggles. . . . And thus the folkish state above all will be created . . . solely by the iron will of a single movement that has fought its way to the top against all. (516–17)

The quotation turned proverb "Der Starke ist am mächtigsten allein" thus becomes a metaphor for the grotesque behavior of Germany under the absolute leadership of Adolf Hitler.

Toward the end of *Mein Kampf* Hitler employs proverbial metaphors that stem from the language of seafaring. Politicians have long referred to the ship of state and its captain.[78] Twice Hitler speaks of the "Ruhe vor dem Sturme" (calm before the storm; see 158 and 194) and concludes the second to the last chapter with the oppositional pair of proverbial expressions "mit dem (gegen den) Strom schwimmen" (to swim with [against] the current) as well as the phrase "einen Damm aufrichten" (to erect a dam):

> Today, it is true, we must brace ourselves against the current of a public opinion confounded by Jewish guile exploiting German gullibility; sometimes, it is true, the waves break harshly and angrily about us, but he who swims with the current is more easily overlooked than he who bucks the waves. Today we are a reef; in a few years Fate may raise us up as a dam against which the general current will break, and flow into a new bed. (666–67)

In the last chapter with its bellicose title "The Right of Emergency Defense" (see 668–87) Hitler employs quite consciously the topos of the ship's pilot. Doubtlessly in 1926 he was already thinking of steering the German ship of state in due time on a new course of National Socialism:

> We might hope . . . at long last to do what would have to be done in the end anyway, "das Steuer des Reichsschiffes herumzureißen" (to pull the helm of the Reich ship about) on some particularly crass occasion, and ram the enemy. This, to be sure, meant a "Kampf auf Leben und Tod" (life-and-death struggle). (673–74)

Here we have the pilot or "Führer" in his proverbial struggle for life or death. Hitler envisioned himself as this captain throughout *Mein Kampf,* and this struggle became a *leitmotif* for his entire existence in his later years. That he actually would bring death to millions of people he probably did not yet imagine in the middle of the 1920s. Or did he? At the time of composing *Mein Kampf,* he wrote with fanatical confidence that his National Socialist movement would be victorious in Germany. With about five hundred proverbs and proverbial expressions on 782 pages of the German edition of *Mein Kampf,* Hitler reaches the high frequency of one proverbial utterance for every page and a half. This is indeed a clear indication that he has made ample use of metaphorical folk speech to underpin his program of National Socialism. In his "philosophical" and rhetorical fanaticism, it was obvious to him that his struggle would eventually make him the indisputable "Führer" of Germany. In this drive to absolute power, he shows a definite preference for the proverbial expression "Herr der Lage sein" (to be master of the situation), as was already mentioned at the beginning of this discussion. It is appropriate, therefore, to close these comments by looking at yet another use of this phrase in which Hitler describes one of his early speeches at a National Socialist meeting. This short passage shows his complex character and his pathological struggle to become the "Führer." It should, however, be noted that at this early time he uses the still unfulfilled proverbial subjunctive: "After about an hour and a half—I was able to talk that long despite interruptions—it seemed almost 'als ob ich Herr der Lage würde' (as if I were going to be master of the situation)" (505). If only he had never become this *master*, who "marched straight to destruction, drawing the dear people behind like the Pied Piper of Hamelin" (149).[79] Even this last quotation out of *Mein Kampf* can once again today be read as an ironic and prophetic statement by the proverbially bankrupt Adolf Hitler.

2

"Make Hell While the Sun Shines"

Proverbial Rhetoric in Winston Churchill's
The Second World War

While literary historians have investigated the use and function of proverbial speech in the works of such major English authors as Geoffrey
Chaucer, William Shakespeare, Charles Dickens, Agatha Christie, and
many others,[1] relatively little attention has been paid to the rhetorical
employment of proverbs and proverbial phrases in political speeches and
writings. A few more recent studies exist on the use of proverbs as effective verbal strategies during election campaigns,[2] as formulaic arguments
during political discussions on television,[3] as part of the political diplomacy of the United Nations,[4] and in captions for political cartoons and
caricatures,[5] but Joseph Raymond's general article on "Tensions in
Proverbs: More Light on International Understanding"[6] from 1956 still
serves as an informative introduction to the political use of proverbs as
ready-made slogans and verbal weapons.

Not much is known about the use of proverbial language by individual politicians. Toward the end of the nineteenth century, Hugo Blümmer looked at the metaphorical style of Otto von Bismarck's (1815–98)
speeches and letters, showing that this important statesman used German
proverbs as well as literary quotations effectively to argue a point, to dis-
arm his opponents, and to add folkloric spice to his political rhetoric.[7]
There are also five short essays by various authors on Vladimir Ilyich
Lenin's (1870–1924) and Nikita Khrushchev's (1894–1971) rhetorical use
of proverbs for propaganda, agitation, and manipulation.[8] In the preceding chapter and in other works,[9] I have shown how proverbs became dangerous tools in the hands of many National Socialists, not only of Adolf
Hitler and Joseph Goebbels, who misused them as anti-Semitic folk wisdom to discredit the Jewish population.

Scholars thus far have paid particular attention to the proverbial
rhetoric of such folk deceivers as Lenin and Hitler. Where, one might well
ask, are the studies on politicians and statesmen like Theodore Roose-

velt, Harry S. Truman, Willy Brandt, Ronald Reagan, and Ross Perot, who all included proverbial wisdom in their political speeches? Several systematic investigations of such public figures of the twentieth century (or earlier times) are necessary to ascertain the permeating presence of proverbs in political rhetoric. Speeches, essays, letters, diaries, memoranda, and autobiographies by these individuals—all must be studied to gain a complete picture of the role that folk speech plays in verbal communication on the highest political level. There is no urgent need to investigate yet another literary author for the inclusion of proverbial materials. But paremiologists would indeed do well to cast their nets over the use and function of proverbs in the public life of major and minor politicians.

A unique person who fits this bill is without doubt Winston S. Churchill (1874–1965), whose long life as a high public servant has been treated in perhaps more volumes than any other individual of this century. The scholarship on Churchill is so vast that it is now barely manageable. There are also his own voluminous writings which range from extremely personal letters to his beloved wife Clementine and their children to highly secretive memoranda and telegrams, from local campaign speeches to major addresses in the House of Commons and parliaments abroad, from journalistic war reports to biographical essays on great contemporaries, and from his novel *Savrola* (1900) to multivolume histories of the two World Wars and of the English speaking peoples. His complete *oeuvre* comprises approximately 40,000 pages, the three main themes of which are "politics, war, [and] history"[10] as he saw, experienced, and interpreted them. There is definitely one more major aspect that unites all of Churchill's speeches and writings, and that is his love of and fascination with the English language as an orator, journalist, politician, biographer, historian, and scholar. Manfred Weidhorn, who has analyzed Churchill's life and works in a number of books, summarizes the verbal power of this multifaceted individual as follows:

> His story of one prominent man's role in many of the crises of the twentieth century, his fascinating if eccentric reading of the events of his epoch, has its literary as well as historical interests. The manner of the narrative is as compelling as the matter, thanks to his often poetic or novelistic imagery, his awareness of history, his agile use of the colloquial and the intimate no less than the literary and the Latinate vocabulary, of understatement, periphrasis, hyperbole, parallelism, antithesis, wordplay, zeugma, "as if" statements; his sustained and sparkling humor directed at idealism, religion, stupidity, at military and political men and mores, at self and, more frequently, political or national opponents; his ability with phrases, sentences, short passages; and his sustained effects, rhetorical or narrative.[11]

There are those professional historians who do not see Churchill as a serious scholar, while others acknowledge quite willingly his encyclopedic historical knowledge as well as his interpretive abilities.[12] It is the fate of any prominent statesman to attract some and to alienate others, and Churchill was liked or disliked throughout his long life. Neither friend nor foe, however, can deny that he was a rhetorical master, who in 1953 won the Nobel Prize for Literature "for his historical and biographical presentations and for the scintillating oratory in which he has stood forth as defender of human values."[13]

As early as 1926, on the occasion of Churchill's fiftieth birthday, A. G. Gardiner characterized the life of this British politician as being "one long speech. He does not talk: he orates."[14] Gardiner also shows with two splendidly employed proverbs how Churchill's verbosity and his insistence on being a major player in European politics precipitated one personal crisis after another just as the political world was challenged by a continuous series of crises:

> It is not true that a rolling stone gathers no moss. Mr. Churchill has gathered a great deal of moss. Not that a stone, whether stationary or rolling, is a suitable symbol for this extraordinary man. He is like a rocket that intermittently dazzles the night sky, disappears, and dazzles it again; flashes now from this quarter, now from that; is always meteoric but never extinguished. The principal difference between Mr. Churchill and a cat, as Mark Twain might say, is that a cat has only nine lives. By all the laws of mortality, Mr. Churchill should have perished a score of times, sometimes in laughter, sometimes in anger, sometimes in contempt; but the funeral has always been premature, the grave always empty. You may scotch him for a moment, but you cannot kill him, and we grow weary of pronouncing his obsequies.[15]

This only too true characterization was written long before Churchill's stormy political career reached its summit when in 1940 he became prime minister and minister of defence, two pivotal posts which he held until 1945 and which enabled him to mobilize Britain and the rest of the free world against the fascist forces in Europe and Japan.

For a period of five years this man of words and deeds was indeed at the proverbial top of his political power and prominence, rallying the British people, those of the British Empire, the United States, and numerous other nationalities to fight the menace of Hitlerism. It would be wrong to argue away his deeds, for on numerous occasions Churchill risked his life crossing the Atlantic to meet with Franklin D. Roosevelt or visiting leaders and troops on the European continent. His organizational skills gained from the multitude of high government offices which he held made it possible for him to oversee the strenuous war efforts. Yet to all of this high activity level must always be added "his rhetorical machinery"[16] which catapulted those around him into dedicated action:

> Day after day, and often night after night, he poured forth words and phrases in tumultuous torrent and inexhaustible abundance—inspiring, exhorting, moving, persuading, cajoling, thundering, bullying, abusing, enraging. In private engagement or public appearance, Cabinet meetings or Commons debate, car or boat, train or plane, dining-room or drawing-room, bedroom or bathroom, his flow of oratory never ceased.[17]

Fortunately most of what Churchill uttered and wrote during those eventful five years of World War II has survived and has been published. Clearly, all of these materials and more in the form of memoranda and notes were available to Churchill when he set out to write his celebrated six-volume personal and yet historical account, *The Second World War* (1948–54). Some titles of the individual volumes—*The Gathering Storm, Their Finest Hour, The Grand Alliance, The Hinge of Fate, Closing the Ring,* and *Triumph and Tragedy*—have become proverbial in a way, attesting to their impressive publishing success and to their author's influential way with words.[18]

There have been a number of general statements regarding Churchill's literary style, but Joseph Miller's early description leads directly into an analysis of the rich proverbial language of these six volumes. It must be noted, however, that Miller as so many other scholars, fails to include the word "proverb" in his list of Churchill's rhetorical characteristics:

> On the whole, Churchill is most inclined to use distinctively English idioms, personalized address, negative statement, mainly loose sentences varied now and then by strikingly constructed periodic ones, rhetorical questions, exclamations, coined maxims, parallel structure, balanced clauses, antithesis, metaphor, epithets, and amplification.[19]

Some thirty-five years later, Manfred Weidhorn in a chapter entitled "An Affair of Sentences" offers a quite similar characterization of Churchill's style. He speaks of Churchill's "comprehensive, flexible, and perceptive use of imagery from the institutions of society and the disciplines of man—from Scripture, marriage, commerce, science, medicine, sports, games, painting, and, especially, the theater."[20] He also refers to the fact that "while some of his metaphors and similes are predictable or pedestrian, others are effectively, even pithily, used, adeptly moving . . . from the literal to the figurative."[21] Weidhorn mentions that "Churchill enjoys racy colloquialisms no less than formal Latinisms," and he also refers to Churchill's inclination toward "epigrammatic statements."[22] Churchill himself was well aware of the importance of imagery, metaphor, pithiness, idiom, colloquialism, antithesis, and epigram in his speaking and writing. At the age of twenty-one he wrote a revealing yet never published short essay on "The Scaffolding of Rhetoric" (2 November 1897), touching on the importance of correctness of diction, rhythm, accumulation of argument, and analogy in political oratory. Especially important are his observations that "all the speeches of great English rhetoricians—except when addressing highly cultured audiences—display an uniform preference for short, homely words of common usage" and "the influence exercised over the human mind by apt analogies is and has always been immense. Whether they translate an established truth into simple language or whether they adventurously aspire to reveal the unknown, they are among the most formidable weapons of the rhetorician."[23]

There is, of course, no doubt that the above statements by scholars and also Churchill's own emphasis at the beginning of his political career on the use of "short, homely words of common usage" indicate, even if indirectly, the important role that proverbial speech plays in political discourse. What is surprising is that commentators on Churchill's oratory and literary style have paid so little attention to his effective use of proverbs and proverbial phrases in his hundreds of speeches and vast writings.[24] This lack of interest is especially surprising given the impressive number of proverbial expressions found in his works. George B. Bryan and I have shown that Churchill employed 3,300 proverbial utterances in his entire published corpus of 36,917 pages.[25] Perhaps Churchill scholars have been strangely silent about his use of proverbs because Churchill himself so very rarely points to language as being proverbial. Although there is one proverbial phrase for every eleven pages of text, George Bryan and I found a mere nine instances in which Churchill made use of the words "proverb," "proverbial," or "proverbially."

But middle courses are proverbially unpopular. (1902)

The French had a proverb, "Drive away nature and it returns at a gallop." (1904)

The proverbial three courses lay open to him. (1906)

The vanity of authors is proverbial. (1914)

It is well said, there is nothing wrong in change if it is in the right direction. . . . does not it justify and prove the truth of the somewhat doubtful proverb that I quoted a few minutes ago to the House? (1925)

That would be one of those hard cases which proverbially do not make good law. (1928)

There is only one word of advice which I would venture to offer him . . . and that is the old Scotch proverb: Don't try to beat two dogs at one time. (1938)

> To one of his former associates he [John Dudley, Duke of Northumberland] wrote, "An old proverb there is, and that most true—a living dog is better than a dead lion." (1956)

> "By woman and land are men lost" ran the Maori proverb. (1958)[26]

Instead, Churchill usually employs such markers as "saying" and "maxim" to introduce a proverb when he wants to state explicitly that he is citing a piece of folk wisdom. His infrequent use of the term "proverb" probably merely indicates a personal preference for other designators and should not be interpreted as an intentional attempt to stay away from calling a traditional statement a proverb. He is well aware of and "knows a good deal about the value of [proverbial] common sense, always applies it when actually handling a crisis, and in his oratory always extols it."[27] Churchill purposely used proverbs and proverbial phrases right from the beginning, and he made ample use of them throughout his life all the way to his last utterances and writings.

George Bryan and I have now put together a complete index of Churchill's citations of proverbial language,[28] and here in this chapter I would like to look at how he used proverbs in one of his major multivolume historical works. The six volumes of *The Second World War* contain 410 proverbial texts on a total of 4405 pages, which yields a ratio of one proverbial phrase for every 10.7 pages. A statistical analysis of the six volumes is summarized in table 2.1. It is interesting to note here, however, that Churchill's major enemy Adolf Hitler used about 500 proverbial phrases on a total of 792 pages of his *Mein Kampf* (1926–27), making this aggressive, polemic, and propagandistic "Bible" of National Socialism and anti-Semitism much more "proverbial" and by extension more manipulatively authoritarian.[29] It is difficult to know for certain why volumes 1, 3, and 4 of *The Second World War* appear to be considerably more "proverbial" than the others, but perhaps it is due to the particular fighting spirit evident in Churchill's attempts to convince the British people to deal with the menace of Hitler's Germany, to combat Hitler and get Soviet Russia and the United States to enter the war, and to describe the

Table 2.1. Proverbial Texts in Churchill's *The Second World War*

Volume	Pages	Number of Texts	Ratio
1	655	92	1:7.1
2	701	40	1:17.5
3	804	78	1:10.3
4	892	107	1:8.3
5	658	37	1:17.8
6	695	56	1:12.4
1–6	4405	410	1:10.7

mighty preponderance of the Grand Alliance. Where Churchill himself becomes more aggressive and emotional in his speeches and writings, he appears to be more inclined to underscore his rhetoric with proverbial wisdom to strengthen his points and arguments. A short proverb or fitting proverbial phrase enables him to hit the nail on the head, as it were, and also indicates his realization that everybody would understand these proverbial colloquialisms when they were juxtaposed to the normal and factual rhetoric of organizing the war effort.

There are a number of proverbial *leitmotifs* which run through these six massive volumes, which are comprised of letters, memoranda, speeches, and telegrams together with Churchill's historical analysis. Not surprisingly, the proverbial twin formula "life and/or death" appears repeatedly in these books to refer to the struggle of Great Britain and its allies against Hitler and his war machinery. Churchill experienced a tremendously uphill fight in convincing the British government of the menace of Hitler in the mid-1930s, and it is in relation to this situation that he uses the "life and death" formula for the first time in a rather subjective way:

> Although the House listened to me with close attention, I felt a sensation of despair. To be so entirely convinced and vindicated in a matter of life and death to one's country, and not to be able to make Parliament and the nation heed the warning, or bow to the proof by taking action, was an experience most painful. (vol. 1, p. 96)[30]

In 1938 Churchill became even more convinced of Hitler's move toward war, and he used the binary formula once again to express his frustration over the continued isolationist policy of the United States in light of the obvious threats of war confronting Europe:

> No event could have been more likely to stave off, or even prevent, war than the arrival of the United States in the circle of European hates and fears. To Britain it was a matter of life and death. No one can measure in retrospect its effect upon the course of events in Austria and later in Munich. We must regard its rejection—for such it was—as the loss of the last frail chance to save the world from tyranny otherwise than by war. (vol. 1, p. 199)

Later in this first volume, Churchill recalls a meeting with Vyacheslav Molotov after having signed the Anglo-Soviet Treaty in the spring of 1942:

> At the garden gate of Downing Street, which we used for secrecy, I gripped his arm and we looked each other in the face. Suddenly he appeared deeply moved. Inside the image there appeared the man. He responded with an equal pressure. Silently we wrung each others' hands. But then we were all together, and it was life or death for the lot. (vol. 1, pp. 288–89)

Also relating to Soviet Russia is another use of this twin formula in a letter by Churchill to President Roosevelt on 8 October 1941. This reference clearly shows Churchill's understanding of the dangerous situation in which Stalin and his Russian people found themselves in view of the German military aggression:

> As things are now, it appears to us virtually out of the question either to conclude an agreement [concerning the sale of wheat] which may seriously affect her [Russia's] interests without consulting her, or to approach her on such a matter at a time when she is engaged in a life-and-death struggle, and when her richest wheatfields are in the battle area. (vol. 3, pp. 739–40)

In yet another use of this *leitmotif,* Churchill refers to the British intervention in Greece in a letter of 5 December 1944 as "the matter is one of life and death" (vol. 6, p. 253), once again alluding to the urgency of the situation. Churchill also made use of the somewhat related somatic binary formula "body and soul" in a statement which he wrote on 17 November 1938 regarding Neville Chamberlain's controversial policy of appeasement:

> *By this time next year we shall know whether the Prime Minister's view of Herr Hitler and the German Nazi party is right or wrong. By this time next year we shall know whether the policy of appeasement has appeased, or whether it has only stimulated a more ferocious appetite* [Churchill's emphasis]. All we can do in the meanwhile is to gather forces of resistance and defence, so that if the Prime Minister should unhappily be wrong, or misled, or deceived, we can at the worst keep body and soul together. (vol. 1, p. 261)

Churchill had a definite predilection toward the use of such twin formulas, most likely because their reduplicative nature helped to increase the strength of a particular statement. What follows is a list of some of these proverbial formulas in chronological order of their appearance in the six volumes of *The Second World War:*

> The wholesale massacre . . . in the German execution camps exceeds in horror the rough and ready butcheries of Ghengis Khan, and in scale reduces them to pygmy proportions. (vol. 1, p. 14)

> . . . the Fleet . . . would have to go on playing hide-and-seek. (vol. 1, p. 344)

> . . . he [Chamberlain] was never more spick and span or cool and determined than at the last Cabinets which he attended. (vol. 2, p. 305)

> . . . we should do everything possible, by hook or by crook, to send at once to Greece the fullest support. (vol. 3, p. 14)

> . . . they [German troops and tanks] badly needed rest and overhaul after their mechanical wear and tear in the Balkans. (vol. 3, p. 323)

It is now or never with the Vichy French. (vol. 3, p. 507)

Please remember how much they [German troops] got by brass and bluff at the time of the French collapse. (vol. 3, p. 508)

This was no time for a constitutional experiment with a "period of trial and error" to determine the "future relationship" of India to the British Empire. (vol. 4, p. 194)

. . . action will emerge from what will otherwise be almost unending hummings and hawings. (vol. 4, p. 473)

The pros and cons of this have to be very carefully weighed. (vol. 4, p. 759)

I [Churchill] have the greatest confidence in you [General Alexander] and will back you up through thick and thin. (vol. 5, p. 448)

This [the friendly relationship between Churchill and Roosevelt] continued through all the ups and downs of the world struggle. (vol. 6, p. 414)

It is interesting to note that Churchill also uses twin formulas to describe Hitler's grasp of power and Germany's move under him toward military power: "Thus did Hitler obtain by hook and crook a majority vote from the German people" (vol. 1, p. 55) and ". . . the German might grew by leaps and bounds, and the time for overt action approached" (vol. 1, p. 66). He also refers to the assassination of Röhm and other early party members during the night of 30 June 1934, employing the phrase "the night of the long knives"[31] which has become an internationally disseminated proverbial expression: "In that 'Night of the Long Knives,' as it was called, the unit of National Socialist Germany had been preserved to carry its curse throughout the world" (vol. 1, p. 79). A dozen pages later, Churchill observes with the accuracy of hindsight: "If Great Britain and France had each maintained quantitative parity with Germany [in military rearmament] they would together have been double as strong, and Hitler's career of violence might have been nipped in the bud without the loss of a single life. Thereafter it was too late" (vol. 1, p. 91).

A certain feeling of fatalism not only is conveyed in many descriptive passages where Churchill employs proverbial language but also pervades these over four thousand pages of war history. Once the free democracies of the world permitted Hitler to gain ultimate power, Churchill resigned himself to the fact that this foe had to be fought on his terms, through the resolve of the British people and the strongest military alliance that could possibly be assembled. There was no way to escape the fate of a major war, and a number of proverbial *leitmotifs* underscore this sense of doom in these volumes.[32] One of these is a proverb that expresses the idea of an inescapable course of events—events that will occur once they become impossible to prevent. This is the classical "The die is cast," said by Julius

Caesar on crossing the Rubicon after coming from Gaul and advancing into Italy against Pompey (49 B.C.). Churchill similarly plunged himself into desperate and daring action when he accepted the position of prime minister in 1940. A man of action who worked best in crisis situations, Churchill conveyed his own grim determination to go to war in three short decisive statements before the war, all expressing this same fatalistic proverb:

> However, the die was now cast. (1929)

> Accordingly the die was cast. (1935)

> But now the die was cast to fight it out. (1938)[33]

The proverb appears seven times in *The Second World War*, indicating Churchill's unshakable resolve to bring Hitler and his allies to their knees:

> The die was cast. (vol. 1, p. 305)

> Anyhow, the die is cast. (vol. 2, p. 431)

> *The Die is Cast* (vol. 3, p. 514, in chap. headnote)

> I did not know that the die had already been cast by Japan or how far the President's [Roosevelt's] resolves had gone. (vol. 3, p. 532)

> But the die was cast. (vol. 3, p. 627)

> The die was cast, and the [British] fleet dispersed before dark to their several destinations. (vol. 4, p. 555)

> At 4 a.m. on June 5 the die was irrevocably cast: the invasion would be launched on June 6. (vol. 5, p. 556)

The fifth and the seventh of these quotations deserve closer scrutiny since they relate on the one hand to Churchill personally and on the other to one of the most crucial decisions of World War II. In his letter of 12 January 1942 to Lord Privy Seal is the contextualized reference showing Churchill's tribulations about flying home to Britain after meeting President Roosevelt in Washington:

> I woke up unconscionably early with the conviction that I should certainly not go to sleep again. I must confess that I felt rather frightened. I thought of the ocean spaces, and that we should never be within a thousand miles of land until we approached the British Isles. I thought perhaps I had done a rash thing, that there were too many eggs in one basket [several high ranking officials were part of this flight]. I had always regarded an Atlantic flight with awe. But the die was cast. Still I must admit that if at breakfast, or even before luncheon, they had come to me to report that the weather had changed and we must go by sea I should have easily reconciled myself to a

voyage in the splendid ship which had come all this way [to Bermuda] to fetch us. (vol. 3, p. 627)

Churchill's humanity—his everyday fears and anxieties—is clearly felt in this passage and distinctly expressed in proverbial terms. The seventh instance of this proverb occurs in Churchill's description of the decision to launch the long-awaited invasion of mainland Europe.

> The hours dragged slowly by until, at 9:15 p.m. on the evening of June 4 [1944], another fateful conference opened at Eisenhower's battle headquarters. Conditions were bad, typical of December rather than June, but the weather experts gave some promise of a temporary improvement on the morning of the 6th. After this they predicted a return of rough weather for an indefinite period. Faced with desperate alternatives of accepting the immediate risks or of postponing the attack for at least a fortnight, General Eisenhower, with the advice of his commanders, boldly, and as it proved wisely, chose to go ahead with the operation, subject to final confirmation early on the following morning. At 4 a.m. on June 5 the die was irrevocably cast: the invasion would be launched on June 6. (vol. 5, p. 556)

It is, of course, generally accepted today that the informed gamble on the weather by Eisenhower and others proved to be a lucky throw of the dice for the Allies who defeated the Germans within the following year. And here Churchill relies on the powerful metaphor of this same proverbial expression to convey the earthshaking nature of the Allies' decision to invade.

Churchill, who had proudly served as the First Lord of the Admiralty, clearly felt at home on the high seas, and it should not be surprising that he enjoyed the rich proverbial metaphors of the English language that relate to the sea and seafaring.[34] Among others Churchill made use of the following expressions:

> The nation was as sound as the sea is salt. (vol. 2, p. 333)

> After shooting Niagara we had now to struggle in the rapids. (vol. 3, pp. 3–4)

> One of the difficulties of this narrative is the disproportion between our single-handed efforts to keep our heads above water from day to day and do our duty. (vol. 3, p. 4)

> This is a lot of sail to carry on so small a hull. (vol. 4, p. 63)

> The Eighth Army under Auchinleck had weathered the storm. (vol. 4, p. 389)

Churchill also uses the sailing expression "to make heavy weather," meaning to make too much out of a small thing (an equivalent expression is "to make a mountain out of a molehill") as a *leitmotif* of sorts to express the idea of going beyond petty details and on to the major task of fighting and winning a war:

> We must be very careful not to damp the ardour of officers in the flotillas by making heavy weather of occasional accidents. (vol. 1, p. 582)

> We must be careful not to make heavy weather over the manning of landing-craft. (vol. 4, p. 804)

> There will be no need to make heavy weather over this [the losses in a naval battle] at all. (vol. 5, p. 199)

Of particular interest is yet another use of a seafaring proverbial expression. In the chapter on "Pearl Harbor" (vol. 3, pp. 537–54), Churchill reports that he received a telephone call from President Roosevelt in which the latter stated: "'They [the Japanese] have attacked us at Pearl Harbor. We are all in the same boat now'" (vol. 3, p. 538). Two days later, on 9 December 1941, Churchill began a letter to Roosevelt by repeating this maritime expression which so aptly expresses the fact that the United States and Britain were now in the same position of fighting Japan and Germany:

> Now that we are, as you say, "in the same boat," would it not be wise for us to have another conference? We could review the whole war plan in the light of reality and new facts, as well as the problems of production and distribution. I feel that all these matters, some of which are causing me concern, can best be settled on the highest executive level. It would also be a very great pleasure to me to meet you again, and the sooner the better. (vol. 3, p. 541)

It is doubtful that either Roosevelt or Churchill knew that he was employing the classical Latin proverbial expression "in eadem es navi" which has been traced back to a letter by Cicero dated to 53 B.C.[35] Yet in the same boat they certainly were now, for just as Britain, "the United States was in the war, up to the neck and in to the death" (vol. 3, p. 539).

As to classical phrases, it should be noted that Churchill as a pupil of Harrow School had not been particularly fond of Latin.[36] Yet he was acute enough to realize that "when they [writers in Latin] arrived at fairly obvious reflections upon life and love, upon war, fate or manners, they coined them into slogans or epigrams for which their language was so well adapted, and thus preserved the patent rights for all times."[37] Even if he did not remember them in Latin, he certainly knew where to find them, as well as other foreign and English quotations and proverbs, in *the* collection of such formulaic language, namely John Bartlett's *Familiar Quotations* (1st ed., 1855). In his autobiography, *My Early Life* (1930), he comments on his discovery of Bartlett's *Familiar Quotations* which "is an admirable work, and I studied it intently. The quotations when engraved upon the memory give you good thoughts."[38] It is of little wonder, then, that he cites foreign proverbs and quotations in their original language or in translation by means of his "phenomenal retentivity"[39] throughout his works, and certainly also in *The Second World War,* as the following examples show:

> Among the other Service Ministers . . . I was "first among equals." (vol. 1, p. 463)

> Please remember in your stresses that . . . *noblesse oblige.* (vol. 3, p. 93)

> She [Japan] would in fact "cut the Gordian knot." (vol. 3, p. 165)

> Goering gained only a Pyrrhic victory in Crete. (vol. 3, p. 165)

> As Napoleon said, *"La bataille répondra."* (vol. 3, p. 293)

> *Bis dat qui cito dat.*[40] (vol. 3, p. 418)

> *Inter arma silent leges.* (vol. 3, p. 428)

> I also remembered that wise French saying, *"On ne règne sur les âmes que par le calme."* (vol. 4, p. 54)

> . . . to prove my sincerity I will use one of my very few [an understatement] Latin quotations: *Amantium irae amoris integratio est.* (vol. 6, p. 409)

> *Les absents ont toujours tort.* (vol. 6, p. 637)

One foreign proverb that Churchill liked to use deserves special comment since it belongs to the German enemy. Its German form is "Es ist dafür gesorgt, daß die Bäume nicht in den Himmel wachsen," which in English translation is "Care is taken that the trees don't grow up to the sky."[41] There is an equally common variant which adds "God" to the basic text as "Gott sorgt dafür, daß die Bäume nicht in den Himmel wachsen" (God takes care that the trees don't grow up to the sky).[42] Churchill does not appear to have known this stronger variant, but he was certainly familiar with the basic message of the proverb, which is that nobody will grow to such a point that someone (God) will not eventually cut him or her down. Thus when Churchill speaks of the indiscriminate night bombing of British cities by the German *Luftwaffe,* he finds solace in the thought that this powerful aggression cannot continue forever in light of the fortitude and bravery of the British fighter pilots:

> There is a useful German saying, "The trees do not grow up to the sky." Nevertheless we had every reason to expect that the air attack on Britain would continue in an indefinite crescendo. Until Hitler actually invaded Russia we had no right to suppose it would die away and stop. We therefore strove with

might and main to improve the measures and devices by which we had hith-
erto survived and to find new ones. (vol. 2, p. 346)

And in due time Hitler's air menace was cut down like a tree that had
grown too tall for its roots. While Churchill used this proverb only once
in *The Second World War,* he integrated it an additional twelve times in
his works published before and afterwards:

The trees do not grow up to the sky. (1926)

Mercifully, "the trees do not grow up to the sky." (1927)

The most hopeful comment . . . is the German saying: "The trees do not
grow up to the sky." (1930)

The trees do not grow up to the sky. (1931)

Once more it has been proved that the trees do not grow up to the sky. (1931)

The trees do not grow up to the sky. (1934)

I comforted myself by the old German saying: "The trees do not grow up to
the sky." (1938)

The trees do not grow up to the sky. (1945)

The Germans have a wise saying, "The trees do not grow up to the sky."
(1949)

But there is a wise saying "the trees do not grow up to the sky." (1951)

But, as has been wisely observed, the trees do not grow up to the sky.
(1956)[43]

The twelfth occurrence, however, especially reveals Churchill's fascination with this German proverb. In a speech on 9 November 1953 in London, he said:

Another old saying comes back to my mind. . . . I think it was Goethe who
said, "The trees do not grow up to the sky." I do not know whether he would
have said that if he had lived through this frightful twentieth century where
so much we feared was going to happen did actually happen. All the same it
is a thought which should find its place in young as well as old brains.[44]

Churchill is correct that Goethe used this proverb in his autobiography
Dichtung und Wahrheit (1811),[45] but while this example of his phenomenal memory is impressive, it is even more important to notice how
Churchill presents this proverb. Even though he points to the source of
the proverb as Goethe—a man born only 125 years before Churchill—
he suggests that the wisdom it speaks is far more ancient. He calls it an
"old saying" and implies that its source—now in his grave—lived at a

time far distant, at least in moral terms, from his own "frightful twenti-eth century." In Churchill's hands the German proverb becomes a uni-versal truth which "should find its place in young as well as old brains" and is elevated to a philosophical statement somewhat reminiscent of the biblical proverb "Pride goes before a fall" (Prov. 16:18). An examination of the standard proverb dictionaries,[46] however, shows that Churchill's wish that the proverb might become universally ingrained in our minds has not born fruit.

Suffering and fighting were, of course, the driving forces behind Churchill's famous statement made in a speech to the House of Commons on 13 May 1940, his first after having become prime minister three days earlier:

> In this crisis I hope I may be pardoned if I do not address the House at any length to-day. . . . I would say to the House, as I said to those who have joined this Government: "I have nothing to offer but blood, toil, tears and sweat." . . . At this time I feel entitled to claim the aid of all, and I say, "Come then, let us go forward together with our united strength."[47]

With this statement Churchill electrified not only members of the House of Commons but also the entire British nation and free peoples through-out the world who heard the radio broadcast. The novelty of his famous phrase, however, rests only in the fact that Churchill made a quadratic and rhythmic structure out of the triad of "blood, sweat, and tears" which he himself had used in *The World Crisis* (1931) to describe the valiant strug-gle of the Russian armed forces during World War I: "These pages . . . record the toils, perils, sufferings and passions of millions of men. Their sweat, their tears, their blood bedewed the endless plain."[48] The order of the three nouns is reversed here, but the preceding sentence mentions the "toils" which were added about nine years later. It must also be noted that John Donne (1572–1631) already in 1611 speaks of "tears, or sweat, or blood," and Lord Byron in 1823 has the rhyming couplet "Year after year they voted cent per cent, / Blood, sweat, and tear-wrung millions— why? for rent?"[49] Churchill might have known these earlier references, and there is also the chance that he might have remembered the classical twin formula of *"sanguis et sudor"* (blood and sweat) which was very popular with Cicero and many other Latin authors.[50] Be that as it may, there is *no* instance in classical Latin literature or anywhere else in English literature for that matter of the rhetorical group of four nouns corresponding to the sweeping "blood, toil, tears, and sweat," and for that reason it is fair to credit him as the source of an expression that has become proverbial.

Churchill understood the power of the words he had yoked together, as shown by his repeated use of the expression. Even so he often confused their order in his later uses of the phrase. Speaking of the war situation to the House of Commons on 8 October 1940, Churchill described how appreciative the French, Belgian, and Dutch people were of the help that they had received from the British forces: "In all my life, I have never been treated with so much kindness as by the people who have suffered most. One would think one had brought some great benefit to them, instead of the blood and tears, the toil and sweat which is all I have ever promised.[51] In a speech on 7 May 1941 to the House of Commons on the war situation, Churchill repeated the reversed order of "tears and toil" in an impassioned promise to lead the free world to victory over Nazi Germany: "I have never promised anything or offered anything but blood, tears, toil and sweat, to which I will now add our fair share of mistakes, shortcomings and disappointments, and also that this may go on for a very long time, at the end of which I firmly believe—though it is not a promise or a guarantee only a profession of faith—that there will be complete, absolute and final victory."[52] This variant is cited once again in a review of "man-power and woman-power" for the war effort in a House of Commons speech of 2 December 1941: "I promised eighteen months ago 'blood, tears, toil and sweat.' There has not yet been, thank God, so much blood as was expected. There have not been so many tears. But here we have another instalment of toil and sweat, of inconvenience and self-denial, which I am sure will be accepted with cheerful and proud alacrity by all parties and all classes in the British nation."[53] In a speech to the House of Commons on 2 July 1942 on the conduct of the war, Churchill finally quoted his original statement correctly by claiming that "I have stuck hard to my 'blood, toil, tears and sweat,' to which I have added muddle and mismanagement."[54] Yet a mere four months later, on the occasion of the British victory at the Battle of El Alamein, Churchill returned to the earlier variant at a Lord Mayor's luncheon in London on 10 November 1942: "I have never promised anything but blood, tears, toil, and sweat. Now, however, we have a new experience. We have victory—a remarkable and definite victory."[55]

The apparent confusion with the order of the four nouns surfaces again in *The Second World War.* Speaking of various policies of the British government between the two world wars, Churchill remarks that "a national Government had been formed under Mr. Ramsay MacDonald, the founder of the Labour-Socialist Party. They proposed to the people a programme of severe austerity and sacrifice. It was an earlier version of 'Blood, sweat, toil and tears,' without the stimulus or the requirements of war and mortal peril" (vol. 1, p. 29). In the remaining three cases of Churchill's repetition of his own phrase, he quotes himself correctly:

"Blood, Toil, Tears, and Sweat" (vol. 2, p. 3, headnote)

After reporting the progress made in filling the various offices, I said: "I have nothing to offer but blood, toil, tears, and sweat." (vol. 2, p. 24, citing original speech of 13 May 1940)

I have never ventured to predict the future. I stand by my original programme, blood, toil, tears, and sweat, which is all I have ever offered, to which I added five months later, 'many shortcomings, mistakes, and disappointments.' (vol. 4, p. 62, citing speeches of 13 May 1940 and 7 May 1941)

It should be noted that while Churchill quotes his original phrase correctly in this last reference, he changes the order of "mistakes, shortcomings and disappointments" from his 7 May 1941 speech. He is also mistaken about the five months' interval mentioned, for it appears that he added the statement concerning various problems a year later.

All of this shows perhaps only that Churchill in his hectic and prolific literary production did not always adhere to his own frequently stated personal maxim "Verify your quotations" (see vol. 4, pp. 604, 616).[56] What is known is that his confusion or improvisations on the order of these terms did not dilute their impact. He had captured in these four terms a powerful expression which went to the root of human suffering and the will to fight back, an expression which would become proverbial.

Finally, we will never know why Churchill published a volume of his speeches with the title *Blood, Sweat, and Tears* (1941),[57] but perhaps his publisher preferred this shorter triadic structure for a "catchy" title. It is ironic that this shorter formulation, which predates him, though he may never have been aware of it, and which may simply have resulted from a publisher's marketing decision, is the phrase which has gained even greater proverbial currency than Churchill's original phrase.

Churchill had no similar difficulty in remembering his phrase the "iron curtain," which he first used in what he called his "Iron Curtain" telegram to President Harry S. Truman on 12 May 1945. In the sixth volume of *The Second World War,* the last book of which is entitled "The Iron Curtain," he states that of all his public statements on the emergent division of Europe, he would rather be judged by this telegram. He then quotes the five paragraphs of this historic document, of which the third begins as follows:

An iron curtain is drawn down upon their front [Russia and Eastern Europe]. We do not know what is going on behind. There seems little doubt that the whole of the regions east of the line Lübeck-Trieste-Corfu will soon be completely in their hands. (vol. 6, pp. 498–99).

In a second telegram to Truman on 4 June 1945, Churchill repeats this phrase to express his concern about the retreat of the American army from central Europe toward the end of the war, "thus bringing Soviet power into the heart of Western Europe and the descent of an iron curtain between us and everything to the eastward" (vol. 6, p. 523). These two telegrams were secret and could not have transformed the "iron curtain" phrase into a dominant slogan of the Cold War period. This feat was accomplished by Churchill in his famous speech on "The Sinews of Peace" which he delivered on 5 March 1946 at Westminster College in Fulton, Missouri. This address, broadcast throughout the world, is a masterful example of Churchill's rhetorical skills,[58] and it includes the following memorable and often cited passage:

> From Stettin in the Baltic to Trieste in the Adriatic, an iron curtain has descended across the Continent. Behind that line lie all the capitals of the ancient states of Central and Eastern Europe, Warsaw, Berlin, Prague, Vienna, Budapest, Belgrade, Bucharest and Sofia, all these famous cities and the populations around them lie in what I must call the Soviet sphere, and all are subject in one form or another, not only to Soviet influence but to a very high and, in many cases, increasing measure of control from Moscow.[59]

The proverbial phrase of the "iron curtain" has inextricably become attached to the name of Churchill, and yet, he could lay no claim to having originated it. He probably knew it as a theatrical term.[60] The iron curtains hung inside the proscenium arch and, in the event of fire, could be dropped to separate the auditorium from the stage. Churchill might also have remembered reading the sentence "an iron curtain had dropped between him [a scientist] and the outer world" in the novel *The Food of the Gods* (1904) by his friend H. G. Wells. There are other earlier references from the twentieth century which refer to an iron curtain separating Russia from other parts of Europe that might have influenced Churchill to capitalize on this fitting metaphor. Ironically, he might even have been "inspired" by Joseph Goebbels who on 25 February 1945 was quoted in the newspaper *Das Reich* as saying: "If the German people lay down their arms, the whole of eastern and south-eastern Europe, together with the [German] Reich, would come under Russian occupation. Behind an iron screen, mass butcheries of peoples would begin . . ." The Nazi propaganda machine had sent this text to the world press on 22 February 1945, but it had already appeared in this English translation in *The Times* on 23 February. There can hardly be any doubt that Churchill read this report and that he quickly noticed that the translator of the German expression "eiserner Vorhang" should have rendered it as "iron curtain" rather than "iron screen."[61] One thing is certain: for Churchill this phrase became a rhetorical *leitmotif* after the Fulton speech, and he used it repeatedly[62] to describe the division of Europe and the menace of the Cold War. Yet despite his apocalyptic gloom about the immediate future of Europe, in a speech on 4 August 1947, Churchill shone a prophetic spotlight on the European stage after the eventual lifting of the iron curtain:

> It is true that an Iron Curtain has descended across Europe, from Stettin on the Baltic to Trieste on the Adriatic. We do not wish the slightest ill to those who dwell on the east of that Iron Curtain, which was never our making. On the contrary, our prosperity and happiness would rise with theirs. Let there be sunshine on both sides of the Iron Curtain; and if ever the sunshine should be equal on both sides, the Curtain will be no more. It will vanish away like the mists of the morning and melt in the warm light of happy days and cheerful friendship. I trust these thoughts will become facts and not merely dreams.[63]

Churchill restated the last sentence of this quotation in a more proverbial form in the first volume of *The Second World War* where he describes his feelings about having been named prime minister on 10 May 1940: "I thought I knew a good deal about it all [the political situation and the war], and I was sure I should not fail. Therefore, although impatient for the morning, I slept soundly and had no need for cheering dreams. Facts are better than dreams" (vol. 1, p. 527).

It happens rather frequently in Churchill's narrative that he uses proverbial language in a personal manner. It must not be forgotten that *The Second World War* and his other historical volumes were not written in an objective scholarly style. Churchill himself is the central persona, and sentences with the "I" pronoun abound, including those that include folk speech:

> I lived in fact from mouth to hand.[64] (vol. 1, p. 62)

> I felt sure his heart was in the right place. (vol. 1, p. 190)

> I do not feel that we are getting to the root of the matter on many points. (vol. 1, p. 361)

> I then talked of the importance of finding a way out: "He that ruleth his spirit is greater than he that taketh a city."[65] (vol. 1, p. 533)

> As usual I put my case in black and white. (vol. 2, p. 376)

> I fear this may be another example of the adage "A stitch in time saves nine." (vol. 3, p. 52)

> I thought it my duty to break the ice. (vol. 3, p. 340)

> I am too busy to chase these rabbits as they deserve. (vol. 3, p. 777)

I was grateful to James Maxton for bringing the matter to a head. (vol. 4, p. 62)

I had a great desire to have something in hand. (vol. 4, p. 167)

Personally I longed to see British and American armies shoulder to shoulder in Europe. (vol. 4, p. 290)

I was to turn the tables upon him. (vol. 4, p. 362)

I slept the sleep of the just till long after daylight. (vol. 4, p. 469)

I think a golden opportunity may be lost. (vol. 4, p. 626)

I thought it well that the President should take the rough with the smooth about British public opinion. (vol. 4, p. 649)

I found it very hard to make head or tail of the bundle of drafts. (vol. 4, p. 726)

I appreciate your point about being able to take a short cut, and having that up your sleeve. (vol. 4, p. 792)

I am very pleased with the way in which you used such poor bits and pieces as were left you. (vol. 5, p. 195)

I have been fighting with my hands tied behind my back. (vol. 5, p. 198)

I feel very much in the dark at present. (vol. 5, p. 278)

I am completely at the end of my tether. (vol. 5, p. 373)

As usual I am optimistic; the tortoise has thrust his head out very far. (vol. 6, p. 240)

I feel also that their word is their bond. (vol. 6, p. 351)

I am very glad you got into Trieste . . . in time to put your foot in the door. (vol. 6, p. 482)

I said we must face the facts. (vol. 6, p. 565)

"Facing the facts"[66] is yet another proverbial *leitmotif* which characterizes Churchill's attempts to convince his allies and opponents to follow his war strategies. To add rhetorical strength to his verbal arguments, he would quite often shift from the subjective "I" to the more collective "we," thus arguing for a united front. A few convincing examples of this shrewd and at times manipulative procedure can be seen in the following list:

The President [Roosevelt] regarded recognition [of the Italian occupation of Abyssinia] as an unpleasant pill which we should both have to swallow, and he wished that we should both swallow it together. (vol. 1, p. 198)

We must just make the best of things as they come along. (vol . 2, p. 451)

We will let bygones go and work with anyone who convinces us of his resolution to defeat the common enemy. (vol. 2, p. 466)

We should have felt more confidence in the success of our policy. We should have seen that he [Hitler] risked falling between two stools. (vol. 3, p. 84)

Why do we want that hanging over our head anyway? (vol. 3, p. 115)

Somehow we had to contrive to extend our reach [of destroyer escorts] or our days would be numbered. (vol. 3, p. 119)

We had to make the best of it, and that is never worth doing by halves. (vol. 3, pp. 361–62)

We were therefore able to be better than our word to the United States. (vol. 3, p. 543)

Thus we all found ourselves pretty well on the same spot [regarding Anglo-American intervention in French North Africa]. (vol. 3, p. 588)

We must see they [de Gaulle and all Frenchmen who regard Germany as a foe] have a fair deal. (vol. 4, p. 566)

We . . . plan a world in which all branches of the human family may look forward to what the American Declaration of Independence finely calls "life, liberty, and the pursuit of happiness."[67] (vol. 4, p. 616)

We may, by "tightening the belt," save perhaps a million tons [of seaborne tonnage of supplies]. (vol. 4, p. 482)

Everything we had touched had turned to gold, and during the last seven weeks there had been an unbroken run of military success. (vol. 6, p. 132)

In the last quotation, Churchill's "we" refers to President Roosevelt and numerous other high officials who met on 13 September 1944, in Washington, D.C. Like Midas in the classical myth, the war efforts of the Allies were bearing gilded fruit if not turning literally to pure gold. Much of this success was due to the deep friendship and absolute trust between Churchill and Roosevelt. Churchill in particular never tired of reflecting and commenting on their unique relationship, and his appreciation of the United States and its people can be found on many pages of *The Second World War* and his other works. When President Roosevelt and General Marshall in the summer of 1942 helped Britain once again, this time by dispatching much-needed engines for tanks, Churchill summarizes his account of this generous act in particular and the British and American relationship during the entire war with the simple proverb: "A friend in need is a friend indeed"[68] (vol. 4, p. 344).

Gratitude led Churchill, in a speech to the House of Commons on 20 August 1940, to formulate one of his most memorable utterances which by now has taken on a proverbial status of sorts. Expressing his appreciation of the British pilots who in the summer of 1940 fended off the German air attacks, he said:

> The gratitude of every home in our Island, in our Empire, and indeed throughout the world, except in the abodes of the guilty, goes out to the British airmen who, undaunted by odds, unwearied in their constant challenge and mortal danger, are turning the tide of the World War by their prowess and by their devotion. Never in the field of human conflict was so much owed by so many to so few.[69]

Churchill was well aware of the quotability of this formulation, and he used it on three subsequent occasions. Reflecting on the entire Second World War, he reminded his listeners during a radio broadcast on 13 May 1945 of the heroic actions of British pilots during the Battle of Britain:

> In July, August and September, 1940, forty or fifty squadrons of British fighter aircraft in the Battle of Britain broke the teeth of the German air fleet at odds of seven or eight to one. May I repeat again the words I used at that momentous hour: "Never in the field of human conflict was so much owed by so many to so few."[70]

Understandably so, Churchill concludes his chapter on "The Battle of Britain" (vol. 2, pp. 281–300) in *The Second World War* (1949) with the proud observation of the appropriateness of his memorable phrase:

> At the summit the stamina and valour of our fighter pilots remained unconquerable and supreme. Thus Britain was saved. Well might I say in the House of Commons [20 August 1940]: "Never in the field of human conflict was so much owed by so many to so few." (vol. 2, p. 300)

Churchill returned once more to this proverbial phrase at the beginning of a broadcast appeal for the R.A.F. Benevolent Fund on 16 September 1951:

> "Never in the field of human conflict was so much owed by so many to so few." With those words in 1940—our darkest and yet our finest hour—I reported to the House of Commons on the progress of the Battle of Britain, whose eleventh anniversary we now celebrate. I repeat my words tonight with pride and gratitude. They spring from our hearts as keenly at this moment as on the day I uttered them.[71]

This last quotation includes yet another famous phrase coined by Churchill. In a major speech to the House of Commons on 18 June 1940, Churchill made it clear to Hitler and Nazi Germany that Britain would fight them to the bitter end, no matter what price or sacrifice. The speech concludes with the following resolution that set the tone for the entire war effort:

Hitler knows that he will have to break us in this Island or lose the war. If we can stand up to him, all Europe may be free and the life of the world may move forward into broad, sunlit uplands. But if we fail, then the whole world, including the United States, including all that we have known and cared for, will sink into the abyss of a New Dark Age made more sinister, and perhaps more protracted, by the lights of perverted science. Let us therefore brace ourselves to our duties, and so bear ourselves that, if the British Empire and its Commonwealth last for a thousand years, men will still say, "This was their finest hour."[72]

Churchill was well aware of the special and memorable formulation of this phrase. After repeating this passage from his speech in his war history, he states that "all these often-quoted words were made good in the hour of victory" (vol. 2, p. 199). In calling Churchill a "phrase forger," Manfred Weidhorn is certainly correct in observing that Churchill "made his rhetoric memorable by these simple, proverb-like utterances."[73]

Yet Churchill's own inclination toward coining "proverb-like" phrases did not prevent him from making use of traditional proverbs whenever they suited his rhetorical purposes. If, on the other hand, a traditional proverb did not quite express what the moment called for, Churchill was not reluctant to change the wording to fit his needs. At times such innovative proverb manipulations actually resulted in powerful statements which appear to carry the authority of traditional wisdom in their messages.[74] Thus, commenting on a speech by Austen Chamberlain in which the chancellor of the exchequer had argued in 1936 that "if you do not stop Germany now, all is over," Churchill simply alludes to the proverb "Actions speak louder than words": "These were brave words; but action would have spoken louder" (vol. 1, p. 153).

It should surprise no one that Churchill delighted in using the proverb "Deeds, not words" as a *leitmotif* throughout his long life. Not that words or rhetoric were not important to the great orator, but the following fifteen citations from his speeches clearly show that they were only a means to the more important end of precipitating action:

The only answer . . . must be by deeds, not by words. (1901)

To back words with deeds, the Commons proceeded. (1938)

It emphasized his reliance on deeds instead of words. (1938)

One of the ways to bring this war to a speedy end is to convince the enemy, not by words, but by deeds, that we have the will. (1940)

In wartime there is a lot to be said for the motto: "Deeds, not words." (1941)

It is a case of deeds, not words. (1941)

. . . I should immediately be answered, "Let us have deeds, not words." (1941)

. . . that, after all, is a matter which deeds, not words, will prove. (1942)

. . . first, it is a time for deeds and not words. (1944)

In these matters, it is not words that count, it is deeds and facts. (1946)

But deeds are stronger than words, and it is the deeds, or misdeeds, of the Socialist Government . . . which have brought about the violent internal antagonism. (1950)

We seek to be judged by deeds rather than by words. (1951)

We ask to be judged by deeds not words. (1952)

We hope to be judged by deeds, and not by words, and by performance rather than by promises. (1953)

Against all their words, we can set deeds. (1959)[75]

One wonders, of course, what Churchill's political opponents might have thought of this last statement, when everybody in Britain knew about his love of words. It must also not be forgotten that Churchill was a man of action, that no assignment ever appeared too much for him, and that he worked untiringly for his government and his people. As Victor Albjerg in his chapter on "The Essence of the Man" has put it so aptly, "Churchill enjoyed work. To him it was not drudgery, but purposeful creativity."[76]

Churchill also used proverbs in his *Second World War* to characterize certain persons or situations. Lord Cranborne, under-secretary at the Foreign Office, is described as "a man in whom 'still waters run deep'" (vol. 1, p. 206); and Churchill even includes the nasty remarks which his Labour Party foes used after he had narrowly escaped a bomb attack during the London Blitz: "Our Labour colleagues [in the Cabinet] facetiously remarked: 'The devil looks after his own'" (vol. 2, p. 307). One can well imagine that Churchill took this ironic slam with a good dose of "devilish" humor. He was, however, much more serious when he used a proverb to vent his frustration with the 1940 Supreme War Council and the War Cabinet over their failure to act quickly in stopping the flow of iron from Narvik (Norway) to Germany. Seven valuable months were lost before a decision was made to send in the British navy:

But in war seven months is a long time. Now Hitler was ready. . . . One can hardly find a more perfect example of the impotence and fatuity of waging war by committee or rather by groups of committees. . . . Had I been allowed to act with freedom and design when I first demanded permission [to stop iron-carrying boats], a far more agreeable conclusion might have been reached in this key theatre, with favourable consequences in every direction. But now all was to be disaster.

> He who will not when he may,
> When he will, he shall have Nay.
>
> (vol. 1, p. 458)

Here Churchill almost seems to pout—to use this proverb as an "I told you so" reprimand of all those who stood in the way of preventive action.

In his countless memoranda to various ministers and generals, Churchill again and again cited proverbs to support his arguments. By using them, he added a folkloric emphasis to otherwise bureaucratic messages—an emphasis that appeals to a sense of shared wisdom. An example is his short memorandum of 27 May 1944 to the Minister of Aircraft Production in which he expresses his perturbation about the minister's proposal "to centralise jet-propulsion development in [a] new Government company. There is a great deal to be said for encouraging overlapping in research and development rather than putting all the eggs in one basket" (vol. 5, p. 629). In another memorandum of 16 November 1944, Churchill informed General Ismay of about twenty eighteen-inch howitzers which he could make available to him for the direct attack of Germany: "Every dog has his day, and I have kept these [very heavy guns] for a quarter of a century in the hope that they would have their chance" (vol. 6, p. 611). What a way to give "life" to these cannons by comparing them figuratively with a "dog"! General Ismay must have chuckled over this proverbial metaphor, but he probably was also in awe (as modern readers of such memoranda are) of Churchill's detailed knowledge of war supplies at this crucial time in the European theatre of war. There appears to be no detail that escaped Churchill. One gets the feeling that he thought of everything, as can be seen from yet another memorandum of 4 April 1945 to Sir Edward Bridges. The war was not even over yet, but Churchill as the shrewd politician and proponent of the British Commonwealth was already planning to transfer some ships to Canada and Australia as a goodwill gesture for their contributions to the war:

> Arrange with the Admiralty to bring up both cases of the transfer of warships to Canada and Australia at some Cabinet meeting to which the Dominion Ministers are summoned. Then make them a full and free presentation there and then across the table. . . . No financial considerations should be adduced. We owe too much to Canada in money alone, and the effect of gestures like this upon both Dominions concerned will be achieved far better than by arguments about trading off the value of the ships against certain financial considerations. This is not a moment for a "penny-wise, pound-foolish" policy. We must either keep the ships or give them . . . now is the time to make the presentation in the most friendly form. Cast your

bread upon the waters; it will return to you in not so many days. (vol. 6, p. 639)

Notice how Churchill supplements the wisdom of the folk proverb with the authority of the biblical proverb (Eccles. 11:1), even though he does not quite remember the original second part as "for you shall find it after many days." Or is he, in fact, altering the proverb on purpose in order to indicate that this benevolent gesture will bear its fruit in return sooner than people might think? In view of Churchill's ability to retain quotations, a case could certainly be made that this not insignificant change was made intentionally. The appearance of the two proverbs in this memorandum shows once again that Churchill is indeed a masterful proverbial strategist and that proverbs do play a role in the diplomatic ups and downs of the world.

This can also be seen in Churchill's effective use of two proverbs in his reflection on the fateful signing of the Non-Aggression Pact between the Soviet Union and Germany on 22 August 1939. The proverbs serve as moralizing tools by Churchill, who had worked hard to keep Stalin from siding with Hitler:

> A moral may be drawn from all this, which is of homely simplicity. "Honesty is the best policy." . . . Several examples of this will be shown in these pages. Crafty men and statesmen will be shown misled by all their elaborate calculations. But this is the signal instance. Only twenty-two months were to pass before Stalin and the Russian nation with its scores of millions were to pay a frightful forfeit. If a Government has no moral scruples, it often seems to gain great advantages and liberties of action, but "All comes out even at the end of the day, and all will come out yet more even when all the days are ended." (vol. 1, p. 307)

In addition to their moralizing purpose, the proverbs also serve here as prophetic statements of "homely simplicity" that dishonesty and treachery will lead to doom.

Other proverbs show Churchill's pragmatism in his dual role as prime minister and minister of defence. In one of his typical memoranda, he raises the question about much-needed war supplies and then gives a bit of "pithy" advice that action should be taken immediately:

> What is being done about getting our twenty motor torpedo-boats, the five P.B.Y. [Flying-boats], the one hundred and fifty to two hundred aircraft, and the two hundred and fifty thousand rifles, also anything else that is going on? I consider we were promised all the above, and more too. Not an hour should be lost in raising these questions. "Beg while the iron is hot." (vol. 2, p. 590)[77]

What an ingenious way to vary a standard proverb in order to express the definite need of getting these war supplies! Churchill clearly was a master of this type of proverb manipulation, his best "creation" perhaps being the following anti-proverb[78] based on the well-known English proverb "Make hay while the sun shines."[79] In a memorandum of 23 June 1941 to General Ismay, Churchill wrote pointedly, "Now that the enemy [Germany] is busy in Russia is the time to 'Make hell while the sun shines'" (vol. 3, p. 690) in gaining air domination over the Channel and France. In its metaphorical simplicity this statement can be seen as a proverbial *modus operandi* not only of warfare as Churchill envisioned it but also of his political life in general.[80] Take advantage of every possible situation and give the enemy "hell" while you can.

In his victory broadcast on 13 May 1945, the text which Churchill uses to conclude *The Second World War,* he used a proverbial expression in his reflections on what was to happen after the war's end. One senses the anxieties of the prime minister who wonders whether he will still be needed now that this long crisis was past:

> I wish I could tell you to-night that all our toils and troubles were over. Then indeed I could end my five years' service happily, and if you thought that you had had enough of me and that I ought to be put out to grass I tell you I would take it with the best of grace. But, on the contrary, I must warn you, as I did when I began this five years' task—and no one knew then that it would last so long—that there is still a lot to do, and that you must be prepared for further efforts of mind and body and further sacrifices to great causes if you are not to fall back into the rut of inertia, the confusion of aim, and "the craven fear of being great." (vol. 6, p. 672)

The victory speech becomes sort of a campaign speech by the ultimate "work horse" which is by no means ready "to be put out to grass," as it were. When, despite his valiant struggle and final victory in the war, he lost the general election later during 1945, Churchill had extreme psychological difficulties in being pushed aside. In defeat and as leader of the opposition, he used his rhetorical power until in 1951 he once again became prime minister. Churchill neither needed nor wanted retirement and used his tongue and pen to the end of his life to help shape the destiny of Great Britain and the world, perhaps also mindful of the proverb that "The pen is mightier than the sword."[81] Towards the end of his long life, even more honors came to him, one of the most coveted being the honorary citizenship of the United States which was bestowed upon him on 9 April 1963. On that occasion President John F. Kennedy summarized Winston S. Churchill's rhetorical grandeur with the statement: "In the dark days and darker nights when England stood alone—and most men save Englishmen despaired of England's life—he mobilized the English language and sent it into battle."[82] It is doubtful that either Kennedy or Churchill recognized the importance that proverbial speech had played in this mobilization. Yet a good twenty years earlier, in a long speech on the war situation to the House of Commons on 27 January 1942, Churchill expressed his thoughts on the rhetorical significance of proverbial folk speech:

> There is no objection to anything being said in plain English, or even plainer, and the Government will do their utmost to conform to any standard which may be set in the course of the debate. But no one need be mealy-mouthed in debate, and no one should be chicken-hearted in voting. (vol. 4, p. 58)

Despite his erudition and vast knowledge that could lead Churchill to very sophisticated heights of the English language, he was always ready "to speak in plain English" and to voice his opinion without fear of the consequences. Speaking plainly and proverbially certainly helped in arousing the peoples of the free world against the tyranny of dictators. There definitely is proverbial truth in the claim that Winston S. Churchill "mobilized the English language and sent it into battle."

3

"It Sure Is Hell to Be President"

Harry S. Truman's Proverbial Plain English

An American presidency may resonate in a few well-chosen and oft-repeated quotations. The voice of Harry S. Truman (1884–1972) echoes across the decades since the end of his administration in 1953 in sentences that have become proverbial: "Give 'em hell, Harry!" "If you can't stand the heat, get out of the kitchen," and "The buck stops here." Characteristic of the man as these sayings may be, paremiological interest in Truman cuts more deeply than these plain words might suggest.

The plain speaking of the man from Missouri achieved the Aristotelian desiderata of clarity as well as appropriateness to speaker and audience. Truman's public persona eschewed the inspirational rhetoric of his contemporaries Franklin D. Roosevelt (1882–1945) and the majestic cadences of Winston S. Churchill (1874–1965). His major speeches and pronouncements as senator and president are textbook examples of correct but largely unadorned grammar and syntax. His family, friends, the press corps, and the crowds that assembled for his "whistle-stop" addresses heard another Truman, a salty, pugnacious man whose diction was rich in imagery and figures of speech, particularly metaphor. There, too, emerged an impressive array of proverbs and proverbial expressions and comparisons.

Throughout his long life, Truman repeatedly stressed his commitment to such basic ethical values as honesty and decency, and frequently he used proverbial language to describe these values and persuade listeners of his sincerity. Here, for instance, he is in 1952 on the campaign trail for Adlai E. Stevenson. He has already ridiculed the Republican presidential candidate, Dwight D. Eisenhower, as a wavering and unprincipled person, and now in vivid proverbial language he contrasts his own brand of honesty:

> I have always thought that honesty is best in politics, just as it is anywhere else. I have got into trouble sometimes by saying just exactly what I thought. You may have heard something about that at one time or another. But I have stuck to my guns, and I know that it pays in the long run.[1]

Truman ingeniously adapts the traditional proverb "Honesty is the best policy" to suit his own rhetorical purposes. The two proverbial expressions "to stick to one's guns" and "in the long run" help convince his listeners that he has always adhered to the wisdom of the proverb and that this course of action has served him well.

Truman repeatedly couched his belief in a strong moral code in proverbial language. In a letter to Nellie Noland dated 29 October 1949, he stresses that we need to educate good teachers whose instruction is based on "moral integrity as well as a.b.c.'s and readin', writin', & 'rithmetic."[2] And in a short memorandum entitled "My Political Career" (July 1954) Truman gives a pragmatic overview of the moral rules he followed as a public servant. Once again he uses proverbial language to express the rigor with which he attempted to adhere to his own ethical code:

> In all this long career I had certain rules which I followed win, lose or draw. I refused to handle any political money in any way whatever. I engaged in no private interests whatever that could be helped by local, state or national governments. I refused presents, hotel accommodations or trips which were paid for by private parties.[3]

Truman was a religious person as well as a moralist and was well versed in the Bible. One biblical proverb he often invoked to underscore a basic moral principle to be followed in the political and social world is "All things whatsoever ye would that men should do to you, do ye even so to them" (Matt. 7:12). He used this "Golden Rule" proverb in a number of variations seven times in his published writings and speeches,[4] thus expressing his strong belief in and commitment to its basic human value. The most revealing example of this ethical *leitmotif* in Truman's writings is found in a 26 February 1952 diary entry:

> But if I could succeed in getting the world of morals associated against the world of no morals, we'd have world peace for ages to come. Confucius, Buddha, Moses, our own Jesus Christ, Mahomet, all preached: "Do as you'd be done by." Treat others as you'd be treated. So did all the other great teachers and philosophers.[5]

History has shown that Truman's "ethical appeal"[6] was in large part due to his simple and unpretentious roots in the rural environment of Missouri in the heartland of middle America. Truman was proud of his ordinary origin throughout his life, and he always felt that his own social background helped him to understand the common people of this country.

Feeling in touch with the common people was one side of the Truman coin, and the other was decisive leadership based on hard work. Two touching letters to his daughter Margaret, an aspiring singer, say a great deal about the work ethic of a man who never lost his healthy sense of humor. On 13 September 1946, the president gives his daughter this proverbial bit of fatherly advice: "Work hard, be a nice young lady and do what you do with all the energy you have and you'll come out on top. Sometimes hard work will get you too far on top—look at your pop."[7] Barely two weeks later, on 25 September 1946, Truman reiterates his point, exchanging the proverbial expression "to come out on top" with "to make the grade": "Keep working and I am sure if you want to badly enough you can make the grade. It takes lots and lots of hard work and concentration. Your dad knows what that means."[8] His work ethic is evident as well in the short letters Truman often fired off to people who in one way or another seemed willing to criticize his actions without offering alternate solutions. This is the case in a letter dated 13 November 1951, to Democratic Congressman George H. Fallon: "It is easy enough to just sit back and throw bricks at the man who has to make decisions. It would be very much better to contribute a little cooperation."[9] It is implied that the president, who works hard and has to make decisions, does not deserve proverbial bricks thrown at him by members of his own party. Otherwise, things can really "get out of hand," as Truman explains in his book *Mr. Citizen,* published in 1960:

> The most dangerous course a President can follow in a time of crisis is to defer making decisions until they are forced on him and thereupon become inevitable decisions. Events then get out of hand and take control of the President, and he is compelled to overcome situations which he should have prevented. When a President finds himself in that position, he is no longer a leader but an improviser who is driven to action out of expediency or weakness.[10]

Notice how in the midst of this textbook paragraph on decision making, Truman breaks into proverbial language to drive home his own willingness to work hard and act decisively after studying the available facts.

Much has been made of Truman's limited education. His opponents have at times belittled him for his lack of a college degree, forgetting that there are other ways to get an education. Truman valued education highly. He had the highest regard for his high school teachers and gained much knowledge through constant reading, especially in history and biography. In the second letter he wrote to the woman who was to become his wife, Elizabeth Virginia (Bess) Wallace (1885–1982), he indicates one particularly telling early reading interest: "I forgot to say I have been reading Mark Twain. He is my patron saint in literature. I managed to save dimes enough to buy all he has written, so I am somewhat soaked in western slang and Mark Twain idioms."[11] As Truman correctly points out, Mark

Twain's writings are filled with idiomatic phrases,[12] and he might to some degree have taken his cue from Twain for his own preference for proverbial language.

As an autodidact acquainted through extensive reading in American and world history as well as in religion and general philosophy, Truman carved out his personal ethos based on the concept of "common sense," a *leitmotif* that figures prominently in his rhetoric and writing throughout his life. He had read Thomas Paine's *Common Sense* (1776),[13] and he made this principle his *modus operandi* in dealing with the many tasks before him. When he was invited to deliver a series of public lectures to the students of Columbia University in 1959, he combined the "common sense" approach to life's problems with that of "good will" and claimed that "[t]here isn't any reason in the world why good will and common sense won't settle it [in this case, the problem of segregation]."[14] And regarding an apparent split in the Democratic Party, he told the students that this can be worked out "if it's approached by people of common sense and good will."[15]

Translating that common sense and good will into language became Truman's trademark as speaker and writer, and his particular linguistic style has come to be known as "plain speaking." Truman refers to "plain language" so often that only a very few examples can be cited here. Here, for example, are his telling remarks concerning the language of the Constitution of the United States:

> I'm one of the greatest believers in the Constitution in the country, I guess, and one of the greatest admirers of what it says and the way in which it says it. I think it's far and away the best government document that's ever been put together by any bunch of men. It says things simply and beautifully; it's written in plain language, and it states exactly what's meant and isn't tangled up with any legal verbiage or any Latin inserts. And when you read it, you can understand it.[16]

Sometimes Truman changes "plain language" to "plain English," as in his claim that "plain Missouri English can't be beaten. (Scratch off the en on beat.)"[17] Frequently he simply uses the phrase "to speak plainly," as in the following statement, explaining how he wished to communicate with the American people:

> I always made it my business to speak plainly and directly to the people without indulging in high-powered oratory. The truth, I felt, is what voters need more than anything else, and when they have that, they can vote intelligently. When they cannot get the facts from other sources, an honest candidate is obligated to go out and give it to them in person.[18]

There appears to be almost no end to Truman's use of the phrase "to make it perfectly plain," which often introduces a statement that is meant to set the record straight, as for example "I would like to make it perfectly plain"[19] or "I thought I made that perfectly plain."[20] To gain as much clarity and to reach as many people as possible, Truman chose plain and simple words, for as he himself explains in one of his typically short sentences, "The simplest words make for the best communication."[21]

His preference for simple language can be seen in a rather touching fashion in some of the letters to Bess in which this straight-shooting common man expresses his love for the woman who meant everything to him. After a rather lengthy courtship, Bess had finally agreed to Harry's marriage proposal, and here is the way he begins his subsequent letter to her on 4 November 1913:

> Your letter has made a confirmed optimist out of me sure enough. I know now that everything is good and grand and this footstool is a fine place to be. I have been all up in the air, clear above earth ever since it came. I guess you thought I didn't have much sense on Sunday, but I just couldn't say anything—only just sit and look. It doesn't seem real that you should care for me. I have always hoped you would but some way feared very much you wouldn't. You know, I've always thought that the best man in the world is hardly good enough for any woman. But when it comes to the best girl in all the universe caring for an ordinary gink like me—well, you'll have to let me get used to it.[22]

A few weeks later, he reminds Bess proverbially that she owes him a letter or two, stating "Remember you said you were a woman of your word. You've no idea how blank a week is without a letter, so you'd better make this one extra bright."[23] When Bess does write to him, especially during his time as a soldier in World War I in France, it is "Another banner day. Got four letters. Hooray! Also a box of candy from Paris on which it said it was sent by order of Miss Bess Wallace, Independence, Kansas City, Mo."[24] Later, after their marriage, and once Truman had taken up residency in Washington, D.C., while Bess stayed behind in Missouri, he writes the following few lines to his wife and daughter Margaret on 5 January 1937: "I just can't stand it without you. If we were poorer than church mice, what difference does it make? There is only one thing that counts with me and that is you and Margie."[25] Obviously this separation was hard for the family, as is expressed in an emotional letter to Bess on 1 February 1937. While he does not use a proverbial phrase in this statement, he nevertheless reflects on the value of sincere communication that meant so much to him in his personal and public dealings:

... I've never cared much how words were combined if their meaning happened to be honest and sincere, and that is all words are for. Maybe you don't know it, but I'd rather lose a hand or have an eye pulled out than make you a moment's suffering or hurt—either mentally or physically. I've seen so much difficulty caused by sheer unthoughtfulness that I've tried all my life to be thoughtful and to make every person I come in contact with happier for having seen me. Maybe that's silly too. I don't know.[26]

Truman's letters are often humorous and frequently call upon proverbial language to deliver the laugh. His 13 September 1946 letter to Bess makes clear that not all of his concerns are presidential and that the occupant of the White House must also deal with mundane matters:

I failed to answer your question about your car. It seems to me that if you can get a good price for it you may as well sell it and buy a bond, and then when we leave the great white jail a new car can be bought. The new cars won't have the bugs out of them for two or three years anyway. Be sure though that no regulations or price ceilings are in any way infringed, no matter how good you may think the friendship of the person you sell to may be. The temptation to take a crack at the first family for pay is almost irresistible and so far we've escaped any factual misdemeanor and I'd like to finish with that reputation. Save the number.[27]

In a much earlier letter dated 10 March 1913, Truman describes his sleeping uncle in the following humorous manner: "My dear uncle is sawing logs on the couch. Every once in a while he hits a splinter and such a choking and scraping of saw teeth [false teeth] you never heard. He holds the record for snoring."[28] In another letter of that period from 23 April 1913, Truman comments with characteristic proverbial exaggeration that "It is raining to beat the band now. I hope it keeps up and then perhaps I can gush over on two sheets. Don't you hope it stops?"[29] Much of Truman's humor is based on simple metaphors and verbal play, usually attesting to his rural upbringing.

Truman's interest in plain language extended far enough that he sometimes added linguistic or folkloristic explanations to his proverbial utterances. Here, for example, is an early letter to Bess, dated 26 November 1912. He begins proverbially but quickly adds an explanatory sentence or two: "I am going to get this one [letter] off on time or bust a hamstring. That is a classic expression because that said string holds the key to the whole set of harness. If it breaks, away go the horses and you stand in the road. Also it is the last piece of harness to break. It is either very rotten when it breaks or the rest of the harness is very strong."[30] He also explained the phrase "suffering from . . . Potomac Fever" the following way: "It was Woodrow Wilson who coined the phrase. He said that some people came to Washington and grew with their jobs, but he said a lot of other people came, and all they did was swell up. Those that swell up are the ones that have Potomac Fever. They're the people who forget who they are and who sent them there."[31]

In a discussion of the Declaration of Independence, he makes the following explanatory comment: "John Hancock signed first because he was president of the Continental Congress, and I'm sure everybody knows the famous story about his signing nice and big so that his signature wouldn't be missed, which is why, of course, a signature is called a John Hancock today."[32] But Truman does not accept every historical phrase that became current in the United States:

> Around that time [under President Polk], a fancy phrase began to be used around the country. The phrase was "manifest destiny," and it expressed the belief of many citizens at that time that our country was destined, I suppose by God, to rule the area from coast to coast.
>
> Well, I don't like that phrase, and I don't think I'd have believed in it if I had been alive during that period; I think we were lucky in having people in the areas around us who wanted to become part of the United States, and I think we were smart in buying up some of those areas around us when we had the opportunity to do so.[33]

Truman, the folklorist, however, is really at work when it comes to the planting proverb, "Twenty-sixth of July, sow turnips, wet or dry," which he used sixteen times between 1923 and 1962.[34] In a letter to Bess on 27 July 1923, Truman writes matter-of-factly: "Well, yesterday you know was turnip day, and the instructions are to sow them wet or dry. If they'd been sown, they'd have been up tomorrow."[35] Almost twenty-five years later, on 26 July 1947, Truman once again writes to Bess as a knowledgeable former farmer and a splendid raconteur:

> This is turnip day. . . . My old baldheaded uncle, Harrison Young, told me that July 26 was the day to sow turnips—sow them "wet or dry, twenty-sixth of July." In 1901 he went to the seed and hardware store in Belton and stated to the proprietor, Old Man Mosely, a North Carolinian, that he wanted six bushels of turnip seeds—enough to sow the whole county to [sic] turnips. Mr. Mosely asked him what he expected to do with so much seed. My old uncle told him that it was his understanding that turnips are 90 percent water. Nineteen hundred one was the terribly dry year. Therefore if the whole farm were planted to [sic] turnips maybe the drought would be broken.[36]

"Turnip Day" caught the nation's attention when Truman as president called a special summer session of the Eightieth Congress on 26 July 1948, trying to get the so-called Do-Nothing Congress controlled by the

Republicans to pass some of his domestic recommendations. Having failed to do so, the shrewd Truman bombarded members of Congress with such sarcastic ridicule that people actually changed their minds about him and voted for him in the fall election. It is generally believed today that this turnip session of Congress helped the underdog Truman beat his opponent Thomas E. Dewey.[37] In a speech on 30 October 1952, in Detroit, Michigan, Truman recalled with terse pride how he had dropped this turnip bombshell on the Republicans four years earlier: "Well, in Philadelphia, about two o'clock in the morning, when I accepted the Democratic presidential nomination, I called a special session of Congress, and I called it the 'Turnip Day' session, because it came on the 26th of July, and that is 'Turnip Day' in Missouri."[38] He had used the proverb as part of a successful political maneuver, but this does not mean he did not respect the folk wisdom it conveyed. In the following 1962 interview with Merle Miller Truman explains in detail the natural significance of this planting proverb:

> Q. Mr. President, you said you were calling that special session for Turnip Day. What's Turnip Day?
> THE PRESIDENT. The twenty-sixth of July, wet or dry, always sow turnips. Along in September they'll be four, five, maybe six inches in diameter, and they're good to eat—raw. I don't like them cooked.
> Q. Turnip greens are pretty good.
> THE PRESIDENT. Well, yes, but the only way to get turnip greens is in the spring. You take out the turnips that you've kept in the cellar all winter and set them out in the garden, and then they come up. You grow them, and the greens that have come up when they're both, oh, about four or five inches long you mix them with dandelions and mustard, and they make the finest greens in the world. Spinach isn't in it. That's what the country people used to have in the spring. Turnip greens with dandelions and mustard and things of that kind.
> But you have to know which is which with plants like that. Plenty of those things are violent poison. You take poke berries, pokeroots. When they're so long, they're good to go into greens, but you wait a little longer, and you might as well order your coffin. Because you're done. They're as poisonous as cyanide.
> Q. How do you find out when to pick them?
> THE PRESIDENT. Your grandmother has to tell you.[39]

Truman remained interested in all aspects of farm life throughout his life, notably regarding the prediction of the weather. He explained this preoccupation by referring to his farming background: "I follow the weather very closely and have done so all my life because I was raised on a farm. . . . When you're on the farm and you have to harvest wheat or sow wheat, or plant corn or gather corn, or decide on what you are going to do with the livestock to be sure that they don't go to town when the weather is cold and lose a lot of weight, you watch the weather all the time."[40] His early interest in the weather is splendidly expressed in yet another early letter to Bess dated 10 June 1912:

> ... [The corn] has to be plowed, you know, whether school keeps or not. We are also anticipating (spelled right?) a hay crop this week too. Would have had it up by this [time] if it hadn't been for the rain. We ought to have dry weather this week, though. You know, the moon changed in the evening. When it comes before dinner it's a sign of rain. Didn't work last year, though. Mark [Twain] says, all signs fail when it's dry so it's best to carry your own bottle.[41]

It should be noted that although Truman credits Mark Twain as being the source, this American author is by no means the originator of the weather proverb "All signs fail when it is dry," which has been recorded in an American almanac[42] in the United States as early as 1729.

In a chapter entitled "Truman at the Rostrum" in his intriguing book on *The Truman Persuasions* (1981), Robert Underhill underlines Truman's inclination toward certain axioms, colloquialisms, and metaphors. While this scholar does not mention proverbial language by that name, he must have had it in mind when stating that "Truman liked to use vernacular expressions, and frequently his words were common but pungent."[43] His affinity for folk speech is also evident in Truman's occasional use of profanity. Throughout his speeches and writings, one can clearly discern a predilection toward expressions employing the words "damn," "hell," and "son-of-a-bitch." As Underhill has correctly pointed out, "[S]o much has been written about Truman's use of profanity that he often is pictured as an uncouth and frequently vulgar person. The picture could hardly be more distorted. There is no doubt that once in a while he did use language ordinarily considered obscene, and because that language was uttered by the president of the United States it offended some persons."[44] Judged by some of his predecessors in office or by Richard M. Nixon's private records, Truman's colloquial language is actually less profane and obscene.

The one book which did much to disseminate the idea that Truman used what is now euphemistically called "adult language" was Merle Miller's appropriately entitled *Plain Speaking: An Oral Biography of Harry S. Truman* (1974). Throughout this book Miller quotes Truman as using many profane expressions, especially also employing the word "ass." It has come to light in the meantime that Miller did not always stick faithfully to the tape recordings of the interviews that he conducted with Truman for this book during 1962. He clearly let his imagination get the better of him at times, and at least some of Truman's questionable utterances must be taken *cum grano salis,* as has been shown in a magazine article called "Plain Faking" by Robert H. Ferrell and Francis H. Heller.[45] Robert Alan Aurthur, however, in his article on "The Wit and Sass of Harry S Truman" (1971), actually corroborates Truman's use of expressions containing the word "ass." His essay is based on his contacts with Truman during 1961–62 while the president was being filmed and interviewed with Miller present as well.[46] Truman most likely let his guard down on occasion and used his share of mild profanities. However, I did not find a single example of such expletives as "shit" or "fuck" in Truman's published works. They are, of course, also not present in Miller's and Aurthur's publications.

Two examples suffice to illustrate Truman's use of such expressions as "to kick someone in the ass" and "to make an ass out of oneself." The first was used in a telephone conversation with White House aide Steven Early on 22 March 1939. The transcript appears to indicate that Truman might not have uttered the word "ass" itself:

> Well, I'm here, at your request, and I damn near got killed getting here by plane in time to vote, as I did on another occasion. I don't think the bill amounts to a tinker's dam, and I expect to get kicked in the —— just as I always have in the past in return for my services.[47]

The second text is a very short, humorous diary note written on 22 December 1950, in which Truman actually plays with both phrases. The second expression is, however, merely alluded to in this pun:

> Frank Land had a dinner for the Red Cross of Constantine. He asked Roy Roberts to speak. Made an ass of himself, and I gave him a kick where it would do the most good to anybody else—but his anatomy is so surrounded with lard that he didn't feel the kick![48]

Again, these texts are nothing but sarcastic or humorous statements without any conscious attempt to be obscene whatsoever. In fact, they appear rather harmless indeed in comparison with the free use of expletives today.

There is no need for revisionism regarding Truman's use of colorful folk speech including a few obscenities. Who is going to begrudge the man the use of the phrase "to be an old fart" in a letter that he dashed off to the *Washington Post* publisher Philip Graham after music critic Paul Hume had published an unfavorable review of one of Margaret's concerts?

> Why don't you fire this frustrated old fart and hire a music reviewer who knows what he's talking about? At least you should send somebody with him to a piano recital who knows the score.

This review is a disgraceful piece of poppycock. You should be ashamed of having printed it. You're not, of course, because the publicity sheets are never wrong.[49]

Truman was always aware of the profane nature of true folk speech. This is documented in a letter to Bess dated 32 [actually 31] May 1911:

Vivian and Mr. McBroom are plowing corn just north of the house and their language is forceful to say the least when they go to turn here at the house. A horse when he is hitched to a cultivator can make a religious crank use profanity. It is not possible to reach him as your hands are full holding the plow, so you have to take it out in strong talk.[50]

Since Truman was courting Bess at that time, he probably did not want to offend her by citing the actual words and phrases used by the frustrated farmers. Later, however, Truman did not shy away from using colorful language in letters to his wife. Here is a quite outspoken letter from 21 August 1940, in which a frustrated Truman vents his feelings in some choice expressions:

Mr. Boyle Clark from Columbia came in to see me this morning. He is Mr. Stark's [Lloyd Stark, governor of Missouri] great friend—wanted to know if I had heard from the gov., and [I] told him I hadn't and didn't want to hear from the S.O.B. and that so far as I am concerned I didn't give a damn what he did or intended to do, and that I hoped he'd tell him just that. Then he wanted to know if I was angry at Stark's followers. I told him I wasn't, but they would all be in the bandwagon anyway [in November] for most of 'em hated the gov. as badly as I do. He said that is a fact and left in a good humor.[51]

In a letter to Ethel Noland dated 2 February 1952, Truman explains how he even gave his vice president the idea of using a few choice words and phrases to overcome his frustrations: "My poor V.P. fidgeted and squirmed and I being a Missourian was highly amused. Finally I said to him 'You tell the old S.O.B. [Winthrop Aldrich, president of Chase National Bank] to go to hell. I didn't want to see him anyway.'"[52] Truman in early 1949 received a letter from the Rev. Raymond B. Kimbrell, pastor of a Kansas City Methodist church, that scolded him for "cussing" in public. The chief executive defended his use of "damn" and "hell" once and for all in a short statement on 12 April 1949: "Public use of emphatic language, in certain cases, is a prerogative the President will never forego. . . . Best of luck to you and may you eventually become a tolerant, honest, good religious leader."[53] Truman must have had second thoughts about his sarcasm at the end of the letter because he never mailed it. He instead stuck to his guns by using "emphatic language" from time to time.

There is another type of emphatic and proverbial language which Truman used primarily as a young man. He fell into the trap of employing stereotypical expressions about African Americans, Jews, immigrants, and others. This formulaic prejudicial language was probably used unconsciously, and in any case, as Robert H. Ferrell has pointed out, "Truman unloaded his prejudices in advance of most of his contemporaries in the United States who learned only through the object lessons of Adolf Hitler."[54] The strongest statement that Truman seems to have made along these lines is the following in a letter to Bess on 22 June 1911:

> I think one man is just as good as another so long as he's honest and decent and not a nigger or a Chinaman. Uncle Will says that the Lord made a white man from dust, a nigger from mud, then threw up what was left and it came down a Chinaman. He does hate Chinese and Japs. So do I. It is race prejudice I guess. But I am strongly of the opinion that negroes ought to be in Africa, yellow men in Asia, and white men in Europe and America.[55]

It is especially in the form of proverbial comparisons that Truman employs prejudicial language. Hundreds of such stereotypes have been collected by folklorists,[56] and in comparison with many of the slurs contained in large collections, Truman's isolated phrases appear quite mild. Nevertheless, here are a few examples to show how Truman, who later fought valiantly for civil rights in the United States, was not above such ever-ready formulas:

> . . . you do have to work like a coon.[57]

> . . . he screamed like a Jewish merchant.[58]

> Byrnes said here I am at Bennett's suggestion all dressed up like a nigga preacher.[59]

> . . . I'm writing this as impudently as a sassy nigger.[60]

> I'm as red as an Indian.[61]

All these citations come from letters to Bess, in which Truman did not have to pay heed to what effects his language might have in public life. In his speeches and formal writing, he refrained from their use and instead delivered a very significant address as senator to the Convention of the National Colored Democratic Association on 14 July 1940 at Chicago with the title "The New Deal for the Negro." This speech includes the following paragraph which expresses Truman's honest thoughts on civil rights:

Ignorance breeds all of the festering prejudices of our human family. The fraternizing sentiments of mankind are products of education. In my opinion, greater educational facilities for the Negro would be a blessing to him and at the same time a great boon to society at large. If white men wish to do better for themselves, it would be well for them to give more definite attention to the education of the Negro.[62]

Proverbial language with stereotypical or obscene connotations thus plays only a small role in Truman's rich repertoire of folk speech. The real "vintage Trumanisms," as special assistant in the White House office Ken Hechler called the president's colorful folk language,[63] are honest-to-God plain expressions of common people. They are, as Robert Underhill has aptly put it, "echoes from language he heard during his youth and early manhood—language patterns which often came from a strong-willed mother who set forth simple wisdoms phrased in a positive style."[64]

Truman made ample use of this proverbial folk speech in his early public addresses in the 1920s as a young politician in Jackson County, Missouri, while his rhetorical style at the same time "was anchored to the bedrock of cold, pure facts."[65] Reflecting on his many speaking engagements in an interview on 12 August 1953, Truman answered the question "What does the typical audience expect from a speaker?" in the following manner:

People don't listen to a speaker just to admire his techniques or his manner: they go to learn. They want the meat of the speech—a direct statement of the facts and proof that the facts are correct—not oratorical trimmings. Of course, the political speaker must remember that the education of the average man is limited. Therefore, he must make his message as simple and clear as possible. Listeners have to feel a bond with the speaker; they aren't likely to if they believe he is a "high-hat" or "show-off." On the other hand, in working for simplicity, one has to avoid "talking down" to the audience.[66]

He followed the principle of straightforward rhetoric based on facts, clarity, and simplicity in all of his official speeches, interspersing them with colloquial language whenever that suited the purpose of adding life to the dry facts. This pattern is clearly visible in an early speech that Truman delivered to the four thousand Democrats assembled at Oak Grove, Missouri, in July 1922. He cites a lot of facts and figures that form the basis of his solution to a number of political issues, but he also makes an emotional demonstration of his concept of loyalty in his praise for his friend and war-comrade John Miles, who had received Truman's vote as the Republican candidate for the office of County Marshall:

You have heard it said that I voted for John Miles for County Marshall. I'll have to plead guilty to that charge along with some 5,000 other ex-soldiers.

> I was closer to John Miles than a brother. I have seen him in places that would make hell look like a playground. I have seen him stick to his guns when Frenchmen were falling back. I have seen him hold the American line when only John Miles and his three batteries were between the Germans and a successful counter-attack. He was of the right stuff and a man who didn't vote for his comrade under circumstances such as these would be untrue to himself and his country.[67]

Truman connects several proverbial expressions to add deeply felt emotion to what he has to say. He obviously is also very much aware that his listeners will react positively to this clear and straightforward language with its rich metaphors known to everybody.

The speeches of Senator Truman follow the same pattern. They are usually so factual that they cannot possibly be considered oratorical masterpieces.[68] Although Truman admired that great rhetorician Cicero, these addresses can hardly hold a candle to that ingenious speaker. Truman was quite aware of this difference:

> I believe an audience approves of Cicero's method, which was to state his case and then prove it. That is what I always try to do. Charlie Ross [President Truman's press secretary] and I used to translate Cicero's orations from the Latin. I guess I have read almost all of his speeches. They are models of clarity and simplicity. I wish I could do half as well.[69]

The high points of his Senate speeches usually come when he ends a paragraph of facts and figures to drive home a point by way of a proverbial phrase. What follows are four contextualized examples of this *modus operandi* from speeches delivered between 1939 and 1944. They are of special interest since they also reflect the stress and emotions of wartime politics. Prior to the start of World War II, Truman, on 16 March 1939, comments on the dangerous world situation and uses a common proverbial expression to declare that America must ever be vigilant:

> If this great Nation of ours were divided into 48 independent governments with 40 different languages and dialects, we'd be having the same trouble that Europe is having. Suspicion of neighbors and neighbor States comes about through ignorance and lack of understanding. I am one who hopes eventually for world peace, but until that time comes I am also one who wants the Nation to "keep its powder dry."[70]

In the following paragraph from a speech of 12 December 1942, Truman warns of too much taxation as the war effort intensifies, and once again finds a well-known metaphorical phrase to underscore his comment:

> New plans for increasing tax revenues are constantly being made. New sources of additional tax revenues are continually being sought, but the tax

burden is becoming increasingly harder to bear. We must always bear in mind that taxation when made too severe destroys the subject upon which it is sought to be levied. If we keep on piling tax upon tax there will come a time when we pile on the last straw that will break the camel's back.[71]

The third example is drawn from Truman's speech of 6 April 1943 on the necessity for rationing during World War II, a proposition that was not eagerly welcomed:

> Let's see what rationing is. First, it is not starvation, long bread lines, shoddy goods. . . . Second, it is American. The earliest settlers of this country, facing scarcities of food and clothing, pooled their precious supplies and apportioned them out to everyone on an equal basis. It was an American idea then, and it is an American idea now, to share and share alike; to sacrifice when necessary, but to sacrifice together, because the country's welfare demands it.[72]

This is impressive political argumentation in its call to patriotism, even though in fact the proverb "to share and share alike" has been traced back to 1571 in England.[73] Its philosophy is thus not only American, as Truman seems to be saying to strengthen his proverbial argument. And finally, there is Senator Truman's speech of 6 March 1944, in which he accurately declares that a turning point of World War II had been reached due to America's valiant participation:

> We are now in the third year of this terrible war. We are spurred by the grim determination to wage this war relentlessly on all fronts and on all seas until all those who have chosen to live by the sword have perished by it. We now have neither the time nor the inclination for self-appraisal. But when the time comes for the historians to write the record of our participation in this great struggle they will undoubtedly state that at this present period we had reached the turning point of the war.[74]

What an effective rhetorical style Truman employs here by consciously drawing on his rich store of biblical proverbs to prophesy eventual victory by the Allies. Although the Bible says, "All they that take the sword shall perish with the sword" (Matt. 26:52), Truman varies the passage to fit his syntax and is obviously also aware that the biblical passage is usually cited as a folk proverb in the form of "He who lives by the sword shall perish by the sword." His listeners doubtlessly understood his powerful message that the war could be and had to be won.

Truman constantly shifts back and forth from using proverbs in their accepted wording to changing them to fit his special rhetorical needs. When he makes changes, he can still count on people's recognition of the traditional text, and this juxtaposition of tradition and innovation results in effective communication.[75] The same is true when Truman merely alludes to a proverb by truncating it. His listeners doubtlessly enjoyed completing the verbal wisdom, and Truman thus succeeded in getting them involved both mentally and emotionally. A few examples of many illustrate this communicative method with adapted proverbs:

> I'd rather . . . be sure someone wasn't killing two birds.[76]

> That gate always reminds me of the camel and the needle's eye.[77]

> We must have a good healthy body if we are going to have a good healthy mind.[78]

> But people like Mike Mansfield . . . can see that acorn as a giant oak tree.[79]

Yet there are also numerous textual examples of Truman's integration of complete proverbs into his speeches and writings. When cited in their traditional wording, these proverbs usually take on the function of supporting an argument, proving a point, and teaching a simple lesson. It is the latter use that plays a major role in Truman's verbal communication. He quite likes himself in the role of teacher, if not preacher, and obviously exact proverbs are suitable to spreading pithy wisdom among the common people. A few representative examples illustrate Truman's mastery of straight proverb use:

> . . . I've been in a position where I have had to act—and actions speak louder than words.[80]

> . . . the chickens usually come home to roost.[81]

> . . . you know hell is paved with "good intentions."[82]

> It is remarkable indeed how time flies and makes you an old man.[83]

There is, however, also a remarkable example of Truman's taking a traditional three-word proverb and simply altering the word order to express a better idea, one that would be appropriate for a democracy: ". . . we will be forced to accept the fundamental concept of our enemies, namely, that 'Might makes right.' . . . We must, once and for all, reverse the order, and prove by our acts conclusively, that Right Has Might."[84] But how surprised would Truman the "phrase forger"[85] have been, if he had known that his anti-proverb[86] "Right makes might" has existed in English since the early fourteenth century.[87]

There is no doubt that Truman comes into his own as "proverbialist" in the numerous short "whistle-stop" speeches that he delivered throughout the country during the presidential campaign of 1948. There is an entire body of scholarly literature by political scientists, historians, and rhetoricians on this method of campaigning from the rear platform of a railroad car and the new type of rhetorical skills that these speeches of few minutes' duration demanded. In his memoirs Truman makes the following matter-of-fact statement regarding these mini-talks:

> The technique I used at the whistle stops was simple and straightforward. There were no special "gimmicks" or oratorical devices. I refused to be "coached." I simply told the people in my own language that they had better wake up to the fact that it was their fight.[88]

While Truman used some notes to comment on local issues, he talked primarily "off the cuff" and was a smashing success. Truman proved that he could be an effective extemporaneous speaker,[89] whose impromptu delivery gave "his speeches a new punch and lift totally lacking when he mechanically read from a manuscript."[90] Cole S. Brembeck has analyzed "Harry Truman at the Whistle Stops" (1952) in great detail and stated that his over three hundred speeches were delivered in the "Missouri vernacular," were "folksy," and made use of "the idiom of village and town, country road and main street."[91] Interestingly enough, nobody has made any direct comment regarding Truman's obvious reliance on rich proverbial speech at the whistle-stops, with the possible exception of Edward Rogge, who includes a list of fifteen contextualized "figures of speech" [some of which are proverbial expressions] in his dissertation, "The Speechmaking of Harry S. Truman" (1958).[92]

Truman himself gives us his own explanation of how the phrase "whistle-stops" originated:

> Robert Taft [Republican Senator from Ohio] started it, and he wished he hadn't. Somebody asked him what was happening on my tour, and he said that I was lambasting Congress at all kinds of "whistle-stops across the country." Of course some of the boys at the national committee picked that right up and got word out to towns all across the country about what Taft had said, and the mayors of those towns didn't like it a bit. It did us no harm at all at the polls in November, of course.
>
> . . . and some of those towns had populations of a hundred thousand people and more, including Los Angeles, of course, and, after that, the whole campaign became what was called a whistle-stop campaign, and I saw to it in my speeches that people remembered what Taft had said about their towns.[93]

A few contextualized excerpts from the many speeches suffice as illustrations of Truman's proverbial "plain speaking" to the American people. Again and again he emphasizes that he wants to speak plainly and to make things perfectly plain. The result is proverbial rhetoric spiced with vivid images that every middle-class American voter could relate to without any difficulty:

So don't forget that on November the 2d, if you believe that the paramount issue in this campaign is the special interests against the people, you will go and vote the straight Democratic ticket, and save the country. That is what I hope you will do. I hope you will join me in this crusade to keep the country from going to the dogs.[94]

And what we are trying to do is sell the world on the idea that peace is the best policy. As old Benjamin Franklin said: honesty is the best policy. If you study that a long time, it has implications. Well, in our day: peace is the best policy for the world.[95]

That [80th] Congress immediately began to turn the clock back. You can't turn the clock back. In the 1920's, we tried our best to turn the clock back, and go back into our shells, go back to 1908. It didn't work.[96]

But it is important for the people of this country to recognize that time has not changed the fundamental outlook of the Republican Party since it was last in power. The leopard has not changed his spots; he has merely hired some public relations experts. They have taught him to wear sheep's clothing, and to pour sweet nothings about unity in a soothing voice. But it's the same old leopard.[97]

This soft talk and double talk, this combination of crafty silence and resounding misrepresentation, is an insult to the intelligence of the American voter. It proceeds upon the assumption that you *can* fool all the people—or enough of them—all the time.[98]

From North to South, from East to West, I am getting reports that States are with us. The people's crusade is rolling along to victory, and it is going to leave the Republican polltakers flat on their faces on November the 3d.[99]

But, keeping quiet on the issues that are important to the people is not my way of doing business. I would rather be defeated for trying to do what is right than to hide my views from the people and get in there under false pretenses. I never sit on a fence. I am either on one side or another.[100]

The more whistle-stops Truman made, the more excited he got about his talk with the people. He sensed that he was on a proverbial roll toward the end of the campaign. Steadily moving forward, he refused "to turn the clock back," as he accused the Republicans of doing. Truman used this proverbial expression forty-six times in 1948, far more than any other phrase, turning it into the battle cry of the entire campaign.[101] In a speech at Elyria, Ohio, on 26 October 1948, he exclaimed confidently, ". . . a good name for this train ought to be, 'The People's Special,' because my campaign is being fought for the benefit of all the people."[102] The voters believed him and elected him against overwhelming odds to his own well-deserved term as president of the United States.[103]

Much has been written about Truman's use of ghost writers for his prepared speeches. The employment of amanuenses has a long tradition with American presidents, and Truman is not unique in this regard. An anonymous magazine report from 10 November 1950 actually went so far as to run the headline "Truman Sets Up a Speech Factory,"[104] over a story on Truman's speechwriting team, which included Clark Clifford, Charles S. Murphy, David D. Lloyd, and George McKee Elsey. All helped in the formulation of Truman's many addresses, but without Truman's ever letting go of his personal control of what was eventually said and how it was worded.[105] Some speeches went through a dozen versions or more, and the president always had the final say with the ultimate approval of the "Boss," as Bess Truman was affectionately referred to in the White House. An anonymous note in the *New York Times* of 27 November 1949 even claims that she is the one "to make sure that the President says the things he wants to say in a homey, native Missouri style."[106] Charles G. Ross, Truman's press secretary, published in 1948 an account of the relationship between Truman and his speechwriters during the 1948 campaign. Although some professional writers were used at times, Ross describes the main team of writers as people who "knew the president, knew his ideas, knew the kind of sentences and words he liked." Even though the speechwriters shared this intimate knowledge of the president, Ross writes that heated arguments still could erupt during speech-revising sessions, and when they did Truman "would grin and say 'All right, you fellows fight it out and I'll decide.'"[107] Ross makes clear that Truman always had the last word. Truman, with typical wit, acknowledged the contributions of his speechwriters in this way: "Did you ever see a marked-up copy of the Declaration of Independence, in which Franklin and the rest of those fellows made inserts? It looks just like one of my speeches when I write one and my people go to work on it, and those changes are usually improvements, too."[108] In his memoirs, Truman describes the relationship more seriously and indicates his own sense of responsibility for his speeches:

> All presidential messages must begin with the President himself. He must decide what he wants to say and how he wants to say it. Many drafts are usually drawn up, and this fact leads to the assumption that presidential speeches are "ghosted." The final version, however, is the final word of the President himself, expressing his own convictions and his policy. These he cannot delegate to any man if he would be President in his own right.[109]

From everything that various administrators and speechwriters of the Truman presidency have said, it can be stated that the colloquial and proverbial language in particular in his speeches appears to be Truman's home-made variety. At least nobody has made any other claim to the contrary, and other writings by the former president bear out this claim. After all, proverbial language can be found in all of his writings and especially in his off-the-cuff speeches.

This also holds true for his numerous news conferences, although they were usually quite short because Truman gave precise and laconic answers. While he did not mince words at these meetings, he had a few favorite expressions that he used to stop persistent questioning by the journalists. His use of "Wait and see" thirty-six times, "I'll cross that bridge when I get to it" thirty-four times, and "Your guess is as good as mine" eighteen times is an indication of how proverbial language can be used to avoid answering a question.[110] They certainly present a welcome alternative to the colorless "No comment," which Truman also interjected often.[111] Two examples suffice to indicate the flavor of his proverbial exchanges with journalists, who actually enjoyed this type of verbal dueling. The first took place on 2 September 1948 and relates to a previous press conference on 5 August 1948, when Truman had declared that the investigation of government employees as to communist leanings was a useless proverbial "red herring":[112]

> Q. It has been charged that you are protecting Communists.
> THE PRESIDENT. Of course, that is just a lie out of the whole cloth, and you know it. I never protected Communists or any other disloyal people. You know, the spies that really caused us trouble during the war were not Russians. Russia was our ally. The spies were Germans and Japanese. I have never heard anything about a search for them. They were our enemies, if I remember correctly.
> Q. That's a pretty good quote, "a lie out of the whole cloth." What about it?
> THE PRESIDENT. Go ahead, quote it. It's true. It's also a plain lie. I never protected a disloyal person in my life.
> Q. It's the quote which makes the statement.
> THE PRESIDENT. Make it a quote. It's all right. You can use it.
> Q. May we quote "just a plain lie"?
> THE PRESIDENT. A lie out of the whole cloth, that's what it is, just a lie out of the whole cloth. I could give it an adjective, but you wouldn't print it. [*Laughter*].[113]

Truman had established a policy that journalists were not allowed to quote him directly, and that is the reason for the repeated question regarding the permission to do so.[114] A similar exchange took place at a news conference on 20 February 1952, which once again ended in congenial laughter:

> Q. Have you any comment on the action of the House Judiciary Subcommittee yesterday in deciding not to give immunity powers to Mr. Morris [Newbold Morris, Special Assistant to the Attorney General]?

THE PRESIDENT. The only reason that those immunity powers were requested for Mr. Morris was to give him an opportunity to do a bangup job. I have no comment to make on the action of the House Committee. They have been very anxious to have a bangup job done, and I tried to give him the power necessary so he could do that sort of job. There wasn't any bug under the chip, or anything of the kind.

Q. What, sir? [*Laughter*]

THE PRESIDENT. There was not any bug under the chip, or anything of the kind.

Q. Bug under the chip?

THE PRESIDENT. That's right. [*Laughter*].[115]

Here one senses the journalists' disbelief of what they are hearing. The president is obviously throwing them for a loop with a folk expression that he realizes they have never heard before (it means something like "a skeleton in the closet"), and he is enjoying it. At the end, there is a good laugh for everyone, and one assumes that this colloquialism made the rounds in Washington.

On 29 March 1952, President Truman decided not to run for a second term. He poured his energy that fall into a new whistle-stop campaign on behalf of the Democratic Party and its candidate Adlai E. Stevenson. During this campaign, he reached another high point in employing proverbs and proverbial expressions for his political aims, although he could not prevent Dwight D. Eisenhower's winning the election. In the following excerpts, Truman delights in manipulating standard proverbs and approaches a mud-slinging campaign style in his ridicule of the Republican Party and General Eisenhower:

To say that the Republicans are the party of low prices is like saying that the shark is man's best friend, or that tigers make nice household pets.[116]

The Republican platform and the Republican candidate for President have nothing to say about this issue [regarding immigration laws]. Their silence speaks louder than words.[117]

Now when you take a man who has spent his whole life in the Army and put him in politics, he's just like a fish out of water. It would be just the same as if I would take the mayor of my hometown and put him in command of NATO in France. He wouldn't be any more at sea than Eisenhower is right now.[118]

If the General's strategy is successful, then the American people are a lot easier to fool than I think they are. The General should take a tip from a truly great Republican, and a man of principle—Abraham Lincoln. He just can't hope to fool all of the people all of the time. They are too smart.[119]

This last truncated use of Lincoln's famous and by now proverbial declaration that "You can fool some of the people all the time, all the people some of the time, but can't fool all the people all the time" with its concluding reference to the smart voters surely must have met with approval by Truman's Democratic audience. Shortly before the election, in a speech on 1 November 1952 in St. Louis, Truman returned to his favorite 1948 campaign expression of "not turning the clock back." This time he summarized his new whistle-stop campaign with the following statement, which also picks up once again the idea of fooling people: "I have talked to the voters, and they have been talking to me. And I do not believe they are going to turn the clock back. The people of this country know the difference between the Democratic Party and the Republican Party—and the Republicans can't fool them."[120] Yet Eisenhower won the election, and the two men never were able to build up a friendly feeling of mutual respect in subsequent years.

Truman had worked very hard indeed at being a decent and effective president, and historians and political scientists alike consider him one of the best leaders this country has ever had. As he ran the country during the tumultuous years of the end of World War II and the beginning of the Cold War, this small man of humble and plain origin grew to fill the shoes of his revered predecessor in the Oval Office. In numerous texts Truman reflects in proverbial language on his strenuous and challenging task of taking over the ship of state after President Franklin D. Roosevelt's death on 12 April 1945. On that day he wrote in his diary:

> I was very much shocked. I am not easily shocked but was certainly shocked when I was told of the President's death and the weight of the Government had fallen on my shoulders. I did not know what reaction the country would have to the death of a man whom they all practically worshipped. I was worried about the reaction of the Armed Forces. I did not know what effect the situation would have on the war effort, price control, war production and everything that entered into the emergency that then existed. I knew the President had a great many meetings with Churchill and Stalin. I was not familiar with any of these things and it was really something to think about but I decided to go home and get as much rest as possible and face the music.[121]

The two proverbial expressions included in this paragraph epitomize Truman's vision of himself as president—a man carrying the burden of the country on his shoulders and facing the music of world politics squarely. As he correctly points out, Roosevelt had left his vice president pretty much in the dark as far as major decisions were concerned. Yet Truman found himself confronted by powerful and experienced world players like Churchill and Stalin. He soon learned to stand his ground against these two political masters, as can be seen from a letter that he wrote to Bess on 20 July 1945 while bargaining with them at the Potsdam Conference outside of Berlin:

> We had a tough meeting yesterday. I reared up on my hind legs and told 'em where to get off and they got off. I have to make it perfectly plain to them at least once a day that so far as this President is concerned Santa Claus is dead and that my first interest is U.S.A, then I want the Jap War won and I want 'em both in it. Then I want peace—world peace and will do what can be done by us to get it. But certainly am not going to set up another [illegible] here in Europe, pay reparations, feed the world, and get nothing for it but a nose thumbing. They are beginning to awake to the fact that I mean business.[122]

This is certainly not a love letter to his bride back home at the White House! Rather it is a plain-talking epistle with five proverbial expressions in it telling his wife how he, small but tough Harry, is telling Churchill and Stalin where to get off, because he really means to take charge at this conference. This is, of course, not a masterfully crafted letter, but it expresses Truman's mood in splendid metaphorical language. To Bess it must have shown that her husband, even though he now was the leader of the free world, had not really changed in his speech or manner.

Other such revealing letters by Truman to Bess not only show that he was able to share with her his private reflections on world politics, but also record the intimate, ordinary, and often proverbial language he used to describe his political concerns. Here is a short excerpt from a letter to Bess, dated 27 September 1947, which contains three proverbial phrases:

> . . . The world seems to be topsy-turvy, but when you read the history after the Napoleonic Wars and the first World War they are no worse, only over more territory.
>
> I can't see why it was necessary for me to inherit all difficulties and tribulations of the world—but I have them on hand and must work them out some way—I hope for the welfare of all concerned.
>
> Russia has at last shown her hand and it contains the cards [George] Marshall and I thought it would.
>
> All we can do is go ahead working for peace—and keep our powder dry.[123]

The "topsy-turvy" world, as Truman described it to Bess, was of course the beginnings of the Cold War that was to dominate international politics for the next several decades. Truman had already in 1945, after arguing with the Soviet Union over how to set up the United Nations, jotted down private notes that express his distrust of communism. In these notes he argues against the dangerous proverb "The end justifies the means" and champions the "Golden Rule" as the right guiding principle for humanity:

> I've no faith in any totalitarian state, be it Russian, German, Spanish, Argentinean, Dago, or Japanese. They all start with a wrong premise—that lies are justified and that the old, disproven Jesuit formula, the end justifies the means, is right and necessary to maintain the power of government. I don't agree. . . . Honest Communism, as set out in the "Acts of the Apostles," would work. But the Russian Godless Pervert Systems won't work. . . . The combined thought and action of the whole people of any race, creed, or nationality will always point in the right direction—"As ye would others should do unto you do ye also unto them."
>
> Confucius, Buddha, Christ, and all moralists come to the same conclusion.[124]

Here at the close he invokes the wisdom of several traditions as supporting the universal authority of the proverbial Golden Rule, an idea which, as I mentioned earlier in this chapter, he returns to some seven years later in his personal diary. Less than a week after his 27 September 1947 letter Truman wrote again to Bess about the deepening Cold War between the former Allies, this time referring with some hope to the same biblical proverb: "Treaties, agreements, or a moral code mean nothing to Communists. So we've got to organize the people who do believe in honor and the Golden Rule to win the world back to peace and Christianity."[125]

The pressures Truman was experiencing in the summer of 1948 can be seen in a short letter of July 10th, in which he thanks Churchill for sending him a copy of his book *The Gathering Storm* (1948):[126]

> I was deeply touched by your good letter of June 7. I am going through a terrible "trial by fire." Too bad it must happen at this time.
>
> Your great country and mine are founded on the fact that the people have the right to express themselves on their leaders, no matter what the crisis. . . .
>
> We are in the midst of grave and trying times. You can look with satisfaction on your great contribution to the overthrow of Nazism + Fascism in the world.
>
> "Communism"—so-called, is our next great problem. I hope we can solve it without the "blood and tears" the other two [world wars] cost.[127]

Surely Churchill remembered many proverbial "trials by fire" in his own long political career, and Truman's truncated quotation of Churchill's "blood, toil, tears and sweat" phrase is a powerful reference to the suffering and destruction that a possible third world war might bring. In speech after speech Truman reiterated his belief in the superiority of a free society to the oppressive Communist system. Once again resorting to a proverbial image in his 9 January 1952 State of the Union message to Congress, Truman drew a definite line between the United States and the Soviet Union:

> This demonstration [he had talked about various measures to advance America's free society] of the way free men govern themselves has a more powerful influence on the people of the world—on both sides of the Iron Curtain—than all the trick slogans and pie-in-the-sky promises of the Communists.[128]

Truman always believed in the inherent good of a democratic system but also noted that it had to be nurtured and protected. Always having the dangers of the Cold War in mind, he wrote and spoke numerous times about the obligations and responsibilities of the citizenry to maintain freedom and democracy in the United States.[129] In a letter to Edward F. McFaddin dated 29 September 1958, he returned to Churchill's proverbial quotation to suggest that these societal and human values need to be earned:

> You see the future of this great country depends entirely on the coming generations and their understanding of what they have and what was done to create it, and what they must do to keep it.
> It took "sweat, blood and tears" to create it and maintain it. Unless the coming generations are willing to make the sacrifices necessary to keep it, this great Republic will go as did the city states of Greece, the Roman republic and the Dutch republic.[130]

A few months later, in a letter of 21 January 1959 to Stanley E. Whiteway, Truman repeats the same thoughts and uses Churchill's formula once again:

> These young people must understand that our great Government was obtained by "blood, sweat and tears" and a thousand years of effort on the part of the great thinkers over that period and blood-letting revolutions and sacrifices by the people. Why, we even had to spend four bloody years whipping ourselves to make the Constitution work. And we are still at it—trying to make it work![131]

Always the historian, Truman at times gives regular history lessons in his speeches and letters. Referring to how civilizations have fared over the centuries, he concludes his letter of 19 December 1959 to James I. Robertson with a wonderfully humorous and yet relevant pun based on a well-known proverbial expression. These final sentences also show that Truman the teacher and moralist can be funny at times, and that he never loses his touch with the expressive power of folk speech:

> We are their [former civilizations] successors. What can we do to prevent our fate from going down the same road? We must—come hell or high water. We have control of hell, and high water has gone by the board—unless the ice caps melt. It is up to this great Republic to profit by history's mistakes.
>
> Let's do it![132]

The phrase "Come hell or high water" was doubtlessly one of Truman's favorites, and he even used it to describe his life in the White House in a letter to Bess dated 7 September 1950: "As usual I'm having hell and high water every day. But I seem to thrive on it."[133] A short diary note of 2 September 1951 describes in vivid terms one of the "little" frustrations of a president. Thank God, however, that there are those proverbial phrases to vent one's feelings:

> The Lord Mayor of London is supposed to call on me today. He didn't show up!
>
> I find that he is in Ottawa, Canada, and that his call is to take place on Sept. 16th!
>
> Well, it is hell when things at the top get balled up.[134]

Who, then, will be surprised to find Truman in his second year at the helm of the country write the simple yet telling sentence to his wife on 10 August 1946: "It sure is hell to be President."[135] One can imagine that this saying has long since become proverbial among our presidents!

The word "hell" plays a dominant role in Truman's basic vocabulary, and this is also reflected in his use of that term in proverbial expressions.[136] In his published works alone we find "to give someone hell"[137] twenty times, "to go to hell" twelve times, "to raise hell" seven times, "Come hell or high water" six times, "Hell is paved with good intentions" three times, "to hell with someone" two times, and other expressions as well.[138] But the phrase "Give 'em hell, Harry" is the one that has truly become proverbial in America. Although Truman did not originate it, he clearly enjoyed being associated with it, since he refers to it nine times in his speeches and writings. He himself has explained several times how he came to use this proverbial campaign slogan. Asked "Why do people in political audiences always call to you, 'Give 'em Hell Harry,'" Truman gave the following answer in 1960:

> Well, that started out in the Northwest, in Seattle, Washington. It was in 1948, and we were holding an enthusiastic meeting there when some man with a great big voice cried from the galleries, "Give 'em hell, Harry!" I told him at that time, and I have been repeating it ever since, that I have never deliberately given anybody hell. I just tell the truth on the opposition—and they think it's hell.[139]

What Truman failed to mention is that this slogan had also repeatedly appeared in political caricatures depicting him as a vigorous campaigner and an outspoken former president.[140] At least three books have used this slogan in their titles: Eldorous L. Dayton's book with the somewhat overstated subtitle, *Give 'em Hell* [sic] *Harry: An Informal Biography of The Terrible Tempered Mr. T.* (1956); Mark Goodman's *Give 'em Hell, Harry!* (New York: Award, 1974); and Samuel Gallu's *"Give 'em Hell, Harry!"* (New York: Dunetz and Lovert, 1975). The slogan was also used as a marketing strategy for a sound recording of some of his speeches.[141]

Truman's "fun" with this phrase came during his whistle-stop tour during the 1952 presidential campaign. People had not forgotten it four years after its origin in 1948, as can be seen from remarks that Truman made in a speech on 4 October 1952:

> Now they accuse me of going up and down the Nation on a whistlestop train, and the slogans that they hurl at me most the time are "Give 'em hell, Harry." That reputation I did not earn. All I do is to tell them [the Republicans] the truth, and that hurts a lot worse than giving them hell.[142]

Two days later, on the rear platform of a train in Salt Lake City, Utah, Truman returned to this rhetorical *leitmotif*:

> You see, nearly every place I go, somebody in the crowd around the street will let out a yell "Give 'em hell, Harry." Well now, I don't strive for a reputation of that kind. I tell the truth on them [the Republicans], and that's a lot better for the country than giving them hell, because they can't stand the truth.[143]

That is pretty strong medicine to which Truman adds a bit of humor in yet another alteration of this effective reaction to an established campaign slogan:

> Everywhere I go I see signs or people yelling "Give 'em hell, Harry." Well now, that is an awful reputation for a good Baptist to get, and I am telling you what I am doing—I am telling the truth and giving you issues, and that is a lot worse than giving the Republicans hell, because they can't stand the truth.[144]

Of course, Truman did in fact give his opponents "hell" at times, especially in his fights with the 80th "Do-Nothing" Congress. When the young President John F. Kennedy experienced his troubles with the Republicans, Truman sat down on 28 June 1962 and wrote him the following letter of advice from an old fighter who based his political program on a bit of spirited hell-giving:

> It looks as if the Republicans haven't changed a bit since 1936. Pres. Roosevelt had his troubles with them—so did I. Mr. President, you are on the right track. Don't let them tell *you* what to do—you tell them, as you have!

> Your suggestions for the public welfare, in my opinion, are correct.
> This is a personal and confidential statement for what it may be worth.
> You know my program was "Give 'em Hell" and if they don't like it give
> 'em more hell.[145]

Three proverbial expressions, and the "hell" one even cited twice, in one short letter is yet again solid proof that Truman had natural talent for using folk speech when and where it really counted. Surely Kennedy appreciated this confidential note by a respected veteran president. For the record, it should be noted that Truman here admits to his program of "giving hell."

In his voluminous *Truman* (1992) biography, David McCullough includes a long chapter entitled "The Heat in the Kitchen" and adds to it as a motto "If you can't stand the heat, you better get out of the kitchen"—a favorite Truman saying.[146] This is somewhat misleading, since Truman by his own admission neither originated the proverb nor used it very frequently. In his published works it appears only twice. In its first occurrence in a speech on 17 December 1952 in Washington, D.C., Truman states clearly where he had picked up this piece of metaphorical wisdom:

> One of the results of this system [of the president's approval powers] gives the President a good many hot potatoes to handle—but the President gets a lot of hot potatoes from every direction anyhow, and a man who can't handle them has no business in that job. That makes me think of a saying that I used to hear from my old friend and colleague on the Jackson County Court. He said, "Harry, if you can't stand the heat you better get out of the kitchen." I'll say that is absolutely true.[147]

Truman reiterated his opinion that this proverb perfectly describes the chores and frustrations of the presidency in his revealing book *Mr. Citizen* (1960), in which the following paragraph concludes his chapter on "Some Thoughts on the Presidency." It is interesting that Truman once again chooses a proverb to summarize everything he has said to describe the position of president of the United States:

> There has been a lot of talk lately about the burdens of the Presidency. Decisions that the President has to make often affect the lives of tens of millions of people around the world, but that does not mean that they should take longer to make. Some men can make decisions and some cannot. Some men fret and delay under criticism. I used to have a saying that applies here, and I note that some people have picked it up: "If you can't stand the heat, get out of the kitchen."[148]

Truman is saying here that he used to quote this proverb, and although it appears but twice in his writings, he obviously must have employed it orally to the point that others started to cite it as well. It is of little wonder then that it appears in *The Concise Oxford Dictionary of Proverbs* (1982) and also in a collection of *Sayings of the Century* (1984). Lexicographers and paremiographers, however, are wrong to name Truman the originator of the proverb.[149] He made it clear he learned the proverb elsewhere, and its author remains unknown. Some warning should also be expressed concerning the ever-popular books of quotations by our presidents. Most of these books do not give any sources, and they perpetuate the general belief that this or that president coined a particular phrase.[150] With regard to the "kitchen" proverb, it must be said that Truman's name is so attached to it by now that for Americans he will no doubt remain its apocryphal source. Robert Underhill has put it best *vis à vis* Truman quotations of all kinds: "Harry Truman was to become one of the most widely quoted of all American presidents. The quotations frequently are from phrases that were not original with him but instead were aphorisms, axioms, and common expressions well known to many persons, but he was able to give old phrases larger dimensions and newer applications."[151] Underhill does not mention proverbs in particular in this statement, and neither does Truman in his own analysis of how he chooses quotable material:

> I don't analyze what methods I am using to support my main contentions. I never decide that I must find a quotation to prove this point or a comparison to prove that point. I just use whatever materials seem to fit. Since I have never studied the niceties of speech composition, I cannot follow a set of rules or principles. Instead, I just go by a sense of "feel."[152]

This natural feeling or inclination led Truman more often than not to employ proverbial speech to drive home his point. It is no wonder that his speeches, especially those off-the-cuff whistle-stop talks, reached the common folk.

In the final pages of this chapter I'd like to take a close look at yet another expression which has undeniably become associated with Truman. As perhaps many Americans know, Truman had a sign on his desk in the White House which stated with proverbial precision, "The buck stops here." This piece of wisdom has entered the general language, it is to be found in phraseological dictionaries,[153] the mass media employ it in advertisements, cartoons, and caricatures,[154] and it has also been used as chapter headings in books on Truman.[155] While the phrase is used by many, it is not clear that they actually understand its finer linguistic and cultural points. Some probably think of "buck" in terms of money, recalling this as a slang expression for a one-dollar bill. However, in this semantic connotation the phrase makes little sense. Actually "buck" is part of a poker player's expression "to pass the buck" or simply "passing the buck," which refers to a marker which can be passed on to another player by someone who does not wish to deal the cards. In its figurative sense, the proverbial phrase has taken on the meaning of passing on a problem or responsibility.[156] The expression has been known since the nineteenth century, Mark Twain having used it in 1871 in *Roughing It:* "I reckon I can't call that hand. Ante and pass the buck."[157] In view of Truman's appreciation of Twain, it is not unreasonable to think that he might have picked up the phrase from this American author.

In any case, Truman refers to the sign on his desk twice in his many speeches. On 31 January 1951, at a dinner for the Democratic National Congressional Committee in Washington, D.C., he talked about the basic duties of a president which, reduced to the lowest common denominator, are that decisions must be made and actions must be taken: "And never a day goes by that . . . I don't have to act. And there's a sign on my desk which says, 'The Buck Stops Here.'"[158] The same theme was picked up by Truman during an address at the National War College on 19 December 1952:

> You know, it's easy enough for the Monday morning quarterback to say what the coach should have done, after the game is over. But when the decision is up before you—and on my desk I have a motto which says "The buck stops here"—the decision has to be made. That decision may be right. It may be wrong. If it is wrong, and it has been shown that it is wrong, I have no desire to cover it up. I admit it, and try to make another decision that will meet the situation. And that is what any President of the United States has to do. Just bear that in mind.[159]

Truman had related similar thoughts to Bess as early as 1918, when he served as a soldier in France. In his letter dated 30 October 1918, he talks about his precarious situation as a battery commander, who, unlike the president of the United States, gets the buck passed from both the bottom and the top: "You know the Battery commander is the man to whom 'the buck' is passed both going up and coming down, and he's got to watch his P's and Q's mighty smartly if they don't succeed in getting something on him."[160] His predilection for folk speech also made him include that fitting second proverbial expression of "watching one's P's and Q's" in this short sentence. There is no doubt that Truman enjoyed proverbial language from his youth to ripe old age.

Another use of the buck-passing phrase is particularly important since Truman employs it to answer that omnipresent question of why he decided to drop the atomic bomb at the end of World War II. Truman seldom entered into philosophical deliberations, and instead of talking about an existential or ethical dilemma, he chose a plain proverbial expression to answer that haunting question in an address on 14 October 1948 in Milwaukee, Wisconsin:

> As President of the United States, I had the fateful responsibility of deciding whether or not to use this weapon [the atomic bomb] for the first time. It was the hardest decision I ever had to make. But the President cannot duck hard problems—he cannot pass the buck.
>
> I made the decision after discussions with the ablest men in our Government [Churchill agreed as well], and after long and prayerful consideration.
>
> I decided that the bomb should be used in order to end the war quickly and save countless lives—Japanese as well as American.
>
> But I resolved then and there to do everything I could to see that this awesome discovery was turned into a force for peace and the advancement of mankind.
>
> Since then, it has been my constant aim to prevent its use for war and to hasten its use for peace.[161]

Truman returns again to this significant proverbial phrase in his "Farewell Address to the American People," which was broadcast from his office in the White House on 15 January 1953. While speaking, he may well have glanced across his desk to the sign with the motto "The Buck Stops Here":

> The greatest part of the President's job is to make decisions—big ones and small ones, dozens of them almost every day. The papers may circulate around the Government for a while but they finally reach his desk. And then, there's no place else for them to go. The President—whoever he is—has to decide. He can't pass the buck to anybody. No one else can do the deciding for him. That's his job.[162]

Robert H. Ferrell, renowned Truman scholar, entitled a chapter of one of his books with the anti-proverb "To Err Is Truman,"[163] thereby citing a proverbial aspersion that was in circulation when Truman's popularity plummeted just as Winston Churchill's had after the war's end. Naturally Truman had his faults, and he certainly committed plenty of errors that precipitated numerous crises.[164] But as this discussion has shown, the classical proverb "To err is human" could just as well be changed to "To act is Truman," or even more appropriately, to the apposite "To speak plainly is Truman." It is fair to say that every president has much to learn from examining the words of Harry Truman, a man who claimed he had "never studied the niceties of speech composition" and whose famous motto "The Buck Stops Here" applied not only to his presidential decisions and acts but also to his words. I repeat here part of a passage quoted earlier in the chapter:

All presidential messages must begin with the President himself. . . . The final version . . . is the final word of the President himself, expressing his own convictions and his policy. These he cannot delegate to any man if he would be President in his own right.

His willingness to take responsibility for his acts and his words inspired in Americans the same kind of trust that Truman himself had in the power and wisdom of plain, and proverbial, speech.

4

"Raising the Iron Curtain"
Proverbs and Political Cartoons of the Cold War

The urgent need to defeat Nazi Germany brought about the unlikely alliance of the Soviet Union and the United States. The strongholds of communism and democracy joined forces against the threat of fascism. While there was some hope that the two political bedfellows of East and West might continue to cooperate after the war in a world where peace was guaranteed by the international efforts of the United Nations, the euphoria over the victory of the Allies soon gave way to a policy of distrust and animosity. The schism between the Soviet and American camps quickly accelerated the geopolitical division of Europe into two halves, the East controlled by the Soviet Union and the West by America and its allies. As mentioned in chapter 2, Churchill recognized this split almost immediately and as early as 12 May 1945, in a secret telegram to President Truman, described the West and East as divided by an "Iron Curtain":

> An iron curtain is drawn down upon their front [Russia and Eastern Europe]. We do not know what is going on behind. There seems little doubt that the whole of the regions east of the line Lübeck-Trieste-Corfu will soon be completely in their hands.[1]

We have looked briefly, in chapter 2, at the origins of the "Iron Curtain" expression and at how it became a predominant metaphor after the Second World War.[2] Here I would like to take a look at a term that is intricately connected with "Iron Curtain": the "Cold War." The quite reliable *Safire's Political Dictionary* explains its origin as follows:

> The phrase was minted by Herbert Bayard Swope [1882–1958], publicist, three-time winner of the Pulitzer Prize, and occasional speechwriter for elder statesman Bernard Baruch [1870–1965]. In 1946, about the time Churchill was speaking of an IRON CURTAIN, Swope used "cold war" in a draft speech for Baruch to describe U.S.-Soviet relations (as contrasted to the recent "hot" or "shooting" war). Baruch felt it was too strong, but used it one year later in a speech at Columbia, South Carolina: "Let us not be deceived—

today we are in the midst of a cold war." He repeated the phrase, by that time picked up and popularized by columnist Walter Lippmann [1889–1974], to the Senate War Investigating Committee on October 24, 1948.[3]

Swope invented the term, but the journalist Lippmann gave it currency in a series of articles that appeared in the *New York Herald Tribune* and in a small but influential book entitled *The Cold War: A Study in U.S. Foreign Policy* (Washington, D.C.: Council on Foreign Relations, 1947).[4] This "war" that never really was declared and that also lacks any victors in the normal sense of that word or a formal peace conference,[5] vacillated for several decades between frost and thaws, but it now has come to an end without ever having developed into a feared third world war. Extremely tense moments, like the Cuban Missile Crisis of 1962, brought the world close to a nuclear nightmare, but in the long run the idea of peaceful co-existence prevailed as each camp kept the other in a state of containment. Throughout this period the Berlin Wall stood as a visual symbol of the Iron Curtain, and when it fell in 1989 the Cold War was understood to be at an end.

Following World War II, people gradually learned to live with the Cold War status quo. Even the two Germanies, divided by the Berlin Wall, lived in mutual recognition. But it was a balance of power maintained at serious financial, political, and psychological costs for both sides. During this time of precarious balance, Mikhail Gorbachev (b. 1931) came to re-place the old guard politicians of the Soviet Union in March of 1985. While he was pushing his programs of *glasnost* and *perestroika*, which re-sulted in increased openness and a fundamental political breakdown of the Soviet political system,[6] President Ronald W. Reagan (b. 1911) was clinging to the old Iron Curtain and Cold War rhetoric, having pronounced the Soviet Union to be an "evil Empire" in a speech on 9 March 1983. But this old Cold War warrior could see the positive changes that Gorbachev was accomplishing in his country, and the two world leaders actually started to form a human bond through personal meetings. Who will for-get the excitement of the Gorbachev era with its sweeping changes toward a freer society that began to influence the entire Soviet Union and the War-saw Pact countries behind the Iron Curtain? Hope for a momentous po-litical change was felt on both sides of the wall dividing Europe, and then came Reagan's speech at the Brandenburg Gate in West Berlin on 12 June 1987. Facing the wall and analyzing East-West relations, he proclaimed the following challenge to Mikhail Gorbachev and his government:

> There is one sign the Soviets can make that would be unmistakable, that would advance dramatically the cause of freedom and peace. General Secre-tary Gorbachev, if you seek peace, if you seek prosperity for the Soviet Union

and Eastern Europe, if you seek liberalization: Come here to this gate! Mr. Gorbachev, open this gate! Mr Gorbachev, tear down this wall![7]

I can still recall watching this dramatic scene on the television news that evening, and how following this speech changes occurred with breathtaking speed, until on 9 November 1989 the Berlin Wall, the horrid symbol of the insanity of the Cold War, came tumbling down. Scholars generally agree that the Cold War ended in 1989 or at least with the collapse of the Soviet Union in August 1991. The titles of their books alone signal the end of an era: for example, William G. Hyland, *The Cold War Is Over* (New York: Times Books, 1990), Michael J. Hogan, ed., *The End of the Cold War: Its Meaning and Implications* (New York: Cambridge University Press, 1992), Allen Lynch, *The Cold War Is Over—Again* (Boulder, Colo.: Westview Press, 1992), and Robert O. Keohane, Joseph S. Nye, and Stanley Hoffman, *After the Cold War: International Institutions and State Strategies in Europe, 1989–1991* (Cambridge, Mass.: Harvard University Press, 1993).[8]

Among these books, *The Cold War as Rhetoric: The Beginnings, 1945–1950* (New York: Praeger, 1991) by Lynn Boyd Hinds and Theodore Otto Windt stands out as one of the few studies on the rhetoric of the Cold War. Its authors, especially in a chapter called "Churchill's 'Iron Curtain' and Beyond," very acutely characterize the uniqueness of this "war" that lacked actual combat in the traditional sense:

> The Soviet-American cold war was a rhetorical war, one fought with words as weapons. But the cold war was more than threats by one nation hurled against another. The rhetoric created the consensus we call the cold war. When one begins studying its origins, one immediately concentrates on public statements: Stalin's "February Election" address, Churchill's "Iron Curtain" speech, Truman's speech to a joint session of Congress in March 1947, Marshall's commencement address announcing the Marshall Plan, and on and on [i.e., speeches by Khrushchev, Kennedy, Nixon, Brezhnev, Gorbachev, and Reagan, among others] through major and minor statements by central figures in the rhetorical drama of the beginnings of the cold war. This rhetoric created a complete and pervasive political reality about events, motives, actions, and policies. In the United States, it created a universal worldview of national and international politics where nothing else than the survival of the American way of life seemed to be at stake. The cold war became all encompassing, not merely a rivalry between two great powers, but a Manichaean struggle between the forces of light and the forces of darkness.[9]

A few other scholars have also discussed the rhetorical nature of the Cold War,[10] but they have failed to touch upon the intriguing role which folk speech, especially proverbial language, has played in the politics of words that made up the ideological and strategic "war games" of the past decades. Politicians, such master rhetoricians as Churchill or Nikita S. Khrushchev included, certainly were more than willing to employ vivid imagery and traditional wisdom in the form of proverbs and proverbial expressions to their anything but cold speeches to add at least linguistic and expressive fervor to their utterances. The phraseological units of the "Iron Curtain" and the "Cold War" were the dominating proverbial *leit-motifs* of this historical period, and doubtless will remain current in metaphorical parlance in the future, but a slew of traditional proverbs employed repeatedly by world political players can also be identified. During the Cold War period, politicians frequently used metaphors in the form of proverbs to add authoritativeness and imagery to otherwise rather bland rhetorical exercises. Proverbial language was easily adapted to the kind of emotionally loaded contrast between good and evil that permeated Cold War rhetoric.

In previous chapters we have noted that politicians have long been aware of the manipulative power of proverbial rhetoric. Marcus Tullius Cicero, the Roman orator and senator, frequently employed legal proverbs such as "Summun ius summa iniuria"[11] (Extreme law, extreme injustice) or picturesque proverbial expressions, like "in eadem es navi"[12] (to be in the same boat), which still today is often used to refer to a collective situation in politics. Otto von Bismarck employed numerous German proverbs and proverbial expressions in his many speeches and letters to argue for a unified national state and socio-economic programs.[13] Vladimir Ilyich Lenin's propagandistic use of proverbs has been analyzed,[14] Adolf Hitler's perverted use of proverbs for the sake of anti-Semitism and military aggression has been scrutinized in chapter 1 of this book and elsewhere,[15] and all of the proverbs and proverbial phrases included in Winston S. Churchill's complete speeches, letters, and many books have been excerpted and studied.[16] There also are some general studies on the use of proverbs in the political rhetoric of various countries,[17] all indicating that such stock phrases are in fact universally found in political discourse at the local, national, and international level.

Even the speeches and discussions at the renowned world institution of the United Nations are not lacking in proverbial language. This is convincingly shown in a large bibliophilistic publication on the *Wit and Wisdom of the United Nations: Proverbs and Apothegms on Diplomacy* (New York: privately printed, 1961), in which Lt. Colonel Victor S. M. de Guinzbourg includes private letters written to him by United Nations personnel containing small lists of proverbs relating to international relations and diplomacy. The book also includes a large collection of proverbs dealing with all aspects of war and peace.[18] The frequent use of proverbs in United Nations debates or speeches was also noticed by R. D. Hogg, one of the simultaneous interpreters at that polyglot institution:

> Many a participant in the intricate and sometimes heated public debates of our time has deemed it necessary to descend, on occasion, from the rarefied heights of conventional abstract language to the more solid ground of the proverb. Used sparingly and with discrimination, the proverb is a vivid, persuasive form of speech. It is a hammer with which to drive home an abstruse theoretical point, a spice to lend piquancy to an argument overladen with unsavoury or indigestible matter. The Russians, who like plain speaking, have an old adage: "Dobraia poslovitsa ne v brob', a priamo v glaz" (A good proverb strikes not the eyebrow, but straight in the eye).[19]

This proverb conjures up an image of that robust Cold War warrior Nikita Khrushchev, who pounded the lectern with his fists in the hall of the General Assembly at the United Nations to underscore his proverbial rhetoric. Khrushchev was so attached to proverbial language that the American journalist James B. Reston entitled a 10 July 1995 *New York Times* article "Khrushchev and Diplomacy by Proverb."[20] Russian diplomats clearly delighted in filling their speeches with proverbs during the early period of the Cold War. In another article in the *New York Times,* this one dated 27 January 1952, journalist A. M. Rosenthal characterizes this phenomenon with the headline "The Bear That Talks in Proverbs" and quotes for readers this same Russian proverb:

> Language experts with time on their hands will be able to prove by the record that the sixth season of the United Nations Assembly here set a new mark for the cultivation and use of proverbs. As is well known, proverbs are old snappy sayings, very pithy, invented in Russia. For about six years now, Russian delegates at the United Nations have been enthusiastically exercising the patent, apparently on the basis of that old Russian proverb about proverbs: "A good proverb strikes not the eyebrow but straight in the eye."[21]

The article cites proverbial use by the early Soviet Foreign Minister Vyacheslav M. Molotov (1890–1986) and his successors Andrei Y. Vishinsky (1883–1955) and Andrei A. Gromyko (1909–89). This proverbial barrage never ceased, and James Reston certainly was on the right track when on 17 February 1985 he published yet another article in the *New York Times* on "Russia's Book of Proverbs."[22] In addition to listing the proverbs that Soviet negotiators are likely to quote at nuclear reduction talks in Geneva, he states quite appropriately that "the Soviet negotiators know these proverbs as well as they know the multiplication tables, and quote them whenever they are in trouble. *Kak izvesto* (as is well known), they always say, there's an old Russian proverb: Keep feet in mud, and not in stars." These examples help demonstrate that proverbs clearly played their strategic and rhetorical role in Cold War politics. They were (and are) useful because they not only hit the nail on the head at the end of a complex debate or negotiation, but they also are exceedingly difficult to argue against or refute if one does not have an opposing proverb ready at hand. No wonder that prior to visiting the Soviet Union Richard M. Nixon beefed up his knowledge of Russian proverbs. An anonymous editorial in the *New York Times* on 19 July 1959 entitled "Reckoning With His Host, Nixon is Packing Proverbs" begins with this telling statement:

> Vice President Richard M. Nixon has been engaged in an intensive program of study to prepare himself for his coming trip to the Soviet Union, an informed source disclosed today.
> He even is preparing to counter Premier Nikita S. Khrushchev on the latter's favorite ground—the proverb. The Vice President has been recalling old and learning new proverbs to use in talks with Soviet officials and, more important, in his many planned public appearances. The Soviet Premier is noted for his frequent use of proverbs. Here are a few he has used in recent talks:
> "Spit in his eye and he'll say it's dew from heaven."
> "Those who fight for a just cause are strong in spirit."
> "The scales will fall from the eyes of the blind; they will have their eyes opened and will see what is white and what is black."
> "Strong friends cannot be parted—even by water."
> "Get rid of the devil and the priest will have nothing to do."[23]

At this time there is still no study of the use and function of proverbs in major debates and speeches at the United Nations having to do with Cold War issues. Such a contextualized analysis of proverbs would doubtless indicate their effectiveness as a powerful verbal tool. Proverbial rhetoric on the political stage of the world has been far too long ignored, and such more or less popular collections as Selwyn Gurney Champion's *War Proverbs and Maxims, East and West* (London: Arthur Probsthain, 1945), Gurdip Singh Bhatia's *Over 1200 World's Military Maxims & Proverbs* (New Delhi: Deep and Deep, 1968), or Edward Fenton's *Peace—It's wonderful! A Small Collection of Olive Branches, Being Memorable Quotations, Verses, and Proverbs About War and Peace* (New York: New American Library, 1971) do not really provide any insights into the functional significance of proverbs in the diplomatic mediation between war and peace.[24]

Keeping this more serious function of proverbs in mind, it is appropriate and fruitful to look at how proverbs have been used by the international press to comment on the fears and anxieties experienced by people on both sides of the Iron Curtain. Many headlines, caricatures, and even advertisements dealing with the "orientational metaphors"[25] of the

"Iron Curtain" and the "Cold War" employed well-known proverbs. To-gether with realistic visualizations of certain world leaders or tanks, rock-ets, and even futuristic illustrations of Star Wars devices, the proverbs take on very serious meanings indeed. Two proverbs, in fact, have devel-oped into proverbial *leitmotifs* of the Cold War, namely the three-mon-key-proverb of "Hear no evil, see no evil, speak no evil" and the classi-cal proverb of "Big fish eat little fish."[26] These proverbs based on animal imagery became stereotypical images for human behavior during this pe-riod and telling commentary on the absurdity of the Cold War mentality. Numerous other instances exist in which proverbs with interpretive com-ments, at times even in the form of an expressive poem, and appropriate pictorializations communicate in a most convincing fashion the political reality through their universally understood rhetorical message.[27] Prov-erbs are thus used to convey the general worldview that was prevalent during this historical period with all of its questionable "perceptions, opinions, attitudes, [and] policies."[28] The worldview was also conveyed, of course, in lengthy and convoluted speeches, in essays, and books, but proverbs used in oral speech acts or on the printed page communicated these opinions and attitudes metaphorically, in but a few words, for everybody to understand and comment on.

It must be remembered that the Cold War is an outgrowth of World War II. In fact, some scholars even feel that the Cold War started in 1917 with the Russian Revolution and the coming to power of communists in the Soviet Union.[29] Proverbs were employed as propagandistic tools dur-ing and after the Bolshevik revolution,[30] and they played a major role in manipulative and authoritative statements designed to demonize the enemy during the Second World War. A month after Great Britain's dec-laration of war on 3 September 1939, the German satirical magazine *Sim-plicissimus* depicted the British national stereotype John Bull in the Ham-let pose holding an olive twig in one hand and the skull of Mars in the other. This "Hamlet John Bull" is trying to decide between peace or war, as the proverbial Shakespeare quotation "Sein oder nicht sein, das ist hier die Frage!" (To be or not to be, that is the question) in the caption makes clear.[31] Barely a year later, with Britain facing the German menace alone, the same magazine published a caricature based on the same motif, but this time depicting a "Hamlet Churchill." Churchill, his head in his hand, and a warfare-reddened sky in the background, states in desperation "Sein oder Nichtsein, das ist jetzt die Frage!" (To be or not to be, that is now the question).[32] The Nazi-controlled German press and its propa-ganda machine were clearly under the impression in the fall of 1940 that England could be defeated, never realizing with what resolve and prowess the British people would rally behind Churchill as their indefatigable prime minister. The Germans' confidence in victory is seen as well in a third caricature that shows a despairing Churchill standing in the rubble of London and citing the classic English proverb "My house is my castle!"[33] In the meantime Churchill mobilized his nation by word and deed, approving with a good bit of British humor various rather comical war-effort posters. A particularly telling example is a poster from 1941 that asked the British people to conserve food: "BETTER POT-LUCK with Churchill today THAN HUMBLE PIE under Hitler tomorrow [-] DON'T WASTE FOOD!"[34] The catchy proverbial structure of this slogan and the inclusion of the two proverbial expressions "to take pot-luck" and "to eat humble pie" made it seem familiar and helped it take root in the British consciousness. The illustration featured two familiar cooking pots, one the formidable head of the prime minister in a jovial mood with his ever-present cigar in his mouth, and the other a sinister Adolf Hitler.

During this same time, in March of 1941, the United States under President Roosevelt began its "lend-lease" economic and military aid to Britain. The U.S. program was ridiculed in Germany's second widely circulated satirical magazine *Kladderadatsch* with a caricature showing Uncle Sam as the American national stereotype sticking his nose into European affairs: "Eine seltsame amerikanische Perversität: Die Nase in fremde schmutzige Wäsche stecken!"[35] (A strange American perversity: Sticking one's nose into foreign dirty linens). The proverbial expression together with the illustration is a clear indication that Hitler's press did not appreciate America's meddling in European matters. Two months before America's declaration of war on 7 December 1941, Roosevelt was depicted as God Almighty in the *Fliegende Blätter,* another major satirical magazine of long standing in Germany and under Nazi control since Hitler's grasp of power in 1933. In this cartoon Roosevelt's help to Churchill and Joseph Stalin is seen as amounting to mere drops in the bucket, or "Tropfen auf einen heißen Stein"[36] (drops on a hot stone) as the German would say proverbially. His aid falling on the hot stone of Europe will not amount to anything is the message of this proverbial caricature. Military outcomes began to reverse in December of 1941 with America vigorously participating in the naval warfare of the Atlantic. Before the end of December, *Kladderadatsch* published a cartoon that shows Roosevelt performing a dance of death in company with the figure of death which is depicted in its customary skeleton shape.[37] Roosevelt, who smiles devilishly and has lost his crutches (a nasty allusion to his disability), is shown to be thinking that the Atlantic has become "Sein Meer" (his sea) despite the skillful German submarines. But the skeleton is laughing as well, and the proverbial caption "Wer zuletzt lacht, lacht am besten" (He who laughs last, laughs best) alludes to the conviction

that Germany will win the battle of the Atlantic. These and other caricatures together with their traditional messages based on proverbs played
their role in demonizing America and its allies, leading Germans to think
that they were invincible and destined to rule the world.

The Germans were not alone, however, in using proverbs to propa-
gandize. American companies effectively utilized proverbial messages to
advertise their involvement in the war effort. The Mallony Metal Company, for example, published a one-page advertisement in *Fortune* in
1942, explaining that light metal was needed for the construction of war
planes.[38] Its headline, "Clouds of Planes with Silver Linings," is an obvious play on the proverb "Every cloud has a silver lining," and a picture
of several effective light-metal war planes is included to emotionalize the
industrial message into a call for the war effort. The Young and Rubican
advertising agency published an even more direct request for civilian participation in the war effort in another large ad in *Fortune* two months
later.[39] The ad publicizes Young and Rubican's contributions to the war
effort, conveying the message that it is a worthy agency, and urges civil-
ians to do the same with a picture of a monkey-wrench accompanied by
the headline "Will you throw this in the Nazi machine?" The illustration
together with the question obviously allude to the proverbial expression
"to throw a monkey-wrench into something," and thus break or destroy
it. Once again a proverb is used to get Americans to do their part to win
the war. Another effective advertisement, this one placed by a paper
company, shows a quill and a sword and carries the headline "The pen
is mightier . . ." The text below the picture quotes General Douglas
MacArthur in a passage where he uses the proverbial expression "The pen
is mightier than the sword."[40] When this full-page ad appeared in *Fortune*
in May of 1943, there was an unrealistic hope that the war might soon
come to an end. But already by June of that year *Time* magazine published
a cover page that showed the boot of Italy, with Sicily as its heel, and a
superimposed worried Benito Mussolini. The caption declared simply
"Mussolini: His heel is in hot water."[41] The cover illustration ingeniously
anticipated, through proverbial indirection, the Anglo-American invasion
of Sicily just three weeks later in July of 1943 and indicated that Americans were beginning to grasp that the war would not be over quickly.

Like their British counterparts, there were also American posters
published by the Office of War Information that took a more comic approach to the war effort. One dating from 1943, for example, shows the
worried face of a man who is bending over while a woman sews up a tear
in the seat of his pants. Clearly he does not fully trust her with the needle. The slogan states "USE IT UP—WEAR IT OUT—MAKE IT DO!"[42] The actual proverb includes a fourth element, "or go without," but keeping this

might have made the slogan too long, or it may have been eliminated because it would have reminded American citizens of how much they were
already sacrificing for the war and how hard life was on the home front.

One final advertising headline in the form of a proverb and its
straightforward text from *Time* illustrates once again how effectively
proverbial wisdom was incorporated in the civilian war effort rhetoric:

> Victory, like charity, begins at home
> . . . Sure we stand up at the anthem, we buy some bonds, we're in war work.
> But you know in your heart the war hasn't even begun for most Americans—
> and too many are not going to let it, if they can help it.
>   . . . Victory begins at home—in your heart and mine, in our minds, *in
> our hands*. Until it begins here, there can be no victory but only horrible
> death in New Guinea, Europe, the cold North Sea. There *can* be no victory
> until we are worthy of it. This war *will not* be won by *some* Americans while
> others profit by it. Not until the last American has surrendered his selfishness
> for the unselfish good of his country will the slaughter of other Americans
> stop.[43]

This is indeed a powerful statement, and there is no doubt that its proverbial title, by its juxtaposition of the words "victory" and "charity," convinced readers to read the entire advertisement.[44]

These examples all show how proverbs in their traditional wording
or in the form of ingenious variants helped to get Americans involved in
the war effort, and a case could be made that such short expressions of
folk speech were to a certain degree as influential as the war rhetoric offered by politicians because everybody could understand proverbs. The
same is true for other verbal folklore genres such as fairy tales, legends,
folk songs, and nursery rhymes. They, or at least easily recognizable seg-
ments of them, were also used in popularizing the war effort as rhetorical
devices that carried the authority of tradition behind them. Folklore is a
major device in human communication, figuring either as a positive force
of traditional knowledge or as a manipulated weapon in the most varied
power struggles confronting humankind.[45] But of all the folklore genres,
proverbs are clearly best suited to be part of this communicative process
because of their differentiated wisdom based on the experience and observation of generations of people from around the entire world.

A few months before the end of the Second World War, on 26 June
1945, fifty countries of the world agreed on the charter of the United Nations in San Francisco. Despite this new effort for cooperation and peace,
it still took the horrific deed of dropping atomic bombs on Hiroshima
(6 August 1945) and Nagasaki (9 August 1945) to force Japan into capit-
ulation, and the Second World War was barely over when the the globe
split into two superpowers, beginning what became known as the Cold

War. Germany and Japan were finally defeated, but the threat of a nuclear war between the United States and the Soviet Union dominated the next four decades, resulting in a number of political crises and an arms race that brought the world repeatedly to the brink of a third world war. The ever-present threat was perhaps best illustrated in an early Cold War cartoon published in the *St. Louis Post-Dispatch* on 31 May 1946 (see fig. 4.1). It shows a lonely person standing on top of the world. Attached to the world is a burning fuse that spells out the word "atom." This singular person doubtless represents the forlorn human race wondering about the fate of the world and humanity. The artist could not have chosen a better caption than the quotation which we have already seen was frequently used by both Hitler and Churchill during the war, Shakespeare's proverbial "To be or not to be."[46] It perfectly expresses the fundamental question of the Cold War.

The ever-present threat of atomic warfare caused the relationship between the United States and the Soviet Union to quickly disintegrate while each nation tried to increase its influence and power. In his speech of 12 March 1947, President Truman declared that communism must be contained, and thus launched what later became known as the Truman Doctrine. On 5 June of the same year, the Marshall Plan was announced in a speech by General George C. Marshall at Harvard University. While this massive humanitarian rescue plan provided much needed food for thousands of Western Europeans, it obviously also established a U.S. power base in that area. A cartoon from 1948 (see fig. 4.2) illustrates this dual mission of the Marshall Plan by showing Uncle Sam delivering a food basket to starving Europeans with the telling caption "Whose Bread I Eat, His Song I Sing."[47] The basket is labeled "From the Land of Freedom," and it is clear that the intent here is to show that America's humanitarian aid is coupled with influence peddling. The proverbial caption says this, however, in a wonderfully indirect way, alluding to the fact that getting bread will mean that Western Europeans will have to accept the American political system and way of life. At least ten years later, in 1959, there appeared a similar cartoon with Uncle Sam looking worriedly into a large bag containing the "Free World Aid Program" while a rather evil-looking communist face frowns about the whole idea of American aid.[48] Its caption, the proverbial expression "Better Late Than Never," effectively argued to Americans for the necessity of continuing foreign aid as a means of simultaneously gaining political influence.

Once America and its new European allies established the North Atlantic Treaty Organization (NATO) on 4 April 1949, the Soviet Union and its allies in Eastern Europe followed suit with their Warsaw Pact on 14 May 1955, thus formalizing the two military and political camps that have

TO BE OR NOT TO BE

May 31, 1946

Figure 4.1

dominated world politics for so long. Anti-Soviet propaganda established itself as quickly in the West as the anti-American slogans spread behind the impenetrable Iron Curtain. A particularly vexing problem for the West was, of course, the clandestine behavior of the Soviets. This was splendidly illustrated by a cartoon from 1950 based on the proverbial

--Justus in the Minneapolis Star-Journal.

"Whose Bread I Eat, His Song I Sing."

Figure 4.2

—*Alexander in* The Philadelphia Evening Bulletin.

"Behind the Iron Curtain."

Figure 4.3

motif of the three monkeys (see fig. 4.3). While a smirking Stalin peers out from behind an Iron Curtain that is imprinted with the hammer and sickle emblem, three comrades sit protectively in front of the curtain in the three-monkey pose, labeled respectively "Speak no facts, see no facts, hear no facts."[49] Naturally a cloud of suspicion hovered over the communist rival in the East, and only a few years after NATO was formed a cartoon succeeded in demonizing the West's enemy. In the background lurks the "Threat of communism" represented by a devil with a pitchfork. In the foreground is the message that too much money spent on defense might bring "Economic and political ruin" to the United States. Between the two stands a bewildered Uncle Sam reading a large poster with the inscription "National Defense: How much do we need? How much can we afford?" And if all of this isn't clear enough, the proverbial caption adds the metaphorical message "Between the Devil and the Deep Sea."[50] The expense of the arms race, of course, became a source of serious controversy for the political leaders of East and West, and its absurd escalation helped in due time to bring an end to the Cold War.

In Germany, where East and West met at a solidly fortified border, the fear of communism or at least the political propaganda against it took on similar forms of demonization. A 1953 election poster of the Christian Democratic Union (CDU) showed a surrealistic communist head at the end of parallel lines representing paths toward the evils of Marxism. The proverbial slogan "Alle Wege des Marxismus führen nach Moskau"[51] (All roads of Marxism lead to Moscow) was based on the classical proverb of "All roads lead to Rome" and indicated the perils and certain decline that awaited anyone intending to vote for the Communist Party. Naturally the poster also added the statement "Darum CDU" (Therefore [vote] CDU). The idea of the evil Soviet Union and communism lurking in the background was frequently used in political cartoons with appropriate proverbial motifs and captions. As the Soviet Union expanded its influence in the Middle East, a cartoonist depicted a dromedary whose smoking hump symbolizes the explosive region. At the end of the rising smoke appear a hammer and sickle, making immediately clear the message that the truncated proverbial caption, "Where There's Smoke . . . ,"[52] is supposed to communicate: the Soviet Union is ready at any moment to stir up problems or to be present where it might possibly increase its power base. This message is equally well illustrated by a cartoon which appeared about thirty years later in 1985 in the national magazine U.S. News & World Report. The caption reads simply "Lebanese Cookbook,"[53] and the cartoon itself shows a row of fish representing the P.L.O., Christians, and Moslems swimming into the mouth of a larger Syrian fish. Underneath this last big fish is a frying pan, expectantly extended by a Soviet military officer. The message, that while various factions attempt to destroy each other, Syria as the biggest fish will devour them all, alludes of course to the proverb "Big fish eat little fish." And because the Syrian fish shall soon fall into the hands of the Soviet Union, one also recalls the proverbial expression "To have other fish to fry." The double proverbial metaphors help to communicate the message about who is the real controlling force in the Middle East. The "big fish eating little fish" motif was also used in a 1983 American cartoon to comment on the relationship between the USSR and Afghanistan.[54] No caption was necessary, since the illustrated proverb clearly shows how the mighty superpower USSR is about to devour a small Afghanistan fish. But just because the West could rely on this proverb to criticize the East does not mean the East could not employ it effectively as well. A cartoon that appeared in 1957 in the French communist newspaper L'Humanité and which was also published in the official communist party newspaper Pravda featured a large American fish bearing dollar signs and the caption "Interdépendance Atlantique."[55] Smaller fish, representing member states of NATO, are swimming into the big fish's mouth, dramatizing their financial dependency on the United States.

The period between 1958 and 1962 might well be called Nikita Khrushchev and John F. Kennedy's Cold War that culminated in the Cuban Missile Crisis in October of 1962. This was, of course, also the time when East Germany with the support of the Soviet Union began to build the Berlin Wall on 13 August 1961. That particular crisis saw Kennedy and NATO back down to avoid a major military confrontation. The German *Simplicissimus* published a cover caricature showing the two Cold War warriors Kennedy and Khrushchev begrudgingly shaking hands and citing that proverbial cliché "Ende gut—alles gut!"[56] (All's well that ends well). Nothing was well, of course, and Khrushchev faced plenty of domestic problems, as was illustrated in a nasty caricature in the British satirical magazine *Punch*. It shows Khrushchev as Marie Antoinette in his parlor with a vodka bottle next to him while the deprived population is shouting for food outside of his window. The caption states sarcastically, "Nikita Antoinette: 'Milk?—Let them drink vodka!'"[57] Later, on 26 June 1963, Kennedy made the following symbolic declaration at the Berlin Wall: "All free men, wherever they may live, are citizens of Berlin. And therefore, as a free man, I take pride in the words 'Ich bin ein Berliner.'"[58] This proverbial utterance did not topple the Berlin Wall, which was not to fall for more than another twenty-five years, but it did indicate to Khrushchev once and for all that he could not bully this young and promising president and that the West was resolved to stand firm in Berlin.

After Kennedy's speech and before the Berlin Wall fell, years of containment and peaceful coexistence with intermittent negotiations went by, with each superpower building up its arsenal of weapons and rigidly defending its realm of influence. Under Richard M. Nixon and Gerald R. Ford a feeling of "détente" was reached, with Secretary of State Henry A. Kissinger doing much of the negotiating. A 1974 Soviet cartoon directed against America might just as well have been published with reversed labels in the United States. It shows a large fish symbolizing the military budget swallowing up smaller fish representing funds for schools, pensions, medicine, science, and other interests (see fig. 4.4). The Russian caption states simply "'Zolotaia' rybka"[59] (The "Gold" fish). The prevalent "big fish eat little fish" motif was used once again five years later by the German cartoonist Horst Haitzinger, illustrating the international aspect of the Cold War with a fish sequence. The small fish Cambodia is being devoured by Vietnam which in turn is being swallowed up by China. These three fish are followed by a large Soviet fish who still has its mouth shut but is ready to join in the uncontrolled rapacity at any time.[60] Under President Jimmy Carter "détente" continued at first, but tensions on the international scene brought about a new inflammation of the Cold War in the late 1970s and early 1980s, especially with Ronald Reagan's becoming

Figure 4.4

president in 1981. A vodka advertisement, of all things, illustrates the increasingly feisty American mood. In 1978 *Playboy* magazine printed an ad that pictured an attractive woman with a bottle of Gilbey's vodka. The proverbial headline and part of the text read as follows:

> EAT YOUR HEART OUT, RUSSIA.
> Maybe Russia invented vodka. But it took Gilbey's American know-how to make vodka a lot better . . . to smooth it, to make it delightfully crisp and clean. Try Gilbey's—the vodka the Russians wish they'd invented.
> GILBEY'S VODKA
> You can't buy a better vodka for love nor rubles.[61]

During this same period of increasing tensions, important negotiations led to controls on major missiles with the signing of the SALT II treaty by Carter and Leonid I. Brezhnev on 18 June 1979. A German caricature published later that year used a biblical proverb as a caption to explain Brezhnev's problem of having plenty of SS 20 long-range missiles but not enough wheat. Brezhnev, surrounded by giant missiles and with a sickle in hand, is trying to cut sparsely growing wheat (see fig. 4.5). The caption reads: "Wie man sät, so erntet man auch" (As you sow, so you reap; Galatians 6:7).[62]

Wie man sät, so erntet man auch. (Bauernregel)

Figure 4.5

Even the world of sports was affected by tensions between East and West when the United States decided on 22 April 1980 to boycott the Olympic games in Moscow because of the Soviet invasion of Afghanistan. Leading up to this decision, journalists analyzed the pros and cons of a boycott in an article in *Time* magazine with the fitting proverbial headline: "Olympics: To Go or Not to Go. The U.S. weighs hitting Moscow where it would really hurt."[63] The boycott took place, and a few months later an alarming cartoon appeared in *The New Yorker,* one which seemed to indicate escalating tensions. In this cartoon, two high-level military officers are shown talking at a cocktail party. One of them spouts the new wisdom that "one bomb is worth a thousand words" (see fig. 4.6).[64] This is, of course a telling parody of the proverb "A picture is worth a thousand words,"[65] but this anti-proverb, as such proverbial perversions have come to be called,[66] is also a clear indication of how some members of the military establishment on both sides of the Iron Curtain viewed the discussions on arms control. The precarious nature of the balance of power between the two superpowers became only too obvious during the 1981 crisis in Poland. That Soviet intervention in Poland was only barely prevented is the message of a drawing by the German cartoonist Horst Haitzinger. He drew the face of a big clock with Poland at the twelve o'clock mark. In the middle of the clock stands a Soviet tank with its large gun pointing at number eleven on the dial. The whole matter thus became an illustration of the German proverbial expression "Fünf vor zwölf" (Five to twelve, meaning, at the eleventh hour).[67]

With Ronald Reagan's inauguration as president on 20 January 1981, and with the aging and failing Leonid Brezhnev's holding on to his stagnating power in the Kremlin, the prospects for avoiding a nuclear confrontation and an escalation into a third world war looked alarming indeed. Reagan's 9 March 1983 assertion that the Soviet Union was "an evil Empire,"[68] is a measure of how quickly the Cold War accelerated between 1981 and 1985. Then, however, with the appearance of Mikhail Gorbachev, events quickly began to move in a different direction with the Reagan administration showing enough flexibility to cope with a truly changing world order. There exists an incredible German caricature from April 1981 that shows Reagan and Brezhnev facing each other as rather ridiculous looking Easter bunnies (see fig. 4.7). Each holds a split-open egg shell in front of him from which a long-range missile protrudes. The caption "Kuckuckseier"[69] (cuckoo eggs) represents a shortened version of the proverbial expression "Jdm. ein Kuckucksei ins Nest legen" (To place a cuckoo's egg in someone's nest). The caricature is thus a double folkloristic play on the belief in the Easter bunny and the proverbial expression, indirectly stating that both world leaders wish that they could be

"And I say one bomb is worth a thousand words."

Figure 4.6. Drawing by Dana Fradon; Copyright ©1980 *The New Yorker* Magazine, Inc.

Kuckuckseier

Figure 4.7

liberated from the nuclear weapons that someone, the Easter bunny or the cuckoo, has mischievously placed in their country. Especially the finger-pointing gesture from Reagan seems to imply that he blames Brezhnev and believes that America has such missiles only because the Soviet Union has them—the famous catch-22 of the arms race. As the arms race gained in momentum and grew more confrontational during the 1980s, cartoons that drew on folklore motifs to illustrate its absurdity appear to have increased as well.

At the same time that tensions between East and West escalated, talk of arms reduction also gained momentum. A slogan from the disarmament movement during the early 1960s reappeared in the 1980s in a German cartoon strip. In the first frame of this strip, someone has just finished writing the well-known slogan "Lieber rot als tot!" (Better red than dead) on an empty wall. The second frame shows another person crossing out this message and replacing it with the inversion "Lieber tot als rot!!" (Better dead than red). In the third frame yet another person crosses out both versions and begins to write a new slogan with the word "Lieber" (Better) which then is concluded in the fourth frame as "Lieber weder noch!!!" (Better neither nor).[70] The cartoon strip offers a welcome relief in perspective from the either/or view of politics, arguing that, in fact, the threat of nuclear war eliminates any real choice between "red" or "dead."

Figure 4.8

Everyone will be dead at the end of this contest. This modern political slogan and its variants probably date back to a much earlier variant used by the Frisians as early as the seventeenth century, when they declared their right to freedom with the slogan "Lewer duad üs Slaw" (Better dead than slave).[71] The modern slogan in both of its versions could be located as actual graffiti quite frequently during the Cold War years, indicating perhaps in a proverbial fashion the frustration that people were experiencing with the propaganda of this time. Joseph Raymond in his unique and enlightening short essay on "Tensions in Proverbs: More Light on International Understanding" spoke already in 1956 of a "paremiological revolt" through which people "voice *personal* tensions in a tone of *generalized* consent."[72] Later in his essay Raymond refers to "proverbs as group symbolic communications,"[73] and that is, of course, exactly the point of these proverbial graffiti.

As has been noted before, the three monkeys and their proverbial wisdom are perfectly suited symbols for the Cold War and the stalemate created by ever-increasing arsenals of weapons on both sides of the Iron Curtain. This was convincingly illustrated in a 1981 German cartoon that shows the traditional monkeys gesturing their well-known message of "hearing no evil, seeing no evil and speaking no evil" (see fig. 4.8).[74] They are sitting in the middle of the globe, while conventional and nuclear weapons are lurking on the horizons of the East and West, ready to strike a major blow at any time. No caption is needed this time, since the message is abundantly clear: the dangerous arms race continues while people everywhere ignore this threat to human life. Two months after this German cartoon was published, yet another famous proverbial symbol was used in a Swiss caricature in August 1981 after Reagan had announced the stockpiling of neutron bombs by the United States. To illustrate the Soviet reaction to this move, the caricaturist drew thousands of conventional tanks facing the West. In the middle of the tanks stands a giant wooden Trojan horse with this sign around its neck: "*Sowjet—'Friedensmarsch' gegen die Neutronenwaffe*"[75] (Soviet—"Peace March" against the neutron weapon). The implication is clearly that the Soviet Union itself has plenty of sophisticated weapons hidden away that will equal America's arsenal any time. The Trojan horse was also utilized in a cartoon by Horst Haitzinger, in which a wooden horse with a head at each end straddles the Berlin Wall dividing "Westeuropa" from "Osteuropa" represented by one soldier each (see fig. 4.9).[76] On the body of the horse is the inscription "EURO-" with the hammer and sickle symbol following the hyphen and forming the second word in this compound. This is a telling depiction of the mistrust on both sides of the Iron Curtain, each fearing the hidden agendas of the other if there ever were to appear a crack in the wall.

Two quite similar cartoons from 1982, one German and one Swiss, also illustrate the prevailing fear of nuclear war, a fear that did not vanish even while the governments of the United States and the Soviet Union were both proposing various arms reduction plans. The German cartoon shows Reagan and Brezhnev sitting at a small conference table and playing chess with rocket-shaped figures (see fig. 4.10).[77] All the while a giant Damocles' sword bearing the symbol of an atom hangs on a proverbially thin thread over their heads. The Swiss cartoon is quite similar: this time Reagan and Brezhnev, holding the world in their hands, are looking up at a modernized sword of Damocles. The sword takes the shape of a nuclear missile swinging once again on a thin thread (see fig. 4.11). As if the proverbial "Damocles' sword" did not make the message clear enough already, the Swiss caricaturist has captioned his drawing with Shakespeare's proverb "Sein oder Nichtsein . . ."[78] (To be or not to be), reinforcing our sense of the precarious situation of humankind in the face of possible annihilation. What is of interest here is that Reagan and Brezhnev appear to be authentically worried as well, which seems to encourage faith in the

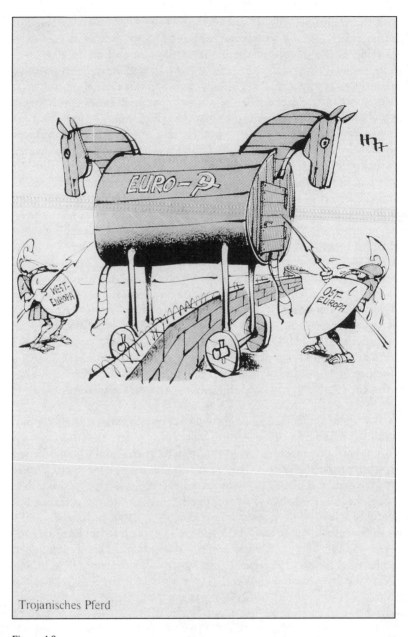

Trojanisches Pferd

Figure 4.9

122

Figure 4.10

Figure 4.11

Nichts gesehen, nichts zu sagen, nichts gehört   Karikatur: H. Hütter

Figure 4.12

idea that they will negotiate arms reductions in earnest. Thus the cartoon not only expresses the prevalent fears of nuclear war and annihilation, with its proverbs carrying the weight of, as Raymond puts it, "vivid expressions of group mind, group remembering, feelings, volitions, and tensions,"[79] it also offers some hope that the absurd eventualities of the Cold War will be escaped through compromise between East and West.

Toward the end of 1982, the two aging world leaders were accusing each other of wanting nuclear war, the feared result of which was gruesomely illustrated once again by the three-monkey motif. But in this Austrian cartoon, the monkeys, or better, the three remaining humans, have been reduced to mere skeletons sitting on the scorched earth after an atomic holocaust (see fig. 4.12). The caption revises the well-known triad to past tense: "Nichts gesehen, nichts zu sagen, nichts gehört" (Saw nothing, had nothing to say, heard nothing),[80] thereby clearly stating that people ignored the imminent danger of nuclear destruction until it was too late. The three monkeys show up again around this time in an advertisement for a new German anthology by authors commenting on the prospects of peace in the world. Once again the monkeys convey a sense of dangerous passivity and irresponsibility. A significant quotation from

Bertolt Brecht is broken into two halves by the illustration of the three monkeys who once again are portrayed in skeletal shape:

> Die weltweiten Schrecken der vierziger Jahre
> scheinen vergessen.
> Der Regen von gestern macht uns nicht naß, sagen viele.
>
> [Illustration of the three figures]
>
> Diese Abgestumpftheit ist es,
> die wir zu bekämpfen haben, ihr äußerster Grad ist der Tod.
> —Bertolt Brecht [81]

(The worldwide horrors of the forties / appear to be forgotten. / The rain of yesterday doesn't get us wet, say many people. / It is this indifference / which we have to fight, for its most extreme degree is death.) There is no doubt that indifference played its role in letting the superpowers continue their escalating arms race to the point of almost no return.

When Brezhnev died on 10 November 1982, Reagan found himself having to deal with a series of new Kremlin leaders. Yet old warriors die hard, and when asked whether he had hopes that relationships between the United States and the Soviet Union might improve with the new leader Yuri V. Andropov, Reagan responded with a short statement on 11 November that included a proverbial quip: "For 10 years détente was based on words from them [the Russians] and not any deeds to back those words up. And we need some action that they—it takes two to tango— that they want to tango also."[82]

It is well known that Reagan was avoiding the dance floor just as much as the Soviets at that time, but his statement popularized the proverb "It takes two to tango" throughout the world in the mass media. This expression, which actually started as a variant of the older proverb "It takes two to quarrel," dates from a 1952 song written and composed by Al Hoffman and Dick Manning called "Takes Two to Tango" and sung by Pearl Bailey.[83] Since that time the tango metaphor has often appeared in headlines in the international press, and has gained currency as a proverb in loan translation in other languages. Not even a month after Reagan made this statement one finds a Swiss cartoon with the proverbial caption "Zum Tango gehören zwei!" (see fig. 4.13).[84] The illustration shows Sir Andropov asking Lady Reagan to tango with both of the world leaders holding on to their missiles, which also are seen ready to be deployed all around them. When Andropov called for a "freeze" in nuclear arsenals on 22 November 1982, another Swiss caricaturist returned to the Trojan horse motif showing the new Soviet leader pulling a "Abrüstung"[85] (Disarmament) horse filled with half-hidden missiles toward the West.

«Zum Tangotanz gehören zwei!»

Figure 4.13

126

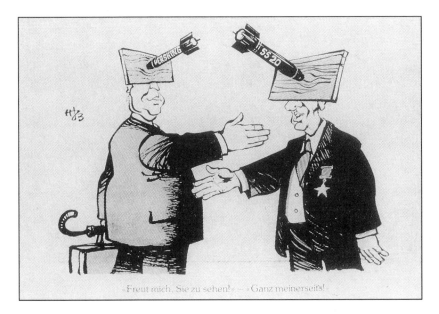

Figure 4.14

There certainly was no tango-dancing during the rule of Andropov until his death on 9 February 1984. Instead Reagan called the Soviet Union an "evil Empire" on 9 March 1983, and each side of the East-West conflict continued to be preoccupied with its various missiles. A Swiss cartoon shows this aggravated situation by transposing the German proverbial expression "Ein Brett vor dem Kopf haben" (To have a board in front of one's head, that is, To be a blockhead) into a politically revealing image (see fig. 4.14). Two representatives, one from the East and one from the West, fail to shake hands. Neither can see the other because each has a wooden board in front of his face, the Eastern board attached by a SS 20 and the Western by a Pershing missile. The caption reads "'Freut mich, Sie zu sehen!'— 'Ganz meinerseits!'" ("Nice to see you!"—"Same feeling here!") and indicates in satirical fashion that this preoccupation with weapons is exactly the reason why the Cold War was getting hotter.[86] This escalation was illustrated in a more grisly fashion in a caricature built around the previously mentioned German proverbial expression "It is five minutes before twelve" (It is the eleventh hour).[87] This time Reagan and Andropov are anxiously staring at a large clock whose indicators, in the shape of Pershing and SS 20 missiles, show that it is indeed five minutes before twelve (see fig. 4.15). We are only minutes away, the cartoon suggests, from the catastrophe of the Cold War turning into an all-too-hot third world war.

Die Weltwoche, Zürich

Figure 4.15

When Reagan announced the so-called "Star Wars" Strategic Defense Initiative (SDI) on 23 March 1983, the Cold War took on a new science fiction aspect.[88] Cartoonists were quick to identify the absurd quality of this expensive new program designed to counter a possible first attack by the "evil Empire." Felix Mussil entitled his 1984 cartoon "Killersatelliten" and returned to the old "big fish eat little fish" motif.[89] But the fish now have become killer satellites going after a military satellite: while a "Killersatellit" is trying to swallow up the "Satellit," it is being devoured by an "Anti-Killersatellit" which in turn is being attacked by an "Anti-Anti-Killersatellit" (see fig. 4.16). Obviously this chain reaction is continuing ad infinitum, showing the grotesque nature of this "Star Wars" game. The general American reaction to the idea of warfare in space was ridiculed by Tony Auth in his 1985 cartoon that showed "Star Wars" enthusiasts looking at the heavens and seeing the stars spelling out the modern proverb "Garbage in, garbage out" (see fig. 4.17).[90] Along this same line is a greeting card that illustrates Reagan and Secretary of Defense Caspar W. Weinberger as each holding a way-out "Star Wars" vehicle. The caption warns "Beware of Geeks bearing gifts."[91] Even though no Trojan horse graces this card, its caption is clearly a parody of the proverb "Beware of Greeks bearing gifts," the verbal counterpart to the Trojan horse image. What is implied, of course, is that Reagan and Weinberger want to sell the idea of "Star Wars" to the Western allies, but such merchandise should

Figure 4.16

be viewed with much suspicion. The ingenious change of the word "Greek" to "Geek" ridicules the entire enterprise, since the slang definitions of "geek" run somewhat like this: "a freak, who performs sensationally disgusting acts that a normal person would not; . . . a degenerate; one who will do anything, however disgusting, in order to satisfy or get money to satisfy degenerate desires."[92] The message is clearly that the "Star Wars" program is an ill-conceived idea.

U.S.-Soviet relations finally began to alter dramatically on 11 March 1985, when Mikhail Gorbachev was elected general secretary of the Soviet Communist Party. The old Kremlin guard was finally gone, and, luckily for the world, Reagan in the remaining years of his presidency showed enough flexibility to deal with this vigorous and innovative new leader. The beginning of the end of the Cold War was in sight, and public opinion definitely required a return to serious arms talks in Geneva. It might also be pointed out that the nuclear accident at Chernobyl made people drastically aware of the dangers of the peaceful and military use of atomic

Figure 4.17. AUTH © 1985 *The Philadelphia Inquirer*. Reprinted with permission of UNIVERSAL PRESS SYNDICATE. All rights reserved.

energy. While an American cartoon of three charred human skeletons in the three-monkey-position and the caption "Soviet Authorities deal with a Nuclear Accident"[93] is a frustrated reaction to the haphazard way in which the Soviets deal with nuclear power plants and their safety, such an illustration clearly also brings to mind the horrific perils that would follow a nuclear attack. The growing public awareness that stricter controls are needed in the management of nuclear power in all of its manifestations was vividly illustrated in an American cartoon based once again on the three-monkey motif. This time the monkeys take the shape of three members of the "N.R.C." (Nuclear Regulatory Commission), whose heads are mere circles with the atomic symbol in the middle.[94] Clearly the cartoon argues that more control and less indifference are mandatory as nuclear power plants proliferate throughout the world.

A nonpolitical advertisement that appeared in *The New Yorker* in September 1986 might well be interpreted as an early sign of hope that the Cold War was drawing to a close. The ad, for the Dexter shoe manufacturer, shows a photograph of a military parade on a rainy day in Moscow's Red Square. The proverbial headline and part of the copy read as follows: "A shoe that's uncomfortable for walking is enough to make anyone see red. When you've got walking to do, an uncomfortable pair of shoes can really rain on your parade. So why don't you walk in shoes that were designed for it?"[95] The proverbial expression "To see red" is a splendid allusion to Red Square and the colorful red banners flying everywhere. It might even refer indirectly to the Soviets (or Reds), in general, who would very much like to have some of the amenities of the capitalist United States, including good shoes. Taking such speculative thoughts a step further, why not also argue that since this ad deals with shoes, that the proverbial expression "To put oneself into the other person's shoes" might just be part of the message as well. Acting out this phrase would, so one should hope, bring about a better understanding for the wishes, needs, anxieties, and dreams of the other side.

On a more tangible level and certainly of extreme importance for arms control was the steady move in 1987 toward the elimination of INF (Intermediate-range Nuclear Forces), which culminated on 8 December in the INF Treaty signed by Reagan and Gorbachev at the Washington Summit. A colorful German caricature by Horst Haitzinger commented enthusiastically on the abolition of intermediate-range missiles from Europe. Reagan and Gorbachev, both dressed in space suits, shake hands and agree that this is "Ein kleiner Schritt für die Menschheit, aber ein großer für uns zwei!" (A small step for humanity, but a large one for us two!).[96] The caption is, of course, an adaptation of astronaut Neil Armstrong's famous statement on stepping on the moon on 20 July 1969: "That's one small step for [a] man, one giant leap for mankind."[97] It will also be remembered that the spaceship which took Armstrong to the moon was called the "Eagle," and Haitzinger has included it in his drawing in the shape of a peace dove with both the U.S. and Soviet flags painted on it and an olive branch in its beak. Proverbially speaking, the INF Treaty was indeed a first small step to some real solutions to the arms race and also toward the end of the Cold War. An advertisement in the Los Angeles Times made this abundantly clear. The giant headline, "The pen is mightier than the sword," expressed proverbial confidence in the power and wisdom of the treaty, enthusiasm that was reinforced by an accompanying photograph that showed Gorbachev and Reagan signing the treaty (see fig. 4.18).[98] Under this photograph runs a brief caption stating simply: "The historic document is signed. The pen is a Parker." This is followed, of course, by a picture of a Parker fountain pen with the trade name in large print. From nuclear missiles to harmless pens, that is the message here, and it is fascinating to observe once again how proverbs are used by the advertising agencies of Madison Avenue not only to make effective ads but also to communicate basic truths with the simple rhetoric of proverbial wisdom.[99]

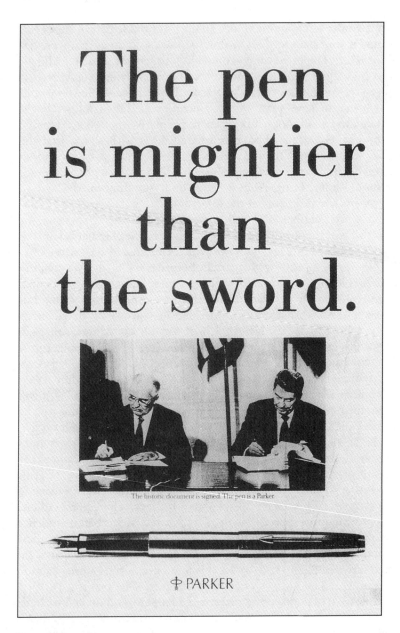

Figure 4.18

Once the INF Treaty was signed, events that signaled the end of the Cold War began to move at a breathtaking pace. With Gorbachev's policies of *glasnost* and *perestroika,* the entire Soviet Union and the Warsaw Pact countries underwent major sociopolitical changes, and arms reduction talks continued. Political scientists agree in general that by mid-1989 the Cold War had basically come to an end. Even so, the Berlin Wall, that ever-present symbol of the Iron Curtain, still divided Germany and thereby Eastern and Western Europe. In a speech on 31 May 1989 in Mainz, Germany, President George Bush reiterated Reagan's earlier request that the Berlin Wall come down so that the division of Europe could once and for all cease to exist. Germany at this time began to play a pivotal role in the final months of the Cold War period. On 10 September 1989, Hungary announced that thousands of East Germans would be allowed to cross the border into Austria and on to West Germany, thus commencing the mass exodus of East Germans to the West. Then, during a state visit on 6–7 October 1989, Gorbachev courageously criticized East German general secretary Erich Honecker and his government for failure to reform, and barely a month later, on 9 November, the Berlin Wall was opened and the Iron Curtain was lifted. Reunification of Germany was inevitable, even though the political leaders of East and West "pussyfooted" around for a while trying to find a workable solution. Once again it was Horst Haitzinger who captured this momentous time through a proverbial caricature. Taking the proverbial expression "Wie die Katze um den heißen Brei gehen" (To walk like a cat around the hot porridge, that is, to beat about the bush, to pussyfoot around) as his starting point, Haitzinger places a hot pot of porridge labeled "Wiedervereinigung Deutschlands" (Reunification of Germany) in the middle of his picture and shows the world's leaders as cats circling it for fear of being burned (see fig. 4.19).[100] This was indeed a hot situation, but with appropriate credit given, above all to Gorbachev, as well as George Bush, Margaret Thatcher, and François Mitterand, Germany became a unified nation again on 3 October 1990.

Many people will remember the television reports of how Germans on both sides of the Berlin Wall chiseled away at the concrete that had separated this city and the world of East and West for twenty-eight years from 1961 to 1989. The Wall as a symbol of decades of paranoia, distrust, and fear was dismantled almost as quickly as it was built. Today only a few isolated feet of it can be seen in Berlin as a reminder of the real Iron Curtain. Where the Wall previously stood, construction crews are eagerly building governmental, commercial, and residential structures for the citizens of reunified Germany. Tourists can still purchase small pieces of the Wall as souvenirs, and I know that I am not the only German living abroad who has carried a tiny section of it back to the United States. Be-

Figure 4.19

fore it fell I walked along this infamous structure during my frequent vis-
its to Berlin, paying particular attention to the graffiti that ornamented it
for miles. Writers of graffiti often cite traditional proverbs or adapt their
underlying structures to innovative messages.[101] The result is a com-
monplace rhetoric which by its anonymity communicates general feelings

in the form of easily recognizable and memorizable slogans or proverbs. Those texts on the Berlin Wall that have a proverbial ring to them clearly express the worldview of tension and frustration that overcame anybody facing this stigmatized structure. There was, of course, a big difference on the two sides of the Wall. While the Western side was covered with graffiti, the Eastern side was naked and blank since people could not reach the Wall due to the barbed wire and mines.

In any case, a few examples of the proverbial graffiti that decorated the Western side of the Berlin Wall will help to summarize the decades of the Cold War as well as the Iron Curtain. One anonymous writer chose the proverb "United we stand, divided we fall"[102] and added the internationally known peace symbol to this message which dates back to classical times and here expresses a joint front against the oppression and lack of freedom in the East. A German graffito spelled out in large letters the subjective wish "Ich will mit dem Kopf durch die Wand" (I want to push my head through the wall).[103] The underlying proverbial expression is precisely "Mit dem Kopf durch die Wand wollen" (To knock [beat; run] one's head against a wall), where the German phrase does not only imply knocking one's head against the wall but also wanting to get quite literally through the wall. This lonely piece of graffiti on a rather sparingly inscribed section of the Wall certainly expressed the common feeling that people experienced whenever they visited the Berlin Wall. But there was also the fitting graffito "The grass isn't greener,"[104] which as an anti-proverb to the traditional text "The grass is always greener on the other side of the fence"[105] succinctly calls attention to the fact that things are not better in the world of communism, as some people in the West argued from time to time. One can also imagine that a British or American student, perhaps, was standing at this Wall who suddenly came to the awareness of how lucky she or he was to live in the free world and felt an overwhelming desire to add this new proverbial truth to the other graffiti on the Wall for all to see.

Another piece of graffiti recalls all the discussions of arms reduction that went on during the Cold War. Earlier in this chapter we saw how the proverb "Charity begins at home" and its variation "Victory begins at home" were used as slogans to accelerate the war effort in the United States during the Second World War. The very fitting additional variation "Disarmament begins at home"[106] which someone scrawled on the Berlin Wall should have reminded negotiators at the various arms reduction conferences all along that both sides had to limit arms, that one side had to start, and that it certainly took two to tango along the disarmament path. Of course, friendship and even love have brought East and West to

Figure 4.20

a better understanding, as the revealing graffito "Love is thicker than concrete," a fitting variation of the proverb "Blood is thicker than water," prophesied on the Berlin Wall in large white (and symbolically innocent) letters (see fig. 4.20).[107]

Reviewing the almost five decades of the Cold War in his book *The Cold War Legacy* (1991), Thomas Naylor includes a significant chapter entitled "The Pot Can't Call the Kettle Black" that ends with the following short paragraph:

> No matter how you slice it, both the Soviet Union and the United States have inflicted a great deal of pain and suffering and bloodshed on a lot of people over the past hundred years or so. Neither side is clean. Maybe in the balance the Soviet Union is a more evil country than the United States? Maybe not. Does it really matter? There is plenty of evil to go around.[108]

There is indeed no sense in one side's placing blame on the other for being more responsible for the Cold War. The proverbial pot should not call the kettle black. While the Cold War was primarily based on a steady increase of arsenals on both sides, there were also distinct Soviet and American worldviews that added an ideological dimension to the state of Soviet-American relations. This is reflected in a pronounced ideological rhetoric, of which the terms "Cold War" and "Iron Curtain" are the two all-encompassing *leitmotifs*. Others are clearly such concepts as democracy, communism, containment, coexistence, détente, *glasnost,* and many more. But in addition to these major terms, there were also political slogans as well as traditional proverbs and manipulated anti-proverbs which characterized the unique ideological rhetoric of this period of history. The whole Cold War could perhaps be summarized by the fourteenth-century proverb "The object of war is peace."[109] Now that the Cold War has run its treacherous course, let us hope that peace will continue to flourish, not only between Russia and the United States but also everywhere on the globe.

5

"The Only Good Indian Is a Dead Indian"

*History and Meaning of a
Proverbial Stereotype*

The interest in the study of national character, stereotypes, ethnic slurs, and racial prejudice as expressed in proverbs and proverbial expressions has a considerable scholarly tradition. Paremiologically oriented folklorists and cultural historians have assembled collections of such invectives, the three standard books being Otto von Reinsberg-Düringsfeld's *Internationale Titulaturen* (1863), Henri Gaidoz and Paul Sébillot's *Blason populaire de la France* (1884), and Abraham A. Roback's *A Dictionary of International Slurs* (1944).[1] Numerous scholarly articles have also investigated the stereotypical worldview expressed in proverbial speech, notably William Hugh Jansen's "A Culture's Stereotypes and Their Expression in Folk Clichés" (1957), Américo Paredes's "Proverbs and Ethnic Stereotyping" (1970); Mariana Birnbaum's "On the Language of Prejudice" (1971), Alan Dundes's "Slurs International: Folk Comparisons of Ethnicity and National Character" (1975), Uta Quasthoff's "The Uses of Stereotype in Everyday Argument" (1978); and my own "Proverbs in Nazi Germany: The Promulgation of Anti-Semitism and Stereotypes through Folklore" (1982).[2] This selected list of publications alone is a clear indication that considerable attention has been paid to proverbial invectives against minorities throughout the world. These unfortunate and misguided expressions of hate, prejudice, and unfounded generalizations are unfortunately part of verbal communication among people, and stereotypical phrases can be traced back to the earliest written records. Proverbial stereotypes are regretfully nothing new, but perhaps people are more willing today to question such dangerous slurs as they become more aware of their psychological and ethical implications. This at least is what a more enlightened citizenry should be hoping for at a time when tensions among political, racial, and ethnic minorities appear to be increasing.

138

Although much is known about proverbial stereotypes among different nationalities and regions, and although numerous studies have been undertaken to study verbal slurs against Jews and African Americans, especially in the United States,[3] very little interest has been taken in the proverbial invectives that have been hurled against the Native Americans ever since Christopher Columbus and later explorers, settlers, and immigrants set foot on the American continent. The 1992 quincentenary celebration of Columbus's voyage sparked numerous scholarly exchanges and publications, many of which examined how the native population suffered terribly in the name of expansion and progress. Native Americans were deprived of their homeland, killed mercilessly or placed on reservations, where many continue their marginalized existence to the present day. Earlier concepts of the "good Indian" or "noble savage," typical of the seventeenth and early eighteenth centuries, quickly were replaced by reductions of the native inhabitants to "wild savages" who were standing in the way of expansionism under the motto of "manifest destiny."[4] Typical of this attitude is the toast recorded in 1779 in the journal of Major James Norris and quoted by Roy Pearce in his valuable book *Savagism and Civilization: A Study of the Indian and the American Mind* (1967): "Civilization or death to all American savages."[5] This early frontier declaration means, bluntly put, change your ways and assimilate the rules and lifestyle of the white conquerors and settlers or die. Anybody resisting this policy was "bad," and once the popular white attitude was geared toward the demonization of the Native Americans, the stage was set for killing thousands of them or driving the survivors onto inhumane reservations. An unpublished and little known dissertation by Priscilla Shames with the title "The Long Hope: A Study of American Indian Stereotypes in American Popular Fiction" (1969) shows how this cruel treatment of the native population is described in American literature,[6] while Dee Brown's best-selling book *Bury My Heart at Wounded Knee: An Indian History of the American West* (1970) gives a more factual account. Brown's book includes a chapter with the gruesome proverbial title "The Only Good Indian Is a Dead Indian," the word "dead" meaning both literal death, and for those who survived the mass killings, a figurative death, a restricted life on the reservation with little freedom to continue the traditional lifestyle.[7]

It is alarming that this hateful proverb, which became current on the frontier not quite a hundred years after Major Norris recorded his threatening toast, is still in use today, astonishingly enough both by the general population and Native Americans themselves. Witness, for example, the title *The Only Good Indian: Essays by Canadian Indians* (1970). How bad must their plight be if the editor, Waubageshig, decided to choose this invective against his own people as a title for a collection of short prose and poetic texts in which these native inhabitants from Canada express their frustration with their marginalized life in modern society. The explanation for the title is given in the introduction as follows:

> Police brutality, incompetent bureaucrats, legal incongruities, destructive education systems, racial discrimination, ignorant politicians who are abetted by a country largely ignorant of its native population, are conditions which Indians face daily. Yes, the only good Indian is still a dead one. Not dead physically, but dead spiritually, mentally, economically and socially.[8]

Yes, this is Canada, but the same picture of daily degradations emerges for Native Americans in the United States. Studies like Ralph and Natasha Friar's *The Only Good Indian . . . The Hollywood Gospel* (1972) have exposed the especially negative stereotypical view of Native Americans in American motion pictures. Even though some movies have shown the "good" Indian, most films are guilty of "the enhancement and perpetuation of stereotype motifs of the Indian as drunken, savage, or treacherous, unreliable or childlike."[9] Similar prejudices can, of course, be observed in other forms of the mass media and everyday verbal communication through the use of jokes, songs, and proverbial slurs.

A third publication that carries part of the proverb "The only good Indian is a dead Indian" in its title is a scholarly dissertation by the folklorist Rayna Green. Herself a Native American, she chose the title "The Only Good Indian: The Image of the Indian in American Vernacular Culture" (1973) for her voluminous and enlightening study. The proverbial title sets the tone—here is a meticulous account of the past and current popular view of Native Americans as expressed by the American population of all age groups, all social classes, and all regions. The result is a shocking stereotypical image that permeates all modes of expression, of which linguistic examples are only a small part. Green includes a few pages on "Sayings, Proverbs, Proverbial Comparisons, and Other Metaphoric Usages"[10] that comment in a stereotypical way about Native Americans.

Other lexicographers and paremiographers have also put together small lists of these invectives. Even a small selection of phrases from these different sources reveals the contempt nineteenth-century Americans felt toward Native Americans. Frequently found proverbial expressions (and the dates of their earliest occurrence where available) are "To go Indian file" (1754, meaning to walk in a single line), "To be an Indian giver (gift)" (1764, to take back a gift), "To sing Indian" (1829, to act as one who defies death), "To do (play) the sober Indian" (1832, to remain sober or drink so little that you are still able to get the knives and do harm), "To play Indian" (1840, to not show any emotions), "To see Indians" (1850, to be in a delirium), "To turn Indian" (1862, to revert to a state of nature), "To be a regular Indian" (1925, to be a habitual drunkard), and "To be on the Indian list" (1925, to not be allowed to purchase liquor). Many proverbial comparisons portray Native Americans as socially or ethically unworthy or unattractive: "As dirty as an Indian" (1803), "As mean as an Indian" (1843), "To yell and holler like Indians" (1844), "As wild (untameable) as an Indian" (1855), "As superstitious as an Indian" (1858), "To run like a wild Indian" (1860), "To spend money like a drunken Indian" (this expression and all of the following stem from the late nineteenth century), "To stare (stand) like a wooden Indian," "Straight as an Indian's hair," "Red as an Indian," "Silent as a cigar-store Indian," "Drunker than an Indian," and "Sly as an Indian."[11]

Turning to *bona fide* proverbs that express slanderous views concerning the Native Americans, Rayna Green observes that the text "The only good Indian is a dead Indian" is "the only genuine proverb with reference to Indians in the [United] states."[12] If only that were true! Unfortunately other proverbs that malign Native Americans have gained currency in the folk speech of this country. For example, there is the disparaging phrase "Indians will be Indians," which dates from 1766 and despite its lack of a metaphor clearly expresses the idea that Native Americans will remain uncivilized savages no matter what improvements the white soldiers and settlers offer to change them.[13] Another proverb that complains of the impossibility of civilizing the original inhabitants of this country is "An Indian, a partridge, and a spruce tree can't be tamed" which was recorded in 1853.[14] And there is also the slanderous proverb "The Indian will come back to his blanket" that was first documented in Oregon around 1945.[15] It implies that even those Indians who have assimilated the ways of the white masters will in due time return to their primitive and traditional ways, or "Indians will be Indians" as a similar proverb maintains. From this same time comes the proverb "Never trust an Indian," first recorded in Kansas.[16] Who will be surprised then that the Hon. Alfred Benjamin Meacham, ex-superintendent of Indian Affairs, had the audacity to write in his book *Wigwam and War-Path; or The Royal Chief in Chains* (1875) that it is irrelevant whether Indians are cheated by the government or not: "It makes no difference. They are Indians, and three-fourths of the people of the United States *believe* and *say* that 'the best Indians are all under ground.'"[17] At another place in his book Meacham poses the rhetorical question "Do my readers wonder now that so many white men, along the frontier line, declare that all good 'Injins are three feet under the ground'?"[18] And one year later, in his book *Wi-ne-ma (The Woman-Chief) and Her People* (1876), Meacham cites yet a third variant of this frontier proverb, namely "All good Indians are four foot [sic] under ground."[19] There can be no doubt about the sad fact that Native Americans were declared proverbially dead by the middle of the nineteenth century, especially following the American Civil War, when U.S. soldiers joined bigoted frontier settlers west of the Mississippi River in a mercilessly carried out campaign to kill off the native population of this giant land.

Such willfully planned and ruthlessly executed destruction of the Native Americans needed its battle slogan, a ready-made catchphrase that could help the perpetrators justify their inhuman treatment of their victims. The proverb which gained currency at that time and which, as we have discussed, can still be heard today is "The only good Indian is a dead Indian." It was indeed a devilish stroke of genius that created this dangerous slur. Its multisemanticity is grotesque to say the least. On the one hand it is a proverbial slogan which justifies the actual mass slaughter of Indians by U.S. soldiers. But it also states on a more figurative level that Indians can only be "good" persons if they become Christians and take on the civilized ways of their white oppressors. Then they might be "good," but as far as their native culture is concerned they would in fact be dead.

Who coined the invective "The only good Indian is a dead Indian" is not known for certain. Although most lexicographers attribute it to a remark allegedly made by General Philip Sheridan in 1869, the *terminus a quo* for this slur can be found in the *The Congressional Globe: Containing the Debates and Proceedings of the Second Session [of the] Fortieth Congress* (1868). During a debate in the House of Representatives on an "Indian Appropriation Bill" on 28 May 1868, Congressman James Michael Cavanaugh from Montana did not hesitate to make the following statement a part of the permanent public record:

> I will say frankly that, in my judgment, the entire Indian policy of the country is wrong from its very inception. In the first place you offer a premium for rascality by paying a beggarly pittance to your Indian agents. The gentleman from Massachusetts [Mr. Butler] may denounce the sentiment as atrocious, but I will say that I like an Indian better dead than living. I have never in my life seen a good Indian (and I have seen thousands) except when I have seen a dead Indian. I believe in the Indian policy pursued by New England in years long gone. I believe in the Indian policy which was taught by the great chieftain of Massachusetts, Miles Standish. I believe in the policy that exterminates the Indians, drives them outside the boundaries of civilization, because you cannot civilize them. Gentlemen may call this very harsh language, but perhaps they would not think so if they had had my experience in Minnesota and Colorado. In Minnesota the almost living babe has been torn from its mother's womb; and I have seen the child, with its young heart palpitating,

nailed to the window-sill. I have seen women who were scalped, disfigured, outraged. In Denver, Colorado Territory, I have seen women and children brought in scalped. Scalped why? Simply because the Indian was "upon the war-path," to satisfy the devilish and barbarous propensities. . . . The Indian will make a treaty in the fall, and in the spring he is again "upon the war-path." The torch, the scalping-knife, plunder, and desolation follow wherever the Indian goes.

. . . My friend from Massachusetts [Mr. Butler] has never passed the barrier of the frontier. All he knows about Indians (the gentleman will pardon me for saying it) may have been gathered I presume from the brilliant pages of the author of "The Last of the Mohicans" or from the lines of the poet Longfellow in "Hiawatha." The gentleman has never yet seen the Indian upon the war-path. He has never been chased, as I have been, by these red devils—who seem to be the pets of eastern philanthropists.[20]

The sentence "I have never in my life seen a good Indian except when I have seen a dead Indian" is, of course, a mere prose utterance that lacks many of the poetic and formal markers of traditional proverbs save for its parallel structure. Yet it is easily noticeable that this subjective sentence contains the clear possibility of becoming shortened into the much more proverbial formula "A good Indian is a dead Indian." From what is known today about the negative attitudes about Native Americans on the frontier and the Indian territories during the second half of the nineteenth century, it can be stated with unfortunate certainty that James Michael Cavanaugh was boldly expressing in the House of Representatives what most Americans felt if not said in as proverbial a fashion.

Indians and death were connected in the frontier worldview, and it should not be surprising that U.S. soldiers and their officers saw the connection as a necessary one. Major William Shepherd expresses this acceptance of the annihilation of Native Americans in his book *Prairie Experiences* (1884):

People who know nothing about Indians look at them at first with curiosity, which soon is mixed with a little contempt; but those who have had much to do with them in wars dislike their presence, and, knowing their habits, are often nervous and apprehensive of treachery. It would be a meritorious deed, from an Indian point of view, for a band to murder a single white man, if it could be done with perfect safety in regard to their skins. . . . The possibility of the Indian being converted to any civilized or useful purposes is a chimera; he will be a wild man, or he will die out; his inherited disposition will prevent his ever being a satisfactory member of a settled community. On the frontier a good Indian means a "dead Indian." Whether the Indians have deserved, or brought on themselves, the injuries they have suffered, and to what extent their treatment might have been ameliorated by honesty in the agents employed by the Government, and by a more humanitarian spirit in the people who have ousted them, can matter little at present. The Indian must go, is going, and will soon be gone. It is his luck.[21]

This cruel passage from 1884 can be contrasted with the thoughts expressed two years later by an Englishman, Vicar Alfred Gurney, in his book *A Ramble through the United States* (1886). Notice that while Major Shepherd's statement that "on the frontier a good Indian means a 'dead Indian'" has not quite yet reached the final proverbial form, the Vicar makes it perfectly clear that Americans frequently expressed the proverbial remark "A good Indian is a dead Indian," thus attesting to the fact that the proverb was well established by 1886:

> The story of Indian warfare is no doubt one of bloodshed, cruelty, and outrage; but, if they resented with the ferocity of savages the intrusion of the white men who appropriated their hunting grounds and gave them no quarter, let it not be forgotten that they responded generously to the appeal of those who, consecrated by the hands of poverty and pain, spoke to them in the Name of a crucified King, and proclaimed the gospel of peace and goodwill. Not yet, I think, are white men civilized enough to handle savages successfully. And of all savages the red man, perhaps, demands the greatest patience, courtesy, and forbearance. Not yet have we learnt to put in practice the divine method, though the experience of ages demonstrates the futility of every other, of overcoming evil, not with evil, but with good. The Government of the United States is at length earnestly endeavoring to do tardy justice to the conquered race; but it was distressing to hear again and again from American lips the remark that "a *good* Indian is a *dead* Indian." For my own part I cannot believe that a people whose dark eyes are so wistful and dreamy, whose speech is so musical, and whose language so full of poetry, can be hopelessly degraded, or doomed to extinction.[22]

Positive as this assessment by a man of the religious order might be at first glance, it does nevertheless endorse the attempts of "civilizing" the Native Americans into Christians, thereby destroying their traditional beliefs and culture. The difference between the soldiers and militant people of the frontier, on the one hand, and the Christian missionaries, on the other, was one of degree, for both groups intended to change or convert the perceived savages by the sword or the word of God.

For the historical survey of the proverb "The only good Indian is a dead Indian," it is of considerable importance to notice that the preceding quoted passages from 1884 and 1886 do *not* associate any particular person with having coined these early proverbial variants. This is also true of the three variants from the 1870s quoted earlier about Indians belonging several feet below the ground. It is a well-established fact that although "conceivably a proverb may for a time be associated with the inventor's name, all ascriptions to definite persons must be looked upon with suspicion,"[23] as Archer Taylor observes correctly in his seminal book on *The Proverb* (1931). And yet, such an ascription of the proverb under discussion here was in fact undertaken by Edward Ellis in his book *The History of Our Country: From the Discovery of America to the Present Time* (1895). In a short paragraph entitled "Sheridan's Bon Mot," Ellis relates the following from an eyewitness account by Captain Charles Nordstrom:

> It was the writer's [Nordstrom's] good fortune to be present when General Sheridan gave utterance to that *bon mot* which has since become so celebrated. It was in January, 1869, in camp at old Fort Cobb, Indian Territory, now Oklahoma, shortly after Custer's fight with Black-Kettle's band of Cheyennes. Old Toch-a-way (Turtle Dove), a chief of the Comanches, on being presented to Sheridan, desired to impress the General in his favor, and striking himself a resounding blow on the breast, he managed to say: "Me, Toch-a-way; me good Injun." A quizzical smile lit up the General's face as he set those standing by in a roar by saying: "The only good Indians I ever saw were dead."[24]

This anecdotal paragraph with Nordstrom's obvious delight in telling the gruesomely "humorous" event appears of questionable authenticity at first. It is, of course, understandable that General Philip Sheridan repeatedly denied having made such a statement, but there is also no doubt that Sheridan was known as a bigot and Indian hater, as the historian Paul Andrew Hutton has shown in a chapter of his book *Phil Sheridan and His Army* (1985) so appropriately called "Forming Military Indian Policy: 'The Only Good Indian Is a Dead Indian.'"[25] It is of interest, however, that Hutton does not quote Sheridan's statement "The only good Indians I ever saw were dead" but rather its more generalized and more powerful proverbial form "The only good Indian is a dead Indian" which became synonymous with the Indian policy of Sheridan and most other generals and soldiers. As Stephen Ambrose puts it so clearly in his account of the parallel lives of the two American warriors, *Crazy Horse and Custer* (1975): "Frontier posts reverberated with tough talk about what would be done to the Indians, once caught, and it became an article of faith among the Army officers that 'you could not trust an Indian.' Sheridan's famous remark, 'The only good Indian I ever saw was dead,' was often and gleefully quoted."[26]

Naturally Sheridan has had his defenders who have tried to disclaim his having coined this proverb, and they are technically correct, for it will probably never be known whether the proverb developed from Sheridan's statement in 1869 or whether his contemptuous utterance was a subjective reformulation of the proverb already in currency. It must be remembered that James Michael Cavanaugh from Montana had made a quite similar statement already in 1868 in the U.S. House of Representatives, and yet no one claims that he originated this frontier proverb. Sheridan's firm association with the proverb may rest entirely on his reputation as a malicious Indian killer, a reputation which would not be erased even if someone someday locates "The only good Indian is a dead Indian" in print before Sheridan's January 1869 statement. Even so attempts have been made to clear Sheridan's name as this proverb's author. In 1904 Brig.-Gen. Michael V. Sheridan, in his new and enlarged edition of *Personal Memoirs of Philip Henry Sheridan,* writes apologetically that "some 'fool friend' in Montana attributed to General Sheridan the expression that 'a dead Indian is the only good Indian,' and, though he immediately disavowed the inhuman epigram, his assailants continued to ring the changes on it for months."[27] (The expression "ring the changes" probably means to play variations on a theme and comes from the art of ringing bells.) Another scholar who tried to defend General Sheridan was Carl Rister, who begins the preface of his book *Border Command: General Phil Sheridan in the West* (1944) with the following remarks:

> Sheridan's foes charged that he had said, "The only good Indian is a dead Indian." It is improbable that he made such a statement. That was not his policy. But he did believe that Indians must be taught that crime does not pay; that, if murder and theft were committed by either red man or white, punishment would be swift and sure. Moral suasion, he argued, could not always be used even among the most enlightened people; courts and law enforcement agencies were necessary. In this, Sheridan had enthusiastic support—not only of his officers and men, but also of the border people. To his enemies, Sheridan was haughty, unbending, and scornful; to his subordinates he was "Little Phil," a man of fiery temperament, caustic, impetuous, savage when his plans were not properly executed, never sparing himself or others, but fair and generous when the occasion demanded. Physically, he was a small man, but every inch a leader, strong and magnetic, honored, loved, and feared.[28]

This attempt to whitewash the former Civil War general who in the late 1860s turned his attention to fighting Indians and who was widely known as an unscrupulous general who strongly believed in placing all Native Americans on well-guarded reservations and punishing those mercilessly who did not follow his round-up orders,[29] fails precisely because the proverb "The only good Indian is a dead Indian," the frontier's motto and one born in the nineteenth-century's Indian wars on the plains, is exactly the sort of thing one would expect General Sheridan to say. If he is not its actual author, his policies against Native Americans encourage us to consider him the proverb's symbolic author.

If General Sheridan did not coin this proverb, its author was also not an even more famous, or rather infamous, Indian fighter who made the following remarks at a speech in January of 1886 in New York:

> I suppose I should be ashamed to say that I take the Western view of the Indian. I don't go so far as to think that the only good Indians are dead Indians, but I believe nine out of every ten are, and I shouldn't like to inquire too closely into the case of the tenth. The most vicious cowboy has more moral principle than the average Indian. Turn three hundred low families of New York into New Jersey, support them for fifty years in vicious idleness, and you will have some idea of what the Indians are. Reckless, revengeful, fiendishly cruel, they rob and murder, not the cowboys, who can take care of themselves, but the defenseless, lone settlers on the plains. As for the soldiers, an Indian chief once asked Sheridan for a cannon. "What! Do you want to kill my soldiers with it?" asked the general. "No," replied the chief, "want to kill the cowboy; kill soldier with a club."[30]

The person who spoke this passage was that "rough rider" who published his racist and expansionist views and an account of his exploits on the American frontier in his acclaimed book *The Winning of the West* (1889)— no one less than Theodore Roosevelt, who became president of the United States five years after delivering these hateful comments!

The fact that Roosevelt included the proverb "The only good Indian is a dead Indian" in a speech in 1886 in the eastern city of New York, far removed from the racial strife at the frontier, is a clear indication that the proverb and its discriminatory message had permeated the American consciousness by that time. Even so it was not until 1926 that Gurney Benham registered Philip Sheridan's "The only good Indians I ever saw were dead" as a political phrase in his *Complete Book of Quotations*.[31] Other lexicographers did the same, with H. L. Mencken in 1960 and Bergen Evans in 1968 attributing it mistakenly but more or less fittingly to another famous Civil War general who had participated in Indian wars, namely William Tecumseh Sherman.[32] The editors of two more recent books of quotations, both published in 1988, obviously realized this mistake and returned the credit to Sheridan.[33] There are, however, also numerous authors of quotation dictionaries who list the actual proverb, "The only good Indian is a dead Indian," rather than Sheridan's phrase. As early as 1934 Burton Stevenson in his *Home Book of Quotations* has it both ways, citing the proverb as the major heading and then referring to Sheridan's actual statement in an explanatory note.[34] This is the first instance in a major reference work of the partial identification of the frontier proverb with General Sheridan. Seven years later the editors of the renowned *Oxford Dictionary of Quotations* (1941) followed suit and went one step further. They merely cited the actual proverb and attached Philip Sheridan's name to it. The subsequent editors of the second and third editions of this classic work published identical entries, thus playing their role in spreading the lexicographical misinformation that Sheridan coined this stereotypical proverb.[35] The American competitor, Bartlett's *Familiar Quotations,* improved on the Oxford editors' entry. Christopher Morley, as the editor of the eleventh edition from 1941, listed Sheridan's remark "The only good Indians I ever saw were dead" for the first time in this important reference work. He repeated the same information in the twelfth edition of 1949, but the unnamed editor of the thirteenth edition (1955) added the following comment after quoting Sheridan's statement: "The phrase is more often heard in the version 'The only good Indian is a dead Indian.'" Emily Morison Beck as the editor of the two subsequent editions of Bartlett's *Familiar Quotations* (14th ed., 1968; 15th ed., 1980) kept the identical entry, thus at least indicating to the readers that there is a difference between General Sheridan's personal quotation and the folk proverb.[36] Yet quotation dictionaries of lesser value and distribution have since 1942 usually just listed the proverb "The only good Indian is a dead Indian" with Philip Sheridan's name attached to it,[37] a phenomenon that indicates how often lexicographers blindly copy from each other.

Obviously paremiographers have also played their role in registering the folk proverb in newer proverb collections. The British scholar Vincent Stuckey Lean listed the early variant "A good Indian is a dead Indian" as an American proverb for the first time in 1902 in his *Proverbs Relating to the United Kingdom . . . together with a few English Estimates of other Nations and Places,* after having found it in Alfred Gurney's *A Ramble through the United States* (1886) which has been discussed above.[38] The next reference comes in 1931, this time by the dean of international paremiology Archer Taylor, who in his book *The Proverb* included the terse statement that "'The only good Indian is a dead Indian' breathes the air of our western frontier."[39] Admittedly that does not say much, but it indicates that Taylor recognized this text as a *bona fide* folk proverb from the American frontier that long had currency throughout the United States without the need for at best an apocryphal attribution to General Philip Sheridan.

In 1944 Abraham Roback included the slight variant "The only good Indian is a dead one" as an American "slogan originating in the Colonial period, when the Indians became a real menace, massacring hundreds of the new settlers" in his *Dictionary of International Slurs.*[40] While Roback is incorrect in ascribing the seventeenth or at least eighteenth century as the time of origin of the proverb, he does at least point to sociopolitical problems that existed between the Native Americans and the early settlers. Samuel Eliot Morison's fascinating book on the early English settlers of Massachusetts, *Builders of the Bay Colony* (1930), cites the nineteenth-century proverbial invective as an appropriate description of tensions that existed between the new English settlers and the Native Americans:

> That same autumn of 1646, the General Court appointed Eliot [John Eliot, 1604–90] one of a committee to select and purchase land from the Indians, at the colony's expense, "for the encouragement of the Indians to live in a more orderly way amongst us." Yet from the start he encountered suspicion and hostility among his own people, whose attitude was always a heavy obstacle to his work. Frenchmen and Spaniards mingled easily with the American Indians; but the English pride of race forbade [this]. Your New England settler quickly acquired what has become the traditional attitude of the English-speaking pioneer: "A good Indian is a dead Indian." To him the native was a dirty, lazy, treacherous beast: "the arrow that flieth by day" and "the terror that flieth by night."[41]

The hostility between New England's settlers and the region's Native Americans may have eased some hundred years later, when influential thinkers like Patrick Henry in 1787 even advocated interracial marriages between Indians and whites. Reflecting on "The Indian Contribution to the American Revolution," Leroy Eid comments that "one often hears that the frontier's motto was 'the only good Indian is a dead Indian.' Perhaps this cliché—born in the nineteenth century's plains wars—was true of some frontiers, but it was not anywhere universally true of the earlier frontiers where whites met vibrant and confident Indian cultures."[42] Nevertheless, it is a known fact that Native Americans were also exterminated or marginalized in the Colonies. Such hostile attitudes and policies are exactly what James Michael Cavanaugh referred to when, as earlier quoted, he said in 1868 in the U.S. House of Representatives: "I believe in the Indian policy pursued by New England in years long gone. I believe in the Indian policy which was taught by the great chieftain of Massachusetts, Miles Standish [1584?–1656; military defender of New Plymouth and Weymouth colony]. I believe in the policy that exterminates the Indians, drives them outside the boundaries of civilization, because you cannot civilize them."[43]

Starting with Burton Stevenson's large volume *The Home Book of Proverbs, Maxims, and Famous Phrases* (1948), the major Anglo-American proverb collections all contain the proverb "The only good Indian is a dead Indian" with the notable exception of *The Oxford Dictionary of English Proverbs* (3d ed., 1970).[44] Smaller regional collections bear witness to the established proverbiality and the currency of this stereotypical frontier wisdom throughout the United States. Folklorist Helen Pearce indicates that this was not the only anti-Indian proverb still in current use by the mid-twentieth century, at least in the western United States. She includes six proverbial invectives with explanatory comments in a list of "Folk Sayings in a Pioneer Family of western Oregon," all of which were in current use in her own family (which originally reached Oregon in the 1850s) when she collected them in the early 1940s:

> There's no good Indian but a dead Indian.
> (This attitude is ungenerous, but it is derived from the experience of some of the early settlers.)
>
> He's an Indian giver.
> (He is a person who gives something and takes it back again; an ungracious giver.)
>
> He's off the reservation.
> (He is running wild; or doing something unusual; or appears very green and unsophisticated. The saying is derived from the sometimes wild behavior of Indians when permitted to leave their reservations and enter the white man's towns.)
>
> He was drunker than an Indian.
> (The pioneers found that Indians did not carry liquor well; hence this pioneer saying about a person obstreperously drunk.)
>
> He works harder than an Indian.
> (Often ironically said in western Oregon, where most of the Indians worked very little.)
>
> Wild as an Indian; sly (or cunning) as an Indian.
> (These are examples of numerous uncomplimentary comparisons.)[45]

The "no good Indian" proverb was also collected in 1963 in Pennsylvania and in 1965 in Illinois,[46] and the Folklore Archives at the University of California at Berkeley contain six additional citations that folklore students collected between 1964 and 1986 in California. The following comments by a fifty-year-old American informant to a student folklore collector in 1969 are quite telling:

> The only good Indian is a dead Indian.
> My informant learned this when she was a young girl [c. 1925] growing up in Carson City, Nevada. There was an Indian reservation near where they lived, and the whites of Carson City were very discriminating toward the Indians and looked upon them as quite inferior. She heard this used by many people in town. It was generally said as a comment after someone else would tell of the latest exploits of some "drunken" Indian. This comment meant that they were only good when they were dead, so all Indians alive are bad. My informant believes that this phrase came out of Indian wars and was first said by either General Grant or Lee, she can't remember which.[47]

While this statement makes clear once again how confused the attribution of a proverb to a certain historical person can get, it is also foremost an alarming testimony of the widespread disrespect of Native Americans. A second text from the Berkeley Folklore Archives, dated from 1977, indicates the persistence of this contempt for Native Americans:

> The only good Indian is a dead Indian.
> Donald [Geddes] admits that this is a very racist statement. He doesn't really believe but can still find the humor involved with it. He remembers that people at college in Palo Alto used to say it a lot, circa 1955. But he didn't think he learned it from anyone in particular. He is sure that he heard it in a discussion concerning Indians, but always in jest.
> I think that Mr. Geddes and his friends believe the saying more than they will admit. It reflects American culture because once long ago the Indians possessed our continent. Then we took it from them. When they protest, a good comeback is "The only good Indian is a dead Indian."[48]

A third student collector obtained the following even more recent information from a Californian informant in 1986. It illustrates how this prejudicial proverb is a deeply ingrained part of the worldview of many Americans:

> The only good Indian is a dead Indian.
> My informant is a native of North Dakota where she tells me there were many Indian reservations. She learned this proverb when she was a very young child (c. 1923). She cannot remember any specific sources for the proverb; it was just something that you would hear at home or at school. People in North Dakota were extremely prejudiced against the Indians because they had the reputation of never working, always drinking. They were not very honest people and were believed by many to be murderers and looters. Indians were not respected by the white people at all. Thus, we can understand the reasoning behind the proverb.[49]

This kind of documentation from various published and oral sources led my co-editors and me to ascribe a general geographical distribution throughout the United States to the proverb "The only good Indian is a dead Indian" in our recent *Dictionary of American Proverbs* (1992).[50] We felt that exclusion of this proverbial slur would not only be scholarly dishonest, it would also have hidden or whitewashed the ugly truth about the persistence of this proverb and the hostility toward Native Americans that it expresses.

Just as this proverb persists in oral communication, so it also permeates written sources from scholarly books to novels, from magazines to newspapers, and even surfaces in cartoons. Looking back toward the turn of the century, one finds in Mary Rinehart's detective novel *The Cir-*

cular Staircase (1908), for example, the grotesque double statement: "Just as the only good Indian is a dead Indian, so the only safe defaulter is a dead defaulter."[51] While the proverb actually serves only to introduce a male character who is obsessed with money, it nevertheless is used to describe this man's dishonesty by comparing him to the stereotypical devious Indian. This early reference also shows already what is to become a pattern in more modern uses of the proverb. Often the proverb is not directly quoted, but rather it is reduced to the formula "The only good X is a dead X," giving its speaker or author a ready-made proverbial slogan that carries all the negative and prejudicial connotations of its original proverbial form. Four years after Rinehart's formulaic use of the proverb, Edgar Burroughs followed suit in his futuristic novel *A Princess of Mars* (1912) by describing the heroine as a woman who despite "her tenderness and womanly sweetness was still a Martian, and to a Martian the only good enemy is a dead enemy; for every dead foeman means so much more to divide between those who live."[52] This variation maintains the victimization of the Native American but generalizes to include enemies of any type.

The proverbial formula "The only good X is a dead X" proved especially adaptable as a slogan against the German enemy during the First and Second World Wars. In his book *Good-bye to All That* (1929), Robert Graves reports the following account by a Canadian-Scot of war atrocities:

> They sent me back with three bloody prisoners, you see, and one started limping and groaning, so I had to keep on kicking the sod down the trench. He was an officer. It was getting dark and I felt fed up, so I thought: "I'll have a bit of game." I had them covered with the officer's revolver and made 'em open their pockets without turning around. Then I dropped a Mills bomb in each, with the pin out, and ducked behind a traverse. Bang, gang, bang! No more bloody prisoners. No good Fritzes but dead 'uns.'[53]

In another British account by the pseudonymous "Bombardier X" with the title *So This Was War!* (1930), the editor Shaw Desmond writes in his introduction to this demythologization of World War I:

> If you believe that "the only good Germans were dead Germans," and that every British Tommy lusted only to kill the Boche, and was without religion, read this boy [the bombardier] who writes: "We may curse and swear, but its only bluster. Deep down in our hearts, we pray. The Germans must pray, too. They're in it, the same as we are. They have mothers, and wives, and children, and the same God as we have. It is very difficult, this War. I don't understand it a bit."[54]

From 1930 there is yet another British variant directed against the Germans: "There's only one good Boche, and that's a dead one."[55] These examples verify that variants of the American proverb were used repeatedly by the British people against their German enemy, as does this statement from Anthony Gilbert's novel *Missing from Her Home* (1969): "We used to say in the First War—the only good German's a dead German."[56] Such variants show, of course, also the regrettable internationalization of the slanderous proverb and its underlying proverbial formula.

During World War II Agatha Christie in her detective novel *N or M?* (1941) includes the following dialogue between a British woman and a German refugee that once again connects the traditional proverb by means of a telling wordplay with the Germans:

> "You're a refugee. . . . This country's at War. You're a German." She smiled suddenly. "You can't expect the mere man in the street—literally the man in the street—to distinguish between bad Germans and good Germans, if I may put it so crudely."
> He still stared at her. His eyes, so very blue, were poignant with suppressed feeling. Then, suddenly, he too smiled. He said:
> "They said of Red Indians, did they not, that a good Indian was a dead Indian?" He laughed. "To be a good German I must be on time at my work. Please. Good morning."[57]

The anti-German variant of the proverb surfaces again in another British war novel, entitled *Green Hazard* (1945) by Manning Coles. It's used in a passage where the speaker casts suspicion on the morals of another character: "Good chap, isn't he, though I find that placid manner rather terrifying sometimes. I know 'the only good German is a dead German,' but he enjoys killing them. I don't. What's a duty to me is a pleasure to him."[58] Especially interesting here is the way in which the speaker sets himself apart from the "placid" killer at the same time that he casually uses a proverbial expression that endorses the necessity of exterminating an enemy. Another, more recent work, C. Day Lewis's autobiographical *The Buried Day* (1960), indicates that British schoolboys knew of this proverbial slogan against the German enemy, even if they did not fully embrace its sentiment: "Certainly, racial hatred was not in the curriculum at Wilkie's [school]. We were not encouraged to think along the lines of 'the only good German is a dead German,' nor were we affected by the adult hysteria which looted shops with German names above them and banned Beethoven from the concert halls. We played English v. German war games, of course, but they meant little more to us than Greeks v. Trojans . . ."[59]

The "no good X but a dead X" formula was also adapted to inveigh against the Japanese enemy during World War II. Consider, for example, this passage from Richard Butler's novel *A Blood-Red Sun at Noon* (1980) about the war in the Pacific: "'Ye believe all the propaganda our side have stuffed into your head—things like bishops blessing the flag and telling you God's on our side, not theirs. Generals telling you that the only good Jap is a dead Jap.'"[60] In the late 1960s there also circulated the anti-Vietnamese variant "The only good gook is a dead gook."[61] And yet another "national" variant of the proverb appears in a book on early Spanish conquests in South America, stating that the native population doubtless thought of many of the intruders in terms of "The only good Spaniard was a dead Spaniard."[62] These examples emphasize how powerful this proverbial formula is as a slogan against any military enemy. Its adaptability as a propagandistic tool against any national stereotype is clearly without limit.

The same adaptability is true for some of the following trivializations of the original proverbial invective. Some of these variants might even seem "humorous" in their absurdity, but it must not be forgotten that the actual proverb of "The only good Indian is a dead Indian" is subconsciously juxtaposed to these seemingly harmless variations, thus continuing the slur against Native Americans in a camouflaged manner. In the following list notice that the texts usually mimick the structure "The only good X is a dead X," but in some cases one of the adjectives is altered:

1933:   The only good poacher is a dead poacher.[63]
1942:   The only good teacher is a dead teacher.[64]
1957:   The only good mouse is a dead mouse.[65]
1964:   The only good raccoon was a dead one.[66]
1968:   The only good cop (pig) is a dead cop (pig).[67]
1970:   The only good snake was a dead snake.[68]
1970:   The only good body's a dead one.[69]
1970:   The only good grades are good grades.[70]
1980:   The only good cow's a dead cow.[71]
1986:   The only good photojournalist is a live photojournalist.[72]
1990:   The only good fish is a fresh fish.[73]
1991:   The only good priest [is a dead priest].[74]

As can be readily seen, these variants express to a large degree anxieties of people, about crime (poachers), success (teacher, grades), illness (fish), authority (cop), or animals (raccoons, snakes, mice). Of the twelve examples cited above, I'd like to look particularly at the "mouse" variant in its literary context. Paul Gallico in his novel *Thomasina* (1957) describes in many pages the art of "mousehole watching" that is being practiced by one of his characters for whom this is "a full-time job":

It isn't catching mice, mind you, that is the most necessary. Anyone can catch a mouse; it is no trick at all; it is putting them off and keeping them down [by locating the mousehole(s)] that is important. You will hear sayings like— "The only good mouse is a dead mouse," but that is only half of it. The only good mouse is the mouse that isn't there at all. What you must do if you are at all principled about your work, is to conduct a war of nerves on the creatures. This calls for both time, energy and a good deal of cleverness which I wouldn't begrudge if I wasn't expected to do so many other things besides.[75]

What I want to call attention to is the way in which this humorous passage, and its humor is undeniable especially if one continues to read another two pages about the challenges presented, incorporates a variant of the traditional proverb which to a careful reader brings to mind the fate of the Native Americans who—just like a defenseless little mouse—were hunted down and killed by superior weapons and strength. Behind the animalistic trivialization of the slanderous proverb and shadowing its humor hovers inescapably the historical truth of human extermination.

The "only good X is a dead X" formula which proved so successful a slogan against enemies at war, whether Native Americans, Germans, Japanese, or Vietnamese, has also been used by white Americans against African Americans. Its fluid capacity to express racial hostility is evident in Joseph Carr's novel *The Man with Bated Breath* (1934), in which a bigoted white man from the southern United States makes the following comment about an African American servant: "'That is one of the houseboys. Honest enough if you discount the saying in these parts that the only honest nigger is a dead nigger."[76] That this proverb about Native Americans has, in fact, been easily transferred to African Americans is documented in George Bernard Shaw's compelling introduction to his drama *On the Rocks* (1934). With Nazi Germany on the rise, he prophetically writes about Germany's plans to establish racial purity and Jewish extirpation in a section entitled "Present Exterminations." Here is his account of "Previous Attempts" by racial and nationalistic purists to rid themselves of unwanted members of society:

> The extermination of what the exterminators call inferior races is as old as history. "Stone dead hath no fellow" said Cromwell when he tried to exterminate the Irish. "The only good nigger is a dead nigger" say the Americans of the Ku-Klux temperament. "Hates any man the thing he would not kill?" said Shylock naively. But we white men, as we absurdly call ourselves in spite of the testimony of our looking glasses, regard all differently colored folk as inferior species. Ladies and gentlemen class rebellious laborers with vermin. . . . What we are confronted with now is a growing perception that if we desire a certain type of civilization and culture we must exterminate the sort of people who do not fit into it.[77]

Shaw, already in 1934, draws attention to the fact that racial fanatics refer to undesirable people as "vermin," thus robbing them of their basic human dignity. The Nazis did exactly that as time went on, degrading in particular the Jewish population with verbal and proverbial invectives to "vermin," as I have shown in my study on "Proverbs in Nazi Germany"[78] mentioned at the beginning of this chapter. In light of what happened in Germany and Europe under National Socialism in the many concentration camps, and in consideration of the harm done to Native Americans and African Americans or any other minority, any variant of the proverb "The only good Indian is a dead Indian" seems unacceptable. This is perhaps especially true of the "harmless" variants, such as the one about mice, because of the subtle way in which they reinforce a worldview that endorses annihilation of the enemy or the inferior or the other.

In closing I would like to take a look at a few more examples of works that have repeated the proverb "The only good Indian is a dead Indian," not only to stress how this slur against Native Americans continues to be in use, an ever ready invective to be cited to keep the painful stereotype alive, but also to show how it rears its head in works aimed at very different audiences. In John Buchan's frontier novel *Salute to Adventures* (1915), a young man indicates his willingness to give the native population the benefit of the doubt by exclaiming, "But they tell me the Indians are changed nowadays. They say they've settled down to peaceful ways like any Christian." An old-timer answers grimly, and without any feeling of reconciliation or understanding about the plight of the original inhabitants of this land: "Put your head into a catamount's mouth, if you please, but never trust an Indian. The only good kind is the dead kind. I tell you we're living on the edge of hell. It may come this year or next year or five years hence, but come it will."[79] Here in a book published twenty-five years after the massacre of Native Americans at Wounded Knee, and aimed at popular audiences, the proverb falls from the lips of a frontier veteran. The old man feels no reconciliation with his former enemies and shows no understanding about the plight of North America's original inhabitants. It is probable that readers felt his distrust was warranted, at least to some degree, by his own violent "adventures" on the frontier and that they gave him the authority to relate this proverb's "wisdom."

Twenty years later brought the publication of a detective novel with a particularly despicable title, Carolyn Wells's *The Wooden Indian* (1935). This book, also aimed at a popular audiences, similarly manipulates the reader to accept the wisdom of the "dead Indian" proverb. In the book a character reacts to "the furious wars they [the Indians] waged" with this piece of wisdom: "I agree with Ben Jonson, or whoever said it, that the only good Indian is a dead Indian."[80] General Philip Sheridan is forgotten. Ben Jonson (1573?–1637), an English playwright and poet, will do. Or for that matter, anyone will do because the wisdom expressed is so obviously true to the speaker. Blind fear and hate make any authority for this proverb acceptable, and the reader is encouraged to accept it on faith as well.

Laura Ingalls Wilder's thousands of young readers found the following passage in her celebrated children's book *Little House on the Prairie* (1935):

> Mrs. Scott said she hoped to goodness they would have no trouble with Indians. Mr. Scott had heard rumors of trouble. She said, "Land knows, they'd never do anything with this country themselves. All they do is roam around over it like wild animals. Treaties or no treaties, the land belongs to folks that'll farm it. That's only common sense and justice." She did not know why the government made treaties with Indians. The only good Indian was a dead Indian. The very thought of Indians made her blood run cold.[81]

Who would have guessed that one of America's classic children's books would play a role in ingraining this proverb and spreading the hateful stereotype of Native Americans to generations of Americans who had nothing to fear from a people who were no longer at war with them, who had never been capable of defeating the far more powerful enemy, whose rich and varied culture was unseen by most descendants of the European settlers, and who for the most part were isolated, hidden away on reservations, from white Americans.

It does not appear that this proverb will soon be eradicated from common parlance, a prediction shared by Maxwell Bodenheim in his book *My Life and Loves in Greenwich Village* (1954): "There is no good Indian but a dead Indian, we are told by the grandsons of men who have been scalped."[82] The image of the Indian savages will always remain among us, passed down from one generation to the next. Surely we have evidence that this is true when we open the slick pages of a 1957 *New Yorker* magazine, so-called bastion of Eastern intellectual sophistication, and find a cartoon that shows several Native Americans around a campfire with one of them observing: "I say the only good Indian is a dead Indian. Present company excepted, of course."[83] We must ask whether this is sophisticated humor or simply a sign that the elite of American society shares the same prejudices of the ordinary Americans who say "That only went to show that the only good Indian was a dead Indian"[84] or "They're the Indians—and the only good Injun is a dead one, you can take that from me."[85] The use of proverbial slurs crosses social and class lines and calls into question how different the people who repeat these slurs really are. For example, what is the difference, one must ask, between jokes composed around this most hurtful slander against Native Americans and the sick humor that produces Auschwitz jokes?[86]

Finally I want to turn to a short story by Mack Reynolds with the suspect title "Good Indian" (1964). In a mere nine pages the author manages to reinvigorate the vile stereotype of this proverb with a vengeance. In Reynolds's story, three Seminoles arrive at the office of Mortimer Dowling, Director of the Department of Indian Affairs, a man who thought that "the last Indian died almost ten years ago." The Indians claim that they have come to negotiate a treaty for themselves and the other fifty-five surviving members of the Seminole tribe, and they are well prepared to do so with LL.D.s from Harvard. After some arguing back and forth, they declare that they want Florida, and at the height of frustration the director suggests that they break for lunch. The narrative picks up again the next morning. The director, who is in absolutely miserable bodily shape, is sitting at his desk. His receptionist, Millie Fullbright, observes how disgusting it was of him to get "absolutely stoned" when he finally had something to do for a change. But the hung-over director only points with his finger at the signed treaty on his desk, upon which the receptionist exclaims in astonishment:

> "Heavens to Betsy, the treaty. And all three of their signatures on it. How in the world did you ever—"
>
> Mortimer Dowling allowed himself a self-satisfied leer. "Miss Fullbright haven't you ever heard the old saying *The only good Indian is a dead—*"
>
> Millie's hand went to her mouth. "Mr. *Dowling,* you mean . . . you put the slug in all three of those poor Seminoles? But . . . but how about the remaining fifty-five of them. You can't possibly kill them all!"
>
> "Let me finish," Mortimer Dowling growled. "I was about to say, *The only good Indian is a dead drunk Indian.* If you think I'm hanging over, you should see Charlie Horse and his wisenheimer pals. Those redskins couldn't handle firewater back in the old days when the Dutch did them out of Manhattan with a handful of beads and a gallon of applejack and they *still* can't. Now, go away and do a crossword puzzle, or something."[87]

The author not only bases his story on the "only good Indian is a dead Indian" proverb, but also alludes, of course, to the other proverbial invective of being "drunker than an Indian." The story turns on a tasteless, despicable, and racially motivated joke at the expense of Native Americans, and its publication shows the tenacity of proverbial stereotypes in today's United States of America.

Six years after Reynolds's story appeared, Dee Brown published his masterpiece *Bury My Heart at Wounded Knee* (1970). Anyone who reads this book, and especially the previously mentioned chapter, "The Only Good Indian Is a Dead Indian," cannot possibly see any humor in this proverb. For far too long has it given justification to the literal and spiritual killing of Native Americans. In its poetic brevity is expressed the national shame of a people whose majority succumbed to the worldview that Native Americans had to give up their identity or be killed. The fact that this tiny piece of folk wisdom is still current today is a very sad comment on this society and its behavior toward Native Americans. As long as there remain prejudices and stereotypes about this minority population, the proverb will not cease to exist. Wherever it is uttered or written, it will expose blatant inhumanity toward the Native Americans. The conscious attempt to refrain from using the proverb "The only good Indian is a dead Indian" might at least help to bring about some changes toward a better life for Native Americans, one of pride and dignity as is befitting for the indigenous people of this great country. Better the proverb die a long overdue death than any Native American suffer by it again.

6
"No Tickee, No Washee"
Subtleties of a Proverbial Slur

The impetus for this investigation into the origin, transmission, and mean-ing of the American proverb "No tickee, no washee" and its variants came from a telephone call that I received in mid-November of 1994 from two lawyers in San Francisco. They were dealing with a lawsuit between two male scientists. The plaintiff, an Asian American, accused his Cau-casian colleague, among other things, of having used the proverb "No tic-kee, no washee" toward him in a derogative and stereotypical fashion. I explained to the lawyers that while a proverb like "The only good Indian is a dead Indian" is clearly a slur due to the fact that it permits no meta-phorical interpretation and directly identifies the slurred minority, things might be a bit different with the proverb under discussion in their law-suit. I pointed out that the meaning of a particular proverb depends on its function in a particular situation, and I came up with some possible contexts in which "No tickee, no washee" might be used metaphorically without any stereotypical intent or meaning. Yet when the lawyers in-formed me that the accused Caucasian had used the proverb several times together with the Chinese gesture of holding his hands together in front of his stomach and bowing his head, it became clear to me that they were in fact dealing with a proverbial slur in this situation, one that the Chi-nese American person clearly found insulting and upsetting.

The lawyers were satisfied that their case involved a true ethnic slur, but from a scholarly point of view, the case they described to me raised the vexing question of whether this proverb is automatically a slur or whether it can be used in certain situations in a metaphorical sense that precludes any stereotypical insult. In other words, can a proverb be both an inoc-cuous statement and a slur? In the case of "No tickee, no washee," evi-dence in the form of dozens of contextualized references from the mass media and literary works as well as field research among academicians and students seems to argue that this proverb does have two faces. Archer Taylor, the doyen of proverb studies, included "No tickee, no washee" in

160

his chapter on "Metaphorical Proverbs" and not in the "Blason Popu-laire" chapter in his seminal book, *The Proverb* (1931), thus clearly seeing in this text a relatively new proverb with wider application beyond the confines of its rather obvious origin from the workplace of the Chinese laundries: "'No tickee. no washee,' i.e. 'without the essential prerequi-site, a desired object cannot be obtained,' with its evident allusion to the Chinese laundryman, bespeaks for itself a more recent origin."[1] While Taylor saw the proverb as a rather general statement, proverb scholar Shirley Arora in a letter to me interpreted its ambivalent nature as follows:

> "No tickee, no washee" becomes a slur only in certain contexts, probably if addressed to or used in the presence of someone—a particularly sensitive someone—of Asian descent, to whom it would imply that (1) Asians can't speak proper English; and (2) Asians are characteristically associated with the menial jobs such as washing clothes. And the stereotype is unquestionably there—not as blatantly offensive as in your Indian proverb, to be sure. Part of the context of any "performance" is obviously the identity of the "audi-ence," and if the audience is hypersensitive, the proverb will be taken as in-sulting regardless of the speaker's intent (but I still think a "sensitive" speaker wouldn't use it in those circumstances).[2]

Even though Arora acknowledges the stereotypical nature of this proverb in certain sensitive contexts, she too recognizes the possibility of making use of its metaphorically expressed wisdom in other situations. One might even venture the assumption that in the state of California, for example, the proverb will perhaps be seen as a slur much more readily due to the larger percentage of Asian Americans there than would be the case in the state of Vermont with its rather minute Asian population. In addition, one might ask whether the proverb in a more sensitive if not politically correct world should be shunned altogether because of its questionable status as a stereotype. Perhaps the following analysis and discussion based on dozens of textual references will be of some help in deciding this moral question.

Folklorists in general and paremiologists in particular have dealt in much detail with the problem of verbal stereotypes.[3] It has long been es-tablished that so-called ethnophaulisms (disparaging remarks against an ethnic group) are universally found in cultures as expressions of ethno-centrism and prejudice.[4] Large and representative collections of such slurs have been assembled, notably Otto von Reinsberg-Düringsfeld's *Interna-tionale Titulaturen* (1863), Henri Gaidoz and Paul Sébillot's *Blason Popu-laire de la France* (1884), and Abraham A. Roback's *A Dictionary of Inter-national Slurs (Ethnophaulisms)* (1944).[5] Basically all ethnic groups are represented with derogative statements in such compilations, the Chinese people being no exception. Roback, for example, includes, among others, the following texts:

> To give a Chinaman a music lesson: to go to the toilet.
> Not to have a Chinaman's chance: to have a very slim chance; practically impossible.[6]
> Chinee: a Chinese (jocose or illiterate).
> To walk Chinese fashion: to walk single file.
> Chinese puzzle: an unintelligible situation.
> Chinese wall: a barrier against enlightenment or the solution of a problem.
> Chinese watermelon: the wax gourd.
> Chink(ie): Chinese.
> Chinkland: China.
> To have a Chinaman on one's back: to crave narcotics.[7]

It should be noted that in these texts, the slur against Chinese people is immediately evident, and that was also the case in a sixty-line poem with the title "Plain Language from Truthful James" which Bret Harte, the popular storyteller of the American West, published in 1870. Better known as "The Heathen Chinee," because of its card-cheating protagonist, Ah Sin, this piece "quickly established itself as the most quoted and recited verse of the post Civil-War years."[8] Even though Harte was being ironical in this poem and was himself a champion of the Chinese population of nineteenth-century California, his popular poem helped to spread the image of the "heathen Chinee" as an ethnic stereotype. The difference and peculiarity of this immigrant group became ingrained in people's minds through the following three lines of the first and last stanza of the poem:

> That for ways that are dark
> And for tricks that are vain,
> The heathen Chinee is peculiar. . .[9]

James Evans has shown that the term the "heathen Chinese" was established in the early 1850s by the white settlers of California to differentiate their Christian faith from the non-Christian religious practices of the Chinese immigrants. The Chinese were, of course, also different in appearance, custom, and language, and thus the term became a universal expression of anti-Chinese prejudice. While the Chinese people were at first considered to be very hard workers in the mines and on the railroad, this positive image changed because they were different and seemingly uninterested in being assimilated into the American society, because they appeared to be immoral and corrupt, and because they degraded labor by working for lower wages than the white population.[10] The prevailing racist views of Chinese immigrants are evident in the prejudicial *Report of the Special Committee of the Board of Supervisors of San Francisco on the Condition of the Chinese Quarter of that City* (1885) which includes the following in a section entitled "The Heathen Chinee":

> The Chinese brought here with them and have successfully maintained and perpetuated the grossest habits of bestiality practiced in the human race. The twin vices of gambling in its most defiant form, and the opium habit, they have not only firmly planted here for their own delectation and the gratification of the grosser passions, but they have succeeded in so spreading these vitiating evils as to have added thousands of proselytes to the practice of these vices from our own blood and race. . . . The lowest form of prostitution—partaking of both slavery and prostitution—they have planted and fostered to a lusty growth among us, and have inoculated our youth not only with the virus of immorality in its most hideous form but have, through the same sources, physically poisoned the blood of thousands by the inoculation with diseases the most frightful that flesh is heir to, and furnishing posterity with a line of scrofulous and leprous victims that might better never have been born than to curse themselves and mankind at large with their contagious presence.[11]

Elsewhere in this slanderous report, the author cites the well-known proverb about the leopard's spots to indicate that the Chinese will never change to become decent members of the American society:

> The proof then, is incontrovertible, that the Chinaman, transported to other lands than his own, is the Chinaman still, with all his native habits and inclinations, with all his filth, with all his clannishness, with all his diseases, with all his hideous vices. No more than the leopard can change his spots, can the Chinaman change; at least until through long generations of contamination of the race which undertakes the task, and the sacrifice of the physical and moral health of a hundred of the individuals of such self-sacrificing race for every Chinaman reformed and christianized.[12]

As discussed in chapter 1 of this book, this is exactly the way the Nazi murderers dealt proverbially with the Jewish population, reducing it through proverbial invectives and stereotypes to subhuman beings infested with disease that must be eliminated in order to save the Aryan race.[13]

Fortunately there were contemporary reports that took the opposite point of view from the board of supervisors of San Francisco. One year after this derogatory report was published, another one entitled *The Other Side of the Chinese Question* (1886) was issued. In it Chinese workers appear in a positive light, as expressed by the testimony of this witness:

> A good Chinese servant will do twice the work of any white servant woman you can have here. He will do housework better in every way, and do a great

deal more. . . . Chinese servants do not work by the hour, eight hours a day, but they work at all times, and are willing. . . . I have a Chinaman in mind now who was employed two years in my daughter's family, until very recently, and he did the work of two servants. I consider that he is worth his weight in gold as a servant.[14]

The extent of discrimination against Asian immigrants, particularly in the second half of the nineteenth century in California, can perhaps best be grasped if one considers that the U.S. government's *Report of the Joint Special Committee to Investigate Chinese Immigration* (1877) runs to a length of 1281 densely printed pages.[15]

There is not space here to review the large amount of literature on the immigration policies of the United States government regarding the Chinese people. But there is no doubt that laws like the infamous Chinese Exclusion Act of 1882, which were based on racist attitudes, damaged the well-being of the Chinese population already present in this country and at the same time prevented decent and good Chinese people from immigrating to America. The widespread anti-Chinese racist views were given unambiguous and proverbial expression in 1878 at the constitutional convention of the state of California by a delegate who also indicated that there was in fact a pecking order in racial stereotypes: "One white man is worth two Chinamen, one Chinaman is worth two negroes, and one negro is worth two tramps."[16] Caucasians maintained a definite "we-they" dichotomy regarding ethnic minorities, with the Chinese more than any other group becoming the proverbial scapegoats for all the ills and evils of the time. The Chinese became known as the "yellow peril," and these other and different Californians were summarily stereotyped as "cunning, treacherous, immoral, vice-ridden, subversive, unscrupulous, inhuman, incapable of acquiring the responsibilities of citizenship, degraded, competing with decent workingmen by laboring for low wages, and altogether unassimilable."[17] The proverbial variant "Once a Chinaman, always a Chinaman"[18] from 1923 appears to express the views of the xenophobic American public well into the twentieth century.

It has been pointed out that racial stereotypes often concentrate on such cultural differences of the out-group as "food, language, or accent, common first names, and common occupations."[19] This holds true for the Chinese population of the nineteenth century, who as immigrants encountered extreme linguistic difficulties. Bret Harte hinted at the so-called Pidgin English spoken by the Chinese laborors in 1870 in "The Heathen Chinee." A short time later (ca. 1872), he took the stereotypical imitation of the limited English linguistic knowledge of the Chinese to ridiculous and incredible levels in his poem "The Latest Chinese Outrage." Again featuring "that heathen, Ah Sin," Harte puts the following Pidgin English phrases into the mouth of this by now stereotypical Chinese laundryman with his equally typical name:

> "You owe flowty dollee—me washee you camp,
> You catchee my washee—me catchee no stamp;
> One dollar hap dozen, me no catchee yet,·
> Now that flowty dollee—no hab?—how can get?
> Me catchee you piggee—me sellee for cash,
> It catchee me licee—you catchee no 'hash;' [sic]
> Me belly good Sheliff—me lebbee when can,
> Me allee same halp pin as Melican man!
>> But Melican man
>> He washee him pan
>> On bottom side hillee
>> And catchee—how can?"[20]

The difficulty that the Chinese population had in pronouncing the "r" sound, its tendency to come out as an "l," together with the Chinese habit of adding the double "ee" sound indiscriminately to many English words were ridiculed *ad absurdum* in the literature and mass media of the time, and there is no reason to think that this did not take place in oral communication as well. It should be noted that this stereotypical language use does not reflect the actual Pidgin English as it was used in Chinese harbors as an effective means of communication between people who spoke in two totally different linguistic forms.[21] The indiscriminate substitution of "l" for "r" and the constant adding of double "ee" to words in many American novels, dramas, and poems during the nineteenth century is clearly a means of humorously or often satirically stereotyping the Chinese. Obviously nobody spoke or wrote as in the following American "Chinese Song of the Shirt to His Cousin at Home" from the last quarter of the nineteenth century:

> Workee, workee
> All same workee
> No time thinkee,
> No time see,
> Me no likee,
> Shy for workee,
> Dampoor ricee,
> Dampoor tea.
>
> Washee, washee,
> All day washee,
> All day gettee,

> One rupee,
> No buy smokee,
> All dam boshee,
> No buy drinkee,
> Poor whiskee.[22]

There is no lack of the "Chinese funny man"[23] in American literature of the time. More often than not it is the Chinese laundryman who is characterized as a humorous if not pitiable figure through his lack of English language ability. James J. McCloskey, in his play *Across the Continent: Or, Scenes from New York Life and the Pacific Railroad* (1870), depicts the Chinaman "Very Tart" as a laundryman who is accused of having put starch into someone's socks. His defense is uttered in the stereotypical Pidgin English: "Me no putee starchee sockee. Me putee sockee starchee." A few lines later he also talks of "shirtee,"[24] thereby providing us with an early reference for this particular word form which is part of the proverbial variant "No tickee, no shirtee." Joaquin Miller, in his novel *First Fam'lies in the Sierras* (1875), includes an entire chapter on a rather ridiculous Chinese laundryman called "Washee-Washee."[25] Two years later Miller published a play-version of this work, listing "Washie Washie.— A Helpless little Heathen" in the cast of characters.[26] The same stereotypical depiction can be seen in Bartley Campbell's play *My Partner* (1879), in which the Chinese character Wing Lee talks in the by now expected fashion. When he is able to produce a lost shirt, he states "Me flaid of bossee, me go downe shaftee—me hidee, me sleepee, me findee shirtee! . . . You got 'em cuffee—me got 'em shirtee."[27]

As expected, Bret Harte includes numerous Chinese laundrymen in his voluminous works. Hop Sing in his play *Two Men of Sandy Bar* (1876) is of particular importance for an understanding of how the proverb "No tickee, no washee" with its "shirtee" and "laundry" variants might have originated toward the last quarter of the nineteenth century. The following speeches certainly include all the ingredients that entered into making this proverb:

> HOP SING. Me plentee washee shirtee—Melican man Poker Flat. Me plentee washee shirt Alexandlee Molton. Always litee, litee on shirt allee time. *(Pointing to tail of his blouse, and imitating writing with finger.)* Alexandlee Molton. Melican man tellee me—shirt say Alexandlee Molton—shabbee?
> . . . .
> HOP SING. Alexandlee Molton. Me washee shirt, Alexandlee Molton; he no pay washee. Me washee flowty dozen hep—four bittee dozen—twenty dollar hep. Alexandlee Molton no payee. He say, "Go to hellee!" You pay me *(extending his hand).*
> . . . .

Hop Sing. Me no likee "to-mollow!" Me no likee "nex time, John!"[28] Allee time Melican man say, "Chalkee up, John," "No smallee change, John,"—umph. Plenty foolee me![29]

Hop Sing's complaint no doubt was common to many impoverished Chinese laundrymen, whose white customers would arrive to pick up their clean laundry and not want to pay for it. They would ask for credit, then not return, and probably deploy the same trick at another Chinese laundry in the immediate vicinity:

> Chinese laundrymen have a method of getting even with customers. When bills are not paid they retain the clothes, and it is sometimes necessary to obtain them by attachment. But the garments are returned in a different condition from that in which they were taken.[30]

Such serious financial losses might have prompted a Chinese laundryman one day to express in utter frustration, "No payment, no wash," which later became the more innocuous "No ticket, no wash." Its Pidgin English form of "No tickee, no washee" was probably picked up by Caucasian customers who continued to enjoy ridiculing the "foreign" laundrymen while at the same time venting their frustrations when they were denied their laundered clothes in the event of having forgotten their ticket receipts.

In 1953 the sociologist Paul C. P. Siu completed a dissertation on the Chinese laundryman which was later published in 1987 as *The Chinese Laundryman: A Study of Social Isolation.* Based on serious field research among Chinese laundrymen and their customers, Siu presented a detailed picture of the social and cultural hardships that this profession entailed. He includes only one reference to the proverb under discussion here, but the remarks by his informant (unfortunately not dated) are most revealing:

> I took a batch of laundry to a Chinese laundryman once in Philadelphia. The Chinese laundryman, short, tubby, somewhat greasy, perhaps it was sweat from his steamy work room . . . steam pipes along the low ceiling . . . works late . . . careful . . . honest, always precise though slow, methodical, calm, doesn't worry if something should go wrong. Probably has a lot of money stored up somewhere, though he leads a humble life, desires little, face expressionless except slight smile infrequently, restrained in conversation . . . still says, "no ticky, no washy; come again Fliday," holds hands together in front of stomach and bows slightly as he says this, smiling slightly . . . usually a tubby wife hovering in the back work room behind the partition . . . with some kids running around . . . whole family lives in the tiny shop . . . she cooks in it, too, in the back, inside room. Usually has a son who is well dressed, a white collar worker in the city . . . comes home frequently . . . all in one family . . . keep in close touch . . . see each other whenever possible

> . . . lots of other Chinese (probably family) constantly dropping into the shop to talk a little or just sit and smoke.[31] (ellipses in original)

Siu calls this an "impressionistic" view of the Chinese laundryman and his family by an "ethnocentric individual who has never tried to understand others different from himself with scientific objectiveness. Consequently anything different from himself would be inferior, funny, or queer."[32] Another informant quoted in Siu's book more directly expressed his feeling that the Chinese were inferior:

> The Chinks are all right if they remain in their place. I don't mind their working in the laundry business, but they should not go any higher than that. After all, there aren't even enough jobs for us whites, without them butting in. Besides, we could never compete with them. They naturally work harder than us, and for much less pay.[33]

The stereotype of the Chinese immigrant as laundryman was in part due to the fact that by 1920 about 30 percent of the Chinese in the United States were employed in laundry work.[34] Betty Lee Sung, in her book *Mountain of Gold* (1967), begins a chapter on "Laundries—A Heaven and a Prison" with an anecdote that reveals how rooted this stereotype was by the 1940s:

> At the first meeting of the United Nations in New York, China's chief delegate to the fledgling international organization had gone to visit a friend in the Hotel Ambassador. Preoccupied with the heavy burden of state matters weighing on his mind, he absent-mindedly rang the wrong door bell. A lady appeared at the door and without a word thrust a bundle of laundry into the astonished ambassador's arms. Before he could protest, the door had banged shut.
>
> Standing with the bundle of soiled clothes in his arms, the ambassador was at first startled and puzzled. Then it dawned upon him that the lady had mistaken him for the laundryman. He rang the bell again and explained.[35]

In her book on the history and nature of Chinese American employment in this country, Sung reiterates the sad fact that "somehow the American mind cannot erase the image of the Chinese as mere laundrymen and restaurateurs. In the experience of almost every adult Chinese American, he has been taken at least three times for one or the other or both."[36]

The first large Chinese hand laundry was set up in 1851 in San Francisco. By 1870, about two thousand Chinese laundries could be found in that city alone, and the Chinese laundry business had started to spread to every major city in the United States.[37] Naturally the stereotype of the laundryman moved right along with the expansion of the trade. Little did prejudiced benefactors of their services know how demanding, strenuous, and painstaking the work was in these laundry establishments. This was especially true before the turn of the century when most Chinese laundrymen were here alone without wives and families, and earning their livelihood by working almost around the clock in the hope of saving up enough money to return to China. An informant gave the following account of this hard lifestyle:

> [To save money for a trip home,] you needed more than a thousand dollars at least. It took about twenty years to save that much money, or at least ten or eight years. How to keep the money was another headache. There were thieves all around in American society, and most Chinese hand laundries [in New York] were operated by a single man, with little defense. If he was found having a thousand dollars in cash in his shop, he could be robbed or killed. Many of them were illiterate and could not even read numbers and sign their names [in English]; and they could understand only a couple of English words, so they dared not go to deposit their money in the bank. Besides, they had no time to go to the bank, since they could only rest on Sundays, and all banks were closed on Sundays. . . . Most hid their money in old clothes, or under the floor or in the wall. . . . Some died before they saved enough money to make the China trip. . . .[38]

A clear social and cultural isolation and marginalization of the Chinese laundrymen resulted in part from their "otherness" and the xenophobia of the American population,[39] but also in part from a serious language barrier. The vast majority of Chinese laundrymen could speak only Pidgin English, with some of them speaking so brokenly that their customers could at best only guess at what they were saying.[40] Very few first-generation Chinese immigrants working in the harsh conditions of the laundries had the time, need, or interest to acquire a functional knowledge of the English language, thereby adding fuel to the proverbial stereotype of their linguistic and by false implication mental inadequacies.

It is against this social and economic background that the origin and dissemination of the proverb "No tickee, no washee" must be understood. Its linguistic form reflects the Pidgin English of Chinese immigrants ridiculed to this day. The so-called laundry ticket has also been the cause for humorous or cynical ridicule by non-Chinese customers. As early as 1872 Mark Twain included a chapter on the "Chinese Population in Virginia" in his book *Roughing It*. Here he belittles the Chinese practice of attaching an identifying ticket to the customer's clothes: "the chief employment of Chinamen in towns is to wash clothes. They always send a bill, like this below [illustration of a laundry ticket consisting of some Chinese symbols], pinned to the clothes. It is mere ceremony, for it does not enlighten the customer much."[41] In his discussion of this infamous "Laundry Ticket," Paul Siu concurs that "perhaps the most amusing feature is the Chinese laundry ticket. Chinese characters are written on it. . . . The American customers of the Chinese laundry can understand only the amount charged on the ticket. . . . A customer calls for his clean laundry by presenting the stub which corresponds to the serial and number of the other half attached to the laundry bundle."[42] In any case, the ticket stub had to be presented in order to obtain one's clean wash. If it could not be produced, then the quite nonmetaphorical answer would be "No tickee, no washee."

While we might never know exactly when this short statement was made for the first time and when it took on proverbial frequency, it should be noted that the English language contains numerous older proverbs based on the structural formula of "No X, no Y" that literally assured the fast adaptation of this new formulation by native English speakers. A few examples of this proverb type are "No cross, no crown," "No cure, no pay," "No fee, no law," "No mill, no meal," "No pains, no gains," "No penny, no paternoster," "No silver, no servant," and "No song, no supper."[43] Burton Stevenson, the first lexicographer to register the proverb "No tickee, no washee" in his massive *Book of Proverbs, Maxims, and Famous Phrases* (1948) lists some of these proverbs and adds the internationally disseminated variant "No money, no Swiss" (from the seventeenth century referring to the venality of Swiss mercenaries, but now indicating that one must pay for what one wants) before citing "No tickee, no washee" from Archer Taylor's book *The Proverb* (1931).[44] The historically oriented paremiographer finds it both interesting and frustrating to note that Taylor's 1931 reference is to date the earliest printed citation of this proverb. No other major proverb collection lists it before that date, and several regional proverb collections from California also fail to mention it.[45] The same is true for many other regional collections as well as the numerous lists of proverbs culled from American literature.[46] In fact, it took more than another forty years before the lexicographer Eric Partridge finally registered the proverb in 1977, a clear indication of how dictionaries of phraseology in general and proverbs in particular lag behind in registering "new" texts: Here is Partridge's definition:

> *no tickee, no washee.* Literally. "No ticket—no laundry." A Chinese laundry's refusal to work without being paid, but soon came to be applied to any situation where credit is unjustifiably asked for or even expected: US: late C19-20.[47]

Several things are important to note here. First, Partridge is well aware of the original literal significance of this proverb, but he hastens to add that it took on a figurative meaning as well. Second, he describes a fairly restricted financial application of the phrase, while Taylor in 1931 had already stated that it refers quite generally to any prerequisite needed to have a desired result of whatever. Finally, it is significant that Partridge surmises that the phrase originated in the late nineteenth century. From what is known and what has been discussed above about Chinese laundries and the language of the early Chinese American immigrants, I would second Partridge's conjecture that the proverb "No tickee, no washee" became current in the last quarter of the nineteenth century.

Another lexicographer, Robert Hendrickson, reaches similar conclusions ten years after Partridge. He too stresses the semantic broadening of the phrase from a rather specific and literal statement to a figurative and metaphorical phrase:

> no tickee, no washee. People have always had a hard time getting their wash back from the laundry without having the receipt for it. The expression was common among Chinese laundrymen starting in the late 19th century or earlier and is still occasionally heard. The words have taken on the new, wider meaning of "no credit without collateral."[48]

Two years later, the prolific reader and distinguished paremiographer Bartlett Jere Whiting included the proverb in his superb collection of *Modern Proverbs and Proverbial Sayings* (1989), citing three references out of detective novels: "No tikkee [*sic*]—no shirtee" (1942) and "No tickee, no washee" (1948 and 1967).[49] Whiting also cites Taylor's 1931 statement as the earliest written reference, which is what my co-editors and I also did in our *Dictionary of American Proverbs* (1992). We were also able to add the following comment by an informant regarding the meaning of the proverb "No tickee, no washee": "If you don't have your ticket, you don't get your wash," a rather literal interpretation, to be sure.[50] Finally, and certainly very significantly, the proverb has recently been registered by P. R. Wilkinson in his *Thesaurus of Traditional English Metaphors* (1993) as being current in Great Britain as well:

> No tickee, no washee [no ticket, no washing, Chinese laundry] That (whatever) is an essential prerequisite.[51]

Here again the proverb is seen as having a narrow literal and a wide figurative meaning, and it is the latter which is of considerable importance in deciding whether the proverb today functions as a stereotype that is offensive to Chinese Americans. In any case, it must be stated that the appearance of the proverb in six proverb collections published between 1948 and 1993 is indeed slim pickings. This meager paremiographical record of the proverb belies its frequent use in literature, the mass media, and oral communication. It also shows that lexicographers and paremiographers are not paying enough attention to new and modern proverbs.[52]

The earliest literary text that I have been able to find thus far stems from the title and lyrics of the song "No Tickee, No Washee" which Ira Gershwin wrote for the Broadway show *Pardon My English* (1933). The song was actually dropped before the show opened in New York on 20 January 1933, and much of it was reworked into "What Sort of Wedding Is This?" The original song ended with the following four lines that were deleted in the later version as well:

> No wedding, no present!
> No tickee, no washee!
> No tickee, no washee!
> Good day![53]

The proverb in its context has no stereotypical significance. Instead it basically repeats in a more figurative wording that without the necessary prerequisite (wedding) there will be no results (present). Richard Shattuck (pseud. Dora [Richards] Shattuck) makes a similar use of the expression in her murder mystery *The Snark Was a Boojum* (1941): "It wasn't reasonable to be angry at Rod, his attitude was right, coldly and properly right. No money, no love. No tickee, no washee. Yet it was all she could do to keep from hating him for being right."[54] Basically the proverb is once again preceded by a statement based on the proverbial structure "No X, no Y" which is then followed by the figurative proverb to drive home the more specific point of the first utterance.

Three additional references discovered by Bartlett Jere Whiting from three popular mystery novels show the proverb being used without any reference to Chinese Americans. Each time the proverb is used as a generalization to express that something is simply not going to be possible because the necessary prerequisite is not there:

> "Yeah—I get you," grumbled Atherton. That put him ahead of the two troopers, who listened to the exchange with only faint interest anyway. "No tikkee [*sic*]—no shirtee."[55](1942)

> "I'd like you on the other side, Corliss."
> "No tickee, no washee!"[56](1948)

> The papers said this morning he committed suicide. What's with the "killed" bit all of a sudden? Okay Buster. Stay clammed up if you like. I can play potsy too. No tickee, no washee.[57] (1967)

Two titles of orchestral music pieces also appear to be without any racial implications. The Walt Whitman High School Dance Band of South Huntington, New York, recorded "No Tickee, No Shirtee" in 1950,[58] and singer Ethel Smith included "No Tickee, No Cha Cha" on a record released in 1955.[59]

But the following two references clearly evoke the stereotype of the Chinese laundryman or Chinese Americans in general. In his autobiography, *Down These Mean Streets* (1967), Piri Thomas does not mention the proverb but alludes to it by stringing together two nonproverbial variants based on the "No X, no Y" structure. The fact that a Chinese doctor is present doubtless suffices to conjure up the actual stereotypical proverb in the mind of the reader:

> I went back to my place on the floor, but it bugged me that the Chinese doctor should know I was hooked. Jesus, did it show so much now? A funny line went through my head: *No stuffee, no druggee; no habit, no junkie,* and I wondered if I really was hooked.[60]

Maxine Hong Kingston does make use of the actual proverb in her acclaimed book *The Warrior Woman* (1976), which recounts growing up as a Chinese American daughter of a woman who works in the laundry:

> In the midnight unsteadiness we were back at the laundry, and my mother was sitting on an orange crate sorting dirty clothes into mountains—a sheet mountain, a white shirt mountain, a dark shirt mountain, a work-pants mountain, a long underwear mountain, a short underwear mountain, a little hill of socks pinned together in pairs, a little hill of handkerchiefs pinned to tags. . . .
> "No tickee, no washee, mama-san?" a ghost [a Caucasian customer] would say, so embarrassing.
> "Noisy Red-Mouth Ghost," she'd write on its package, naming its clothes with its name.[61]

Kingston's passage clearly reveals how insulting this proverb can be to Chinese Americans, if it is used in a derogative manner toward the very person who has to slave over the soiled laundry. She corrects the misconception that the proverb is used only in a general figurative sense and offers evidence of its remaining power to inflict a painful stereotype.

A comprehensive on-line search on the LEXIS/NEXIS database reveals a similar split in understanding and use of the proverb as a literal stereotype or a figurative statement. This database offers full-text coverage for hundreds of legal and news resources: newspapers, magazines, wire services, newsletters, journals, reports, broadcast transcripts, and court documents, among other sources. Even though the database goes back only as far as the end of the 1970s, it yields thirty-four valuable contextual references to this proverb from sources published between 1979 and 1994. Ten of these references deal in one way or another with Chinese matters, while twenty-four are free of any ethnic or racial implications. Some of the texts of the first group simply identify the proverb as being of Chinese origin, while others explicitly reflect its stereotypical nature:

Alexandria schools did require proof of full immunization yesterday before admitting students. Donald Dearborn, an assistant superintendent for the city's schools said: "to use an old Oriental phrase, 'No tickee, no entrance.'"[62] (1979)

Mayor Ed Koch [of New York City] was begging for an analysis when he attacked certain public-school teachers for mispronouncing the word "ask," as in "I axed the Mayor why he cannot resist making racist insults in a city seething with ethnic tensions?" . . . Koch can't complain publicly about people's pronunciation without demeaning the society in which they live. No tickee no washee! Pasta fazool! Oy gevalt! It's either funny or it's mean, and the Mayor wasn't kidding.[63] (1985)

Initially, Judge Hurst showed no sympathy. "It's like the old Chinese laundry saying—'no tickee, no shirtee.'"[64] (1986)

Naming ski runs can get tricky. One of the slopes in the brand new Oriental Bowl on the back of Vail was named No Tickee, No Washee. Protests from offended Asian customers rushed an expensive change on already printed trail maps to Genghis Khan.[65] (1989)

He said Anthony Brown, of the accountants Grant Thornton, wanted receipts for everything, including bus tickets. "He said it was like a Chinese laundry—no tickee no laundry." I thought that strange for an accountant.[66] (1989)

Wasn't I the smart one not to go into the [money] pool? "The Chinese have a word for this exact occurrence: 'No tickee, no shirtee.' One of the boys put it another way to fit my situation. I quote: 'No tickee, no poolee money, Big Ben.'"[67] (1989)

Its puns [in the movie *A Salute to Rocky and Bullwinkle*] are not only predictable but infrequently funny and delivered in a painfully crude rendition—literally—of the no-tickee, no-laundee Chinese accent (only one of a number of now-winceable stereotypes).[68] (1990)

In an adventure taking place in Shanghai, Rocky and Bullwinkle are chased not only by their customary foes, the Soviet agents Boris and Natasha, but by "a huge sinister Chinese." A confederate of the bumbling communists runs a Chinese laundry, demanding "No tickee, no shirtee"—while Mr. Ward makes light of the threat of an atomic bomb disguised as a wrist watch.[69] (1990)

. . . another wetback, Charlie Chan, [soap-head] coolie dishwasher and [sic] a stinking [Chinky] restaurant. [throws table] [imitating obsequious servant] Wash your shirt, Mister White Man, please? No tickee, no shirtee? On a one from column A and one from column B. Me happy to be in the railroads; me happy to dig mines for you; Mister White Man![70] (1993)

Mr. Chu is best and even valuable when he turns professional. Two plain wooden cases with glass tops hold a fertile documentary display he calls "No

Tickee, No Tomorrow." Included are comparison charts circulated in the late 19th century to show how Chinese men differed from other Asians. Tell-tale signs were important, for Chinese were forbidden to immigrate to the United States. Mr. Chu also calls attention to major Asian-American athletes whose contributions he feels have been under-recognized.[71] (1990)

Of these ten contextualized references, half definitely reflect the racial stereotype that Chinese Americans in particular associate with this proverb. The stereotype clearly ridicules the accent of some Chinese Americans, and also promulgates the image of the subservient Chinese fit only to do menial chores in the old laundry establishments. These examples indicate that use of the proverb to inflict a derogatory stereotype is current still, and it is to be hoped that growing awareness of the historical mistreatment of Chinese Americans will lead more people to reject its use.

The twenty-four other references provided by my LEXIS/NEXIS search do not show any signs of this proverb being used in a derogatory fashion. In them, the proverb operates as a figurative statement that has gone beyond its obvious origins in the "sweatshops" of the Chinese laundries. People who use it as a multifunctional and multisemantic metaphor do not associate it with the Chinese population and thus do not consider it a racial stereotype at all. Even its obvious linguistic reference to stereotypical Chinese speech patterns is not questioned, and it is interpreted as a standard proverb which by definition is applicable to many situations, of which only a literal understanding places it in the Chinese American environment. Most people who use the proverb in this way are simply not aware of its stereotypical background and meaning. They use it naively and innocently and offer it as a concise statement of a bit of wisdom based on experience.[72] The following examples of the proverb in their contexts do not exhibit any intentional stereotyping. I am compelled to point out, however, that the use of this proverb, even if innocent of any derogatory intent, does indicate a certain insensitivity at a time when people are striving to become more aware of ethnic and racial prejudices and the harm and pain they cause. Here are the additional twenty-four references:

". . . I dropped the [airline] tickets in the Farragut West Metro station [and people helped to search for them]." But no tickee—at least until Patrick phoned his wife. "She told me that the tickets had already been returned . . ."[73] (1982)

According to Tara Hamilton, executive assistant to the director of the D.C. Department of Transportation, the watchword in the District is: no taggee [tags for car identification], no tickee.[74] (1982)

"Nobody has tenure," says senior associate Robert G. Neumann, a former ambassador to Afghanistan and Saudi Arabia. "The general understanding is 'No tickee—no laundry.'"[75] (1982)

". . . Broadway shows are so damn expensive we modern dancers just can't afford to go and see them. Ergo, 'no tickee, no laundry.'"[76] (1985)

Michael O'Hara explained why. "Our position was, 'No tickee, no laundry,'" he said. In other words. either ABC paid on time, or it would not be permitted to televise the Games at all.[77] (1985)

The no-tickee no-money concept is neither new nor necessarily suspect. Certain federal obligations have been auctioned at original-issue discount for decades.[78] (1986)

If Peter's job is to create and to address change while honoring the restaurant's traditions, it is not always easy. The day the new computer system came in was a manager's nightmare. This was a total system . . . no tickee, no lunchee.[79] (1986)

The executive doesn't benefit unless the shareholder does. No tickee, no washee, right? Wrong, says KCR. No tickee, we give you new tickee.[80] (1988)

. . . Polan defended the provision Friday, saying the secretaries' salaries must come from the savings generated in each category. "No tickee no washee," Polan said.[81] (1989)

"The Air Force has decided to do the whole thing on simulators, with NO flight testing. No tickee, no shirtee. I no longer support continuation of the AMRAAM project."[82] (1989)

Virginia Gov. Gerald Baliles said states have increased spending on anti-drug efforts and asked why the federal government doesn't withhold aid from foreign nations that do not fully cooperate in drug investigations. "In other words, 'no tickee, no laundry,'" Baliles said.[83] (1989)

But the money [for the Contras] is actually guaranteed only through November, when the White House must get letters of approval from four congressional committees. No tickee, no money.[84] (1989)

Perles was particularly effusive on the subject of advice to players. "We tell them birds of a feather flock together. You want to know what people think of you—look at the guy next to you," Perles said. "We try to tell them no tickee, no washee—that's old second World War slang. And then we summarize by saying people who live in glass houses shouldn't cross bridges before their eggs hatch. That covers them all, brother."[85] (1989)

"If they want to have all that money [for waste management] that you have allocated, I ought to have the authority to say, 'Hey, no tickee, no laundry.'"[86] (1989)

A man's closest friend died and the burial was scheduled for Super Sunday. "Now I would be a pallbearer and would have to tape the game. Instead my friend's son insisted his dad would want me at the game. . . . He said: 'You go on to the game, I'll stay home and tape the funeral.'" No tickee, no perspective.[87] (1990)

There had been furious arguments about what the book was going to be: Holt wanted a juicy kiss and tell, while Mr. Meese wanted a more statesmanlike opus in the Clark Clifford mold. No dirty laundree, no tickee, said Holt. Shame on you Holt![88] (1990)

. . . won a burrito at Enchilada Heaven, or something like that. Drat it, I got in free. No tickee, no burrito.[89] (1990)

"I guess the corporations bought up the tickets [for a sports event], but our instructions were no tickee, no washee."[90] (1991)

. . . Russians play against the Canadians, but, alas, "he had no money," said Fitzgerald. "I said, 'No money, no tickee.'"[91] (1992)

No tickee, no Gretzky [headline]. At Edmonton's Northlands Coliseum, ticket sales for Games 3 and 4 of the semifinal continued to lag yesterday, even though Wayne Gretzky and four other former Oilers play for the Los Angeles Kings.[92] (1992)

Judge in Lotto Case: "No Tickee, No Pay" [headline]. Judge Lewis Hall rules that Tampa resident Nina Miller, who says she lost $6.7 million Lotto ticket, is not eligible to collect unless she finds winning ticket.[93] (1992)

"No tickee, no washee. You work with what you've got," [Quinn] Redeker says. "I write day and night anyway. I write in restaurants a lot."[94] (1993)

It was a case, Prince Philip might have said, of "No tickee, no washee."[95] (1993)

That Marcia Simon spits it right out, doesn't she? No tickee, no laundree. How come Marcia Simon, contest director, is scaring me half to death in a cover letter while the enclosed Publishers Clearing House "Ironclad Guarantee" is telling me in a soothing way: "No Strings Attached to Our Prizes."[96] (1994)

It is obvious from this group of twenty-four contextualized texts that the proverb is currently employed with much "poetic" license, that is, people often cite it with new twists and reversals. Also noticeable is that the proverbial variants of "No tickee, no laundry (laundree)" and "No tickee, no shirtee" are used, but the standard form remains "No tickee, no washee" without any hints at its origin as an ethnic slur. While the "laundry," "shirtee," and "washee" versions should call forth reminiscenses of their stereotypical character, it is doubtful that the same can be claimed for the so-called manipulated "anti-proverbs" in this list.[97] "No tickee, no burrito" and "No tickee, no perspective," for example, merely allude to the actual proverb and have little if any anti-Chinese sentiment in them.

It is, however, disturbing to see the use of the proverb in two legal briefs. In "Great American Ins. Co. v. Katani Shipping Co.," the United States Court of Appeals for the Ninth Circuit handed down an opinion on 7 July 1970 that reads in part: "Katani's agent in the Northern District of California entered into general average bonds with and secured money deposits from the plaintiffs in California under a claim of right plus the coercive threat of "'no tickee, no laundly.'"[98] It is amazing to find the inclusion of a racial slur in the linguistic variant of "laundly" instead of "laundry" in this federal court opinion. Also of interest is the opinion handed down on 20 March 1985 by Judge Teague for Court of Criminal Appeals of Texas in the case of "William John Pacheco v. The State of Texas":

> In so concluding [i.e., that the legal fee must be paid in advance], I believe that the court of appeals placed too much emphasis on that old adage that most criminal defense lawyers espouse and subscribe to, i.e., "no tickee—no washee." Although there is much merit to the proposition that every criminal defense attorney should adhere to the adage that "you either get your fee up front or you won't get it at all," see "Innovative Ways to Finance a Criminal Defense," Vol. 71, *American Bar Journal,* March, 1985, I am unable to believe that such an adage can supersede or interfere with the constitutional right of a defendant to appeal his conviction.[99]

Judge Teague might well have refrained from using this particular proverb to describe the monetary instead of legal priorities of certain lawyers. He is clearly using a stereotype of one minority to stereotype a particular professional subgroup. In any case, had he known his proverbs, he could have much more appropriately cited the proverb "No fee, no law" which has been registered as early as 1597.[100] Had he used it, he would certainly have hit the proverbial nail on the head with a much more relevant metaphor.

What light can folklorists shed on this proverb regarding its possible origin and its literal/figurative meaning in modern contexts? Folklorist Robert Georges told fellow folklorist and proverb scholar Shirley Arora that "he knew the 'No tickee, no washee' proverb very well from when he was growing up in a town just outside Pittsburgh that actually had a Chinese laundryman. According to Bob, the proverb was used derisively, although he also said that since that time he has heard it used many times in a more neutral, even positive sense. He had no suggestion to make regarding an origin, but did say that his memory of hearing it used goes back to the thirties."[101] Clearly the proverb was in common use in the

1930s, and Georges also corroborates the negative and positive ambivalence of the use and meaning of the proverb.

Shirley Arora reported in a letter to me that "my own familiarity with the proverb came from my father, who was of Ohio farming stock. He was not a great user of proverbs, but he used this one with some frequency, enough to make me remember it. (This would have been back in the early forties or so.) His version was 'No tickee, no washee.' I can't recall any specific incident, unfortunately, but it was with the general meaning of having to come up with something necessary in order to get what you want."[102] In the same letter, Arora presents two additional references that are of interest since they show the use of the proverb and its variants by members of other minorities in California:

> One, from 1983, was by the former administrative assistant in our Department [of Spanish and Portuguese at UCLA], a woman of Mexican American background who at the time was about 60 years of age (English was her dominant language, although she was bilingual.) Interestingly, she created her own nonce-variation to fit the context, which was the university requirement that an airplane ticket stub be presented in order to get travel reimbursement; in her words, "No tickee, no checkee." The other, more recent occurrence (1990), was by a woman in New Mexico who was probably about 35 to 40 years of age. . . . Her version was a bit different: "No tickee, no laundry," a rather odd combination of "pidgin" English and a completely standard English term.

References cited earlier have, however, indicated that the variant "No tickee, no laundry" is not as "odd" as Arora thinks. We have also seen that at times the linguistically more stereotypical versions "laundly" or "laundee" were substituted, but even the ending of the standard noun "laundry" rhymes with "tickee" and could thus become an acceptable variant.

This is, of course, also true in the case of the second major variant "No tickee, no shirtee" which, interestingly enough, Shirley Arora chose as part of the title of her fascinating article "'No Tickee, No Shirtee': Proverbial Speech and Leadership in Academe" (1988). This study shows that proverbial speech does in fact play a considerable role in the oral communication among professors. She collected 159 texts during various committee meetings attended by sixteen full professors over a period of two years at the University of California at Los Angeles. In the analysis of her "field research," Arora explains that the intellectually sophisticated professors used the proverbial texts for the purposes of instruction, persuasion, commentary, humor, and impression of familiarity. Obviously traditional proverbial language is very much alive and well in Academe, including the proverb "No tickee, no shirtee":

The proverb used in the title of this paper . . . had the distinction of being the only one used on three separate occasions, several months apart, by two different individuals. As employed here, "No tickee, no shirtee" is a kind of proverbial synonym—one might even say euphemism—for the notorious "Publish or perish," which may itself be considered an academic proverb. The intent of the speaker in each instance was clearly to remind other committee members of a recognized facet of academic life, the prescribed relationship between performance and advancement. . . . So why this proverb instead of the harsher but perhaps even better-known "Publish or perish"? One of the noticeable characteristics of "No tickee, no shirtee" as a proverb is, I suggest, its conspicuously nonacademic nature, residing both in its implicit attribution to a nonacademic personage—the stereotypic Chinese laundryman—and in its reproduction of what is assumed to be the kind of "pidgin English" that such an individual would employ. This nonacademic nature makes the proverb stand out in stark contrast both to subject context—academic achievement—and to the situational context—the academic discourse in which it is embedded. The contrast attracts attention and therefore gives extra emphasis to the statement, and the language itself—together with the proverbial form—serves to imply that the principle enunciated by the proverb is a general truth, applicable not just to the academic world but to the "real" world as well—a principle that even the "man on the street" or the laundryman in the next block would recognize and approve of. I have no way of knowing how many committee members had actually heard of the proverb before; it was known to me from my own childhood as "No tickee, no washee," and I had always associated it vaguely with the California gold rush and the influx of Chinese immigrants that took place at that period. But the structure and language of the saying clearly labeled it as proverbial, and I would be willing to wager that even those who had not heard it before identified it as a proverb and reacted to it in those terms. The same would, of course, be true of "Publish or perish"—but this phrasing of what is essentially the same principle has more negative overtones and so far as I am aware is used primarily in a critical sense, as an indictment of the existing system rather than a defense of it. "No tickee, no shirtee" softens the statement; it suggests, in effect, not that one may or should perish, but perhaps—by association with another well-known phrase—that under certain circumstances one could lose one's shirt.[103]

This long quotation of a master paremiologist is of extreme importance in understanding the multiple uses and functions of this proverb in different situations. But while Arora refers briefly to "the stereotypic Chinese laundryman," she does not, at least not in this particular use of the proverb, interpret it as having stereotypical or racist undertones. She even singled it out for the title of her study due to its frequent use by the committee members. One wonders, however, how the proverb would have been received if the committee had had a Chinese American member. Might the professors in that case have avoided using the text? In any case, Arora informed me in a letter that all three occurrences of the proverb "were in the context of 'No research, no promotion' (or merit increase)," [104] and there were no ethnic innuendos present whatsoever.

There is one further scholarly reminiscence to be mentioned, this one by the phraseologist Jonathan E. Lighter, well-known for his seminal *Historical Dictionary of American Slang* (1994). In a letter to me he writes the following:

> I recall, clearly and unmistakably, learning the phrase from my grandmother (born in New York City 1888) when I was a small child about 1953 or '54. The form she used was "No tickee, no shirtee. . . ." My impression only is that I have seen printed examples of "No tickee, no washee (or shirtee)" dating from before 1931—perhaps as early as the 1890s. I would be very surprised, however, to see an example in print earlier than 1880. [105]

Wish I could find one of those written references from before 1931! I completely agree with Lighter that the proverb's origin might go back as far as the fourth quarter of the nineteenth century. Yet that still remains to be shown by someone more fortunate than I have been. All that I can say here is that I certainly have looked through large amounts of possible sources.

But let us now turn to the holdings of the Folklore Archive at the University of California at Berkeley. This otherwise superb depository of folklore materials houses a mere four references to the proverb, a disappointingly small number when one considers that the proverb probably originated in California. Two informants cite the variant "No tickee, no laundry" and came across it in the 1940s:

> The informant was born and raised in the city of San Francisco in the area where there were an abundant number of Chinese laundry outlets. She remembers walking through the Marina district of San Francisco to visit these laundry mats [sic] to pick up the family linens, towels, shirts and sheets. The informant was ten years of age at the time she heard this said by her mother. The year was approximately 1941 in the City. The informant said that there is some truth to this proverb. She is well aware that the man at the laundry mat [sic] will not give his customers their clothes unless they bring him a receipt. Therefore, it is wise not to lose your laundry ticket. [106] (1941)

> My mother learned this from her father when she was under ten years old (c. 1949). This expression means if you don't meet the requirements you won't get what you desire. My mother said that since both she and my grandfather grew up in San Francisco, which has a large Chinese population, that many things they said poked fun at the Chinese. My mother said if people forgot their claim ticket they could not pick up their laundry from the Chinese laundry. My mom said my grandfather would use this to indicate [the]

lack of [a] necessary requirement. This could be money or brains. . . . This is clearly blason populaire because of the reference to Chinese laundries. It makes fun of the person who demands the claim check before they give you your laundry back. The phrase reads tickee, not ticket, to clearly indicate anger towards this Chinese person who will not give the laundry back without the stupid little claim ticket. However, it seems that the phrase encompasses more than just extemporaneous requirements, like a claim check for one's laundry, but also important requirements. Like much folklore only people who have contact with Chinese laundries will understand this blason populaire.[107] (1949)

While the first informant interprets the proverb very literally but without any indication of its stereotypical background, the second informant understands both the literal and figurative meanings of the proverb. Above all, the proverb is seen as a *blason populaire* which, if directed at the Chinese, becomes a linguistic slur. At the same time the student collector points out that the ethnic slur will, however, only be understood by persons who know its connection with Chinese laundries. That is the crux of the problem with this proverb: it is one thing to use it consciously as a slur toward a Chinese or Chinese American, but is it or does it even function as a slur when being used quite innocently in a figurative sense by someone who knows nothing about the proverb's origin?

The remaining two references of the basic proverb "No tickee, no washee" collected by Berkeley folklore students are quite revealing along this line of thought. Their informants encountered the proverb in the 1970s, and they appear to be quite aware of its stereotypical nature:

This proverb warns that it is impossible to reach a desired end without first fulfilling certain means. It is based on the fact that you can not pick up your laundry ("washee") without first showing your receipt ("tickee"). I learned this proverb *circa* 1970, when I was ten years old. I think I learned it in Piedmont, but I can not remember from whom. It is such a common saying I could have learned it from many sources, including the television. At that time I did not realize that this proverb is a blason populaire. Now I realize that it satirizes the broken English used by Chinese. Many people of this background are in the laundry business, and in fact have used this saying to express its literal meaning during business hours. I would use this proverb almost anywhere except around Chinese people. This is not a very strong blason populaire, but I would avoid any possible conflicts by expressing myself in another way.[108]

This student's recollection and thoughts clearly indicate that the proverb is seen as a common saying which is a stereotypical phrase if taken literally and when directed against the Chinese people. But the student also would be quite willing to use the expression in its figurative sense as long as Chinese people were not present—again a definitely ambivalent stance by a person who knows both the dangerous and innocuous nature of the proverb.

The fourth text recorded by a student collector is unique in that it includes the proverb as an ethnic slur in a racist children's rhyme encountered by the informant *circa* 1975:

> "Name Chingy Wong Chong
> Coming from Hong Kong, Coming from Hong Kong.
> Little boatie,
> Sailed to 'Merikie,
> 1814, hanging out a sign,
> Say no tickie, no washie, your laundly."

This rhyme exhibits many traits found in society but mainly expressed through little children. The rhyme shows the racism that still exists in America. It has often been said that children will say what their parents are often too afraid to say because they don't know any better. This rhyme is a good example of that. It is a direct attack at the ideas of Chinese laundries and their newness in this country. It exhibits a lot of hostility. The use of a boat shows the idea that immigrants are regarded as being "fresh off the boat." The spelling of laundry shows how Chinese are supposed to have trouble saying their r's.[109]

The racist tone of this rhyme is apparent and certainly inappropriate. But it is typical of the unfortunate group of such children's rhymes that spread ill-conceived racial prejudices among young children, often employing proverbs to increase their authoritative claims.[110] While this rhyme is a blatant slur that allows no figurative reading, matters are not so clear-cut with the continued use of this proverb in modern society, where it occupies an ambiguous position.

In order to ascertain what young American students think of this proverb, I asked Alan Dundes at the University of California in Berkeley to distribute a one-page questionnaire (kindly designed by him) to his large American Folklore class in February 1995. Because of the ethnic mix of students at Berkeley, his class seemed to me well suited to help measure how well known this proverb is and how it is currently used, while my own students in Vermont, who are almost all Caucasians, might not produce as accurate an indication. Of Dundes's over 400 students, 184 completed the questionnaire with 133 (72 percent) indicating that they did not know the proverb "No tickee, no washee." Of those students 87 (65 percent) are Caucasian, 38 (29 percent) Asian, 6 (4.5 percent) African American, and 2 (1.5 percent) did not indicate their ethnicity. It is somewhat amazing that almost two-thirds of the students had never heard of the proverb, including a substantial number of Asian students. However, a similar picture would probably arise with some basic proverbs of the English language. It is a fact that students today have a rather limited knowledge of proverbs, something that relates to the decline in cultural literacy in general.[111] There is no doubt that traditional folklore is also falling by the wayside. It might, of course, justifiably be argued that in the case of "No tickee, no washee," it does no particular harm if young people in the United States are not acquainted with so suspect a piece of wisdom.

Of the 51 (28 percent) students who are familiar with the proverb, 35 (69 percent) are Caucasian, 13 (25 percent) Asian, 1 (2 percent) African American, and 2 (4 percent) did not indicate their ethnicity. The percentages regarding the ethnicity of the students who know the proverb are basically the same as for the students who are not acquainted with it, giving this survey a representative character especially in comparing the evaluation of the proverb by Caucasians and Asians. It is not possible to cite all the comments which the students quite eagerly provided to the five questions asking for explanatory comments, but a representative sample sheds much light on the status of this proverb today:

Approximately when and where did you first hear the proverb?

One seventy-five-year-old student recalls hearing the proverb the first time in 1928 in New York City, giving us finally a slightly earlier date than Archer Taylor's citation of the proverb in 1931. A student who came across the proverb in 1936 also resided in New York at that time. Most of the other student respondents recall hearing the proverb first in California: three students in the 1950s, two in the 1960s, ten in the 1970s, fourteen in the 1980s, twelve in the 1990s, and eight having no specific time recollection. One student writes "Today is 1/24 1995. Ironically, I *just* heard it [the proverb] yesterday for the first time, at home, from my husband." There are two more students who encountered the proverb in the state of New York, and one student each came across it first in Alaska, Arizona, Florida, Maryland, Massachusetts, Michigan, Oregon, and Vermont. The proverb is thus clearly disseminated throughout the United States.

Have you ever used the expression yourself? If so, under what circumstances? Can you remember particular occasions when you (or someone else) used it?

Only eight of the fifty-one students (or 16 percent) recall ever having used the proverb. Such explanations as "When I was asking for verification of something and the person offered no proof," "No grade without homework being turned in [as a teacher]," "As youngsters we used this to mean that if you don't have the goods you won't get the rewards," and "When I want to tell someone that if they don't have something they don't get anything else" are proof for the fact that the proverb is usually used in a figurative sense. It is interesting to note that one student who recalls having worked for a clothing store employed the proverb in its original use and meaning: "For alteration pick ups, we used claim tickets. If someone didn't bring their claim check, I, or one of my coworkers, would say 'No tickee, no laundry.'" There is also the comment "Yes, just recently, to tease a Chinese friend (he didn't understand)." That same person answers the later question of whether the expression is in any way offensive or insulting with: "Perhaps, but not to me. It could imply a certain stiffness or lack of ease." Obviously this person has not awakened to the sensitive issue of ethnic slurs and should not be surprised to lose the Chinese friend. One does not tease a friend of another ethnic group with stereotypical proverbs.

There is, finally, also the interesting case of a Chinese American student who has used the proverb (all others have not). She used it "in conversations with friends in which I was trying to be sarcastically 'un-P.C.' (i.e., not politically correct). I used this phrase to characterize Chinese immigrants' speech & occupations, as represented by common stereotypes." In answering the question whether the proverb might be a slur, she writes "Yes, to Chinese Americans or Chinese, if the phrase is used in an insulting manner, or is intended to hurt or degrade these groups." Here is a person who as a Chinese American is clearly aware of the stereotypical nature of this proverb. Yet, as a member of this minority, she feels free to use it to make a point. She also seems to feel that the use of the proverb is quite legitimate as long as it is not used to offend or insult the Asian population. Another Chinese student comments: "I remember my dad saying it [the proverb] sort of as a joke. My mom didn't seem very amused." Stereotypical proverbs clearly are not particularly appreciated in the ethnic group that they depict, not even if used in a joking fashion.

If you know the expression, but cannot remember any specific instance of actual usage, could you make up a hypothetical situation in which the expression might appropriately be used?

Many students didn't bother with this question, probably because they are not used to citing the proverb in normal communication to start with. While they "know" the proverb, they are, as the previous question has shown, only infrequent users of it. But most answers given take a rather figurative view of the proverb: "I imagine it would be used in a situation where someone is unprepared for something and the consequences that result from this are unpleasant or undesirable," "Involving some sort of exchange of materials for services between family members," "If you don't have your receipt, you don't get your stuff," "In order to express a situation in which a token (e.g., money, tickets, etc.) is necessary to obtain a service," and "At the library checking out books; you forgot your card and ask them to look up your account by name. The person refuses, saying, 'No tickee, no washee.'" Four students do, however, also recall the association of the proverb with the Chinese laundry. One of them cites possibilities for its figurative and literal meaning: "If someone wanted you to do something for them without offering anything in return, you would say this to them. Literally, I guess a Chinese dry cleaner would say it to you if you didn't pay first and you wanted him to wash your clothes." One of the Asian students (from Korea) also is aware of the two semantic possibilities: "In a Chinese laundry? (Stereotypically, I mean). Otherwise, it could be used when a person needs a claim ticket to get something." Notice also the comment that "The speaker is making derogatory remarks about someone of Asian, specifically Chinese, descent," by a Caucasian student who is very much aware of the stereotypical potential of the proverb.

In terms of usage, presumably the expression can be used literally, but do you believe it could also be used metaphorically (that is, in situations where actual "tickees" and "washees" were not involved)?

Only about half the students answered this question, but they all did so in the affirmative, indicating that the proverb does have an existence as a nonbiased statement: "Yes; in any situation where some form of documentation or authentication was required for the exchange of goods," "Any situation where bureaucracy or hierarchy is in place. No form/stamp/approval code, etc., no product/service/go-ahead," "In any situation which requires an exchange of one item for another," "A tickee could stand for studying for an exam and washee could stand for a good mark," and very much to the point "Nothing is for free."

One student's remark, "I think it is never literal. I have never heard anyone say that to me at the dry cleaners, and I don't think I would. It's always metaphorical," is overstating things a bit in light of previously discussed examples. Nevertheless, it must be pointed out that numerous people whom I have interviewed here in Vermont only want to see the proverb in its metaphorical sense. A native Vermonter would, of course, also have hardly any idea of Chinese laundries and, unfortunately, comes in contact only very rarely, if at all, with Chinese Americans. Only at the present time does Vermont experience a slight increase in its Asian population (about 4300 or 0.8 percent of the entire population; primarily refugees from Vietnam).[112] In any case, the comment of yet another student expresses how many Vermonters and plenty of other Americans would answer this question: "Of course [the proverb is metaphorical]—and I think some use it without a knowledge of its origin." It would be difficult to attack people who use this proverb innocently in a metaphorical way and who are not aware of its stereotypical origin as being insensitive or even racist.

It should also be noted that five of the thirteen Asian students at Berkeley recognize the metaphorical nature of the proverb, seeing more in the proverb than its racial implications. While one student simply states "yes," the other four answer more elaborately: "'Tickee' could be replaced with money and 'washee' with any service," "If you haven't got the right paperwork then you are screwed for the rewards (i.e., financial aid)," "To deny entrance to somewhere," and "Perhaps as a metaphor for sexual favors?—i.e., 'washee'-sexual act. Also, for other circumstances where something is necessary in exchange for something else." To these students the proverb seems quite appropriate as a metaphorical expression, at least.

Do you consider the expression in any way offensive or insulting? If so, to whom? and why?

Only five of the fifty-one students (10 percent) answered this question with a short and straight "no," with the other forty-four (86 percent; two students did not respond) definitely recognizing the problematic nature of this proverb. Among them are eleven of the thirteen Asian students (two did not respond), who understandably are particularly sensitive to the origin of the proverb in the Chinese laundry environment.

With regard to the answers of the thirty-one Caucasian students, it can be stated that thirteen of them look at this proverb as an insult to the Chinese or Chinese Americans because it ridicules their supposed difficulty with the English language. A few representative responses would be: "It [the proverb] seems sarcastic against an Asian accent or form of speech," "It makes fun of a dialect and stereotypes them [Chinese Americans] in an unflattering light," "It characterizes them [Chinese] as having bad command of English as well as [being] predominantly employed in the laundry business," "Making fun of their English via this stereotypical enunciation and stereotypical job categorization," "It makes fun of their [Chinese and Chinese Americans] speech and it infers the low status of the laundry worker," and "It is stereotyping them [Chinese] as having heavy accents and owning dry cleaning businesses." As can be seen, some of the answers link the linguistic and professional stereotypes together, but there are also answers which deal exclusively with the Chinese laundry environment: "It is the stereotype of Asian Americans running dry cleaners/wash houses," "It refers to a stereotype—the Chinese laundryman," and "It is offensive to Chinese Americans who ran laundry services. It's an ethnic slur." It might be noted that the student who wrote the last comment also remarks that she found the proverb in Maxine Hong Kingston's novel *The Woman Warrior* which was discussed earlier in this chapter.

Three of the Caucasian students have only over time become aware of the fact that the proverb can be a slur. Their revealing statements point to the complexity of coming to terms with the problems that this proverb represents to the ethnically sensitized person. A seventy-year-old student writes: "Haven't used it [the proverb] in years because we have all (?) been sensitive to using ethnic expressions just in case they might be offensive." Another adult student, this one fifty years old, observes: "Now it is certainly an ethnic slur, but then our awareness was not attuned to the discriminating aspects." And a somewhat younger student (twenty-eight years old) states: "At this point my answer is yes [the proverb is a slur]. As a youth I would not have. I was raised without ethnic biased attitudes. But with the pressure for respect between groups of various cultures, I would not want to insult anyone of Asian descent." Here then are three persons who have consciously put an end to the use of this proverb in their verbal communication—a laudable decision to be sure by people who have become aware of the possible harm that this proverb might inflict on other human beings.

And how do the answers by the eleven Asian students who responded to this question relate to all of this? Their comments also refer to the linguistic and professional stereotype that the proverb evokes: "I find it [the proverb] offensive to Chinese and other Asian cultures in that it makes fun of the language used by the immigrants," "It carries the stereotype that all Chinese are laundry shop workers. It makes fun of the accent," "It is offensive to Asian people making fun of their accent and the fact that most work in or own cleaners," "[Offensive] to Chinese Americans or Chinese, if the phrase is used in an insulting manner, or is intended to hurt or degrade these groups," and "I do find it offensive as an ethnic slur and stereotype. It ranks right up there with pulling the corners of your eyes up (or down) and making 'ching, chang, chong' noises." There is, finally, a twenty-four-year-old Chinese American student who takes a rather liberated (or is it flippant?) view of the problematic proverb: "I guess it *can* be construed as offensive to Chinese Americans, the Chinese laundryman stereotype & all. But I *personally* do not take offense . . . of course, keep in mind that I'm a very cynical, unpolitically-correct individual."

No matter in what spirit this last remark was written, it does seem to summarize the various points of view regarding the proverb "No tickee, no washee" and its variants that have been discussed in these pages. There is no doubt that to the Chinese and Chinese American population of this country the proverb is an ethnic slur, especially if it is directed in a willfully insulting fashion to them individually or as an ethnic group. Yet these very people who are directly involved are also willing to see that the proverb can be used metaphorically, that it has its use and place as a nonstereotypical expression. Reactions by Caucasians and other minorities agree with this interpretation of the double-edged nature of this proverb.[113] If it were in our power, then should we purge the language of this proverb altogether? From my careful reading of all the references reviewed here and others not cited because of space limitations, I would say that there might be no need for such a drastic action. In Chapter 5 I argued that the nonmetaphorical proverb "The only good Indian is a dead Indian" deserves to be erased from our language (and yet it is gaining more and more international currency!), but the "No tickee, no washee" proverb presents a different problem. I applaud those people who have consciously stopped using the proverb, but I do not think that certain supercharged politically correct people should condemn people too quickly who use the text figuratively, often even in a varied form.

Here is a small example of what I have in mind: in November 1994 a student from Middlebury College came to visit me here at the University of Vermont. When I told him that I was working on this particular proverb, he told me with much excitement what had happened to him on the previous day taking the Greyhound bus from Middlebury to Burlington. As he was fumbling around for his ticket, the bus driver teasingly said, "No tickee, no ridee."[114] Does this incident prove the slur is alive here in wintery Vermont? Should the driver have quoted instead the nondescript proverb "If you don't have a ticket, you don't ride?"[115] I honestly and humbly don't think so. There is no need to go to such extremes in my opinion. No law is required to forbid the figurative use of the proverb "No tickee, no washee" and its variants, but care should be taken not to offend any Asian person with its improper use. We don't want to legislate so-called political correctness. What we want is respect and understanding for people of all ethnic backgrounds. It won't do anybody any good to purge this proverb if that does not result in more love in our hearts for our minority population. Language in general and proverbs in particular are difficult if not impossible to legislate, but if this study succeeds in getting people to use (if at all) this proverb with care and thought, my labors will not have been in vain.

Notes
Bibliography
Indexes

Notes

Chapter 1. "As If I Were the Master of the Situation"

An earlier version of this chapter was first published in *International Folklore Review* 10 (1995): 35–53.

1. See Michael Kinne, "Zum Sprachgebrauch der deutschen Faschisten: Ein bibliographischer Überblick," *Diskussion Deutsch* 14 (1983): 518–21.

2. See Utz Maas, "Sprache im Nationalsozialismus," *Diskussion Deutsch* 14 (1983): 499–517; U. Maas, *Als der Geist der Gemeinschaft eine Sprache fand: Sprache im Nationalsozialismus. Versuch einer historischen Argumentationsanalyse* (Opladen: Westdeutscher Verlag, 1984); and Carola Sachse et al., *Angst, Belohnung, Zucht und Ordnung. Herrschaftsmechanismen im Nationalsozialismus* (Opladen: Westdeutscher Verlag, 1982).

3. See Karl Kraus, *Die dritte Walpurgisnacht,* ed. Heinrich Fischer (München: Kösel, 1952), 208, 211. It should be noted here that translations of all secondary literature are my own. For additional comments concerning the use of proverbial texts during this period, see Wolfgang Mieder, "Karl Kraus und der sprichwörtliche Aphorismus," *Muttersprache* 89 (1979): 97–115; also in W. Mieder, *Deutsche Sprichwörter in Literatur, Politik, Presse und Werbung* (Hamburg: Helmut Buske, 1983), 113–31. Of interest is also Andrea Hoffend, "Bevor die Nazis die Sprache beim Wort nahmen: Wurzeln und Entsprechungen nationalsozialistischen Sprachgebrauchs," *Muttersprache* 97 (1987): 257–99.

4. Kraus, *Die dritte Walpurgisnacht,* 241.

5. See Victor Klemperer, *LTI: Notizbuch eines Philologen* (1st ed., 1947; Köln: Röderberg, 1987), 16, 166–67.

6. Hans Jacob, "An ihrer Sprache sollt Ihr sie erkennen: Die Gleichschaltung der deutschen Sprache," *Das Wort* 1 (1938): 81–86. The Bible proverb is used as a powerful *leitmotif* throughout Jacob's article and, at the very end, is cited with an imperative exclamation mark. Its use indicates how urgently Jacob was trying to activate the German population to deal critically with the language and deeds of the growing number of National Socialists.

7. All quotations of Hitler's speeches are cited from the standard edition by Max Domarus, *Hitler: Reden und Proklamationen 1932–1945,* 2 vols. (Neustadt a. d. Aisch: Schmidt, 1962–63), vol. 1, p. 244. All the translations into English are my own.

8. See Cornelia Berning, *Vom Abstammungsnachweis zum Zuchtwort: Vokabular des Nationalsozialismus* (Berlin: Walter de Gruyter, 1964); Werner Betz, "The National-Socialist Vocabulary," in *The Third Reich,* ed. Maurice Baumont, John Fried, and Edmond Vermeil (New York: Frederick Praeger, 1955), 784–96; Siegfried Bork, *Mißbrauch der Sprache: Tendenzen nationalsozialistischer Sprachregelung* (München: Francke, 1970); Rolf Glunk, "Erfolg und Mißerfolg der nationalsozialistischen Sprachlenkung," *Zeitschrift für deutsche Sprache* 22 (1966): 57–73, 146–53; 23 (1967): 83–113, 178–88; 24 (1968): 72–91, 184–91; 26 (1970): 84–97, 176–83; and 27 (1971): 113–23, 177–87; Heinz Paechter, *Nazi-Deutsch: A Glossary of Contemporary German* (New York: Frederick Ungar, 1944); Wolfgang Sauer, *Der Sprachgebrauch von Nationalsozialisten vor 1933* (Hamburg: Helmut Buske, 1978); and Eugen Seidel and Ingeborg Seidel-Slotty, *Sprachwandel im Dritten Reich* (Halle: Verlag Sprache und Literatur, 1961).

9. Quoted from Cornelia Berning, "Die Sprache der Nationalsozialisten," *Zeitschrift für deutsche Wortforschung* 18 (1962): 109. Berning's long article contains more explanatory information than her book cited in note 8 above; it can be found in the following volumes of this journal: 16 (1960): 71–149, 178–88; 17 (1961): 83–121, 171–82; 18 (1962): 108–18, 160–72; 19 (1963): 92–112. Klemperer, *LTI,* 246, also quotes this statement by Goebbels.

10. All page numbers given in parentheses in the text are from the following edition of the English translation of *Mein Kampf:* Adolf Hitler, *Mein Kampf,* trans. Ralph Manheim (1st ed., 1947; Boston: Houghton Mifflin, Sentry ed., 1962). Here and in other quotations from this book, italics indicate Hitler's use of spaced type. I thank my friend Prof. George B. Bryan for lending me his copy of this book and for helping me with the translation of some of the proverbial language which Ralph Manheim failed to render into equivalent English. Thanks is also owed to my friend Prof. Veronica Richel for her help with some of the translations of proverbs and quotations. The English quotations are all from this book, but where necessary I attempted a more colloquial translation of the German proverbial language. Reading *Mein Kampf* in the German original reveals Hitler's frequent use of proverbial language much better than this otherwise excellent translation.

11. Compare this similarly condescending statement by Hitler: "The receptivity of the great masses is very limited, their intelligence is small, but their power of forgetting is enormous. In consequence of these facts, all effective propaganda must be limited to a very few points and must harp on these in slogans until the last member of the public understands what you want him to understand by your slogan" (180–81). See also Walther Dieckmann, "Zum Wörterbuch des Unmenschen: Propaganda," *Zeitschrift für deutsche Sprache* 21 (1965): 105–14.

12. See Lutz Winckler, *Studie zur gesellschaftlichen Funktion faschistischer Sprache* (Frankfurt am Main: Suhrkamp, 1970), 90.

13. For this see above all the excellent study with some examples by Sigrid Frind, "Die Sprache als Propagandainstrument in der Publizistik des Dritten Reiches, untersucht an Hitlers 'Mein Kampf' und den Kriegsjahrgängen des 'Völkischen Beobachters'" (diss., Free University of Berlin, 1964), esp. 41–45, 137–41.

14. Quoted from George Steiner's article "The Hollow Miracle" (1959) in

G. Steiner, *Language and Silence: Essays on Language, Literature and the Inhuman* (New York: Atheneum, 1967), 99.

15. For the use of metaphors in the Nazi language see Konrad Ehelich, ed., *Sprache im Faschismus* (Frankfurt am Main: Suhrkamp, 1989), 154–57; Detlev Grieswelle, *Propaganda der Friedlosigkeit. Eine Studie zu Hitlers Rhetorik 1920–1933* (Stuttgart: Ferdinand Enke, 1972), 156–59; Seidel and Seidel-Slotty, *Sprachwandel im Dritten Reich*, 9–11; and Margareta Wedleff, "Zum Stil in Hitlers Maireden," *Muttersprache* 80 (1970): 107–27 (esp. 116–17).

16. See Bork, *Mißbrauch der Sprache*, 91–95; Walther Dieckmann, *Sprache in der Politik* (Heidelberg: Carl Winter, 1969), 108; Frind, "Die Sprache als Propagandainstrument," 70–73; Sigrid Frind, "Die Sprache als Propagandainstrument des Nationalsozialismus," *Muttersprache* 76 (1966): 129–35 (esp. 132); Jürgen Henningsen, *Bildsamkeit, Sprache und Nationalsozialismus* (Essen: Neue Deutsche Schule Verlagsgesellschaft, 1963), 14–16; and Gerhard Voigt, "Bericht vom Ende der 'Sprache des Nationalsozialismus,'" *Diskussion Deutsch* 19 (1974): 445–64 (esp. 447).

17. Grieswelle, *Propaganda der Friedlosigkeit*, 149.

18. Quoted from Georg Büchmann, *Geflügelte Worte. Der Zitatenschatz des deutschen Volkes*, ed. Gunther Haupt and Werner Rust (28th ed.; Berlin: Haude and Spener, 1937), 641–50.

19. See Theodor Heuß, *Hitlers Weg. Eine historisch-politische Studie über den Nationalsozialismus* (Stuttgart: Union Deutsche Verlagsgesellschaft, 1932), 84–85; Bertolt Brecht, "Über den Satz 'Gemeinnutz geht vor Eigennutz,'" in B. Brecht, *Gesammelte Werke in 20 Bänden*, ed. Elisabeth Hauptmann (Frankfurt am Main: Suhrkamp, 1967), vol. 20, pp. 230–33 (written between 1933 and 1939); Ernst Bloch, "Die Fabel des Menenius Agrippa oder eine der ältesten Soziallügen," in E. Bloch, *Politische Messungen, Pestzeit, Vormärz* (Frankfurt am Main: Suhrkamp, 1970), 172–76 (written 1936); and Frind, "Die Sprache als Propagandainstrument," 71.

20. My friend Hans-Manfred Militz (Jena) mentioned this fact to me in a letter dated 14 February 1985.

21. Ruth Klüger, *weiter leben. Eine Jugend* (Göttingen: Wallstein, 1992), 119. The translation is yet again my own. For an English review of this significant book, see Ursula Mahlendorf, "Ruth Klüger: *weiter leben*," *World Literature Today* 67 (1993): 607–8.

22. See Friedrich Wolf, *Gedichte, Erzählungen 1911–1936*, ed. Else Wolf and Walther Pollatschek (Berlin: Aufbau-Verlag, 1963), 85–86.

23. See Wolfgang Mieder, "Proverbs in Nazi Germany: The Promulgation of Anti-Semitism and Stereotypes through Folklore," *Journal of American Folklore* 95 (1982): 435–64; now also in W. Mieder, *Proverbs Are Never Out of Season: Popular Wisdom in the Modern Age* (New York: Oxford University Press, 1993), 225–55.

24. See Kraus, *Die dritte Walpurgisnacht*, 123.

25. Domarus, *Hitler*, vol. 2, pp. 1828–29.

26. See Frind, "Die Sprache als Propagandainstrument," 23.

27. Bork, *Mißbrauch der Sprache,* 92.

28. Ibid., 50–51.

29. See Kirsten Gomard, "Zum Sprachgebrauch im Dritten Reich," *Augias* no. 2 (1981): 27–45 (esp. 33–34).

30. See Klemperer, *LTI,* 28–29.

31. See Kenneth Burke, "The Rhetoric of Hitler's 'Battle,'" in K. Burke, *The Philosophy of Literary Form* (New York: Vintage Books, 1957), 187. It is interesting to note that Burke wanted to warn his American readers through this essay of the menace of Hitler and his dangerous National Socialists, requesting that they read *Mein Kampf* for themselves in order to prevent a similar situation in the United States: "Let us try also to discover what kind of 'medicine' this medicine-man has concocted, that we may know, with greater accuracy, exactly what to guard against, if we are to forestall the concocting of similar medicine in America" (164). A shortened (1933) and then a complete (1939) English translation of *Mein Kampf* were published for this purpose both in England and the United States. The book was also translated into numerous other languages, so that the effort to understand and oppose it ironically made it one of the world's most widely published books. See C. Caspar, *"Mein Kampf—A Best Seller," Jewish Social Studies* 20 (1958): 3–16; Werner Maser, *Hitlers "Mein Kampf." Entstehung, Aufbau, Stil und Änderungen, Quellen, Quellenwert, kommentierte Auszüge* (München: Bechtle, 1966), 30–35; Karl Lange, *Hitlers unbeachtete Maximen. "Mein Kampf" und die Öffentlichkeit* (Stuttgart: Kohlhammer, 1968), 109–11, 126–27, 167–70; and James J. Barnes and Patience P. Barnes, *Hitler's "Mein Kampf" in Britain and America: A Publishing History 1930–39* (Cambridge: Cambridge University Press, 1980).

32. Lange, *Hitlers unbeachtete Maximen,* 30–31.

33. See Maser, *Hitlers "Mein Kampf,"* 26–29.

34. See also Cornelius Schnauber, *Wie Hitler sprach und schrieb. Zur Psychologie und Prosodik der faschistischen Rhetorik* (Frankfurt am Main: Athenäum, 1972).

35. Hitler also used this twin formula in his speeches of 27 January 1932, 10 February 1933, and 6 October 1939, in order to explain his racial ideology; see Domarus, *Hitler,* vol. 1, p. 86 and p. 205; vol. 2, p. 1389. See also yet another use of the expression in *Mein Kampf:* ". . . a time when the Reich was highly interested in colonies, but not in its own flesh and blood at its very doorstep" (11–12).

36. As mentioned in note 10, I have used italics throughout this chapter to indicate Hitler's frequent use of "spaced type" to emphasize certain words, sentences, or entire paragraphs.

37. For the role of the press during the Nazi regime see Joseph Wulf, *Presse und Funk im Dritten Reich. Eine Dokumentation* (Gütersloh: Sigbert Mohn, 1964).

38. See also the use of this expression in Hitler's anti-Semitic speech of 24 February 1943, in which he speaks of the "extermination of Jewry in Europe" and claims that its nature will be made clear "with one stroke to the entire German people"; quoted from Domarus, *Hitler,* vol. 2, p. 1992.

39. Quoted from Ulrich Ulonska, *Suggestion der Glaubwürdigkeit. Untersuchungen zu Hitlers rhetorischer Selbstdarstellung zwischen 1920 und 1933* (Ammersbek bei Hamburg: Verlag an der Lottbek, 1990), 87. See also E. Epping, "Die NS-Rhetorik als politisches Führungsmittel" (diss., University of Münster, 1954).

40. Domarus, *Hitler*, vol. 2, p. 2161.

41. Ibid., 2163.

42. Ibid., 2185. See also Wolfgang Mieder, "'Sein oder Nichtsein'—und kein Ende: Zum Weiterleben des Hamlet Zitats in unserer Zeit," in W. Mieder, *Sprichwort, Redensart, Zitat: Tradierte Formelsprache in der Moderne* (Bern: Peter Lang, 1985), 125–30.

43. Hitler uses the proverbial comparison "as plain as one's hand" rather frequently in order to express something quite obvious; see also *Mein Kampf,* 313, 407, 424, 559. It must, however, be pointed out here that Ralph Manheim always translates this metaphor by the nondescript phrase "it is obvious."

44. For Luther's interest in and use of proverbs see above all J. A. Heuseler, *Luthers Sprichwörter aus seinen Schriften gesammelt* (Leipzig: Johann Barth, 1824; rpt. Walluf: Sändig, 1973); James C. Cornette, "Proverbs and Proverbial Expressions in the German Works of Luther" (diss., University of North Carolina, 1942); Dietz-Rüdiger Moser, "'Die wellt wil meister klueglin bleiben . . .': Martin Luther und das deutsche Sprichwort," *Muttersprache* 90 (1980): 151–66; and Berthold Weckmann, "Sprichwort und Redensart in der Lutherbibel," *Archiv für das Studium der neueren Sprachen und Literaturen* 221 (1984): 19–42.

45. See *Mein Kampf,* 154, 246, 259, 499, 505, 506.

46. See Büchmann, *Geflügelte Worte,* 649.

47. Domarus, *Hitler,* vol. 1, p. 533. See also the discussion of "Sportsprache" (language of sports) during National Socialism in Berning, "Die Sprache der Nationalsozialisten," 18 (1962): 108–11; and Bork, *Mißbrauch der Sprache,* 16–17.

48. Additional examples of proverbial expressions from the Bible in *Mein Kampf* include, among others, "das tägliche Brot" (the daily bread, 153); "im Schweiße seines Angesichts" (in the sweat of his brow, 77); "das goldene Kalb" (the Golden Calf, 128); "Laß die linke Hand nicht wissen, was die Rechte gibt" (the left hand should not know what the right hand giveth, 313). For biblical proverbs as such see Carl Schulze, *Die biblischen Sprichwörter der deutschen Sprache* (Göttingen: Vandenhoeck and Ruprecht, 1860; rpt. ed. by Wolfgang Mieder; Bern: Peter Lang, 1987). See also Manfred Ach and Clemens Pentrop, *Hitlers "Religion": Pseudoreligiöse Elemente im nationalsozialistischen Sprachgebrauch* (München: Arbeitsgemeinschaft für Religions- und Weltanschauungsfragen, 1977).

49. See also the characterization of Hitler himself as a "Vogel Strauß" (ostrich bird) in Domarus, *Hitler,* vol. 2, p. 1335.

50. This essay was first published on 27 May 1932 in the *Berliner Börsen-Courier;* also in Herbert Jhering, *Der Kampf um das Theater und andere Streitschriften 1918–1933,* ed. Ludwig Hoffmann (Berlin: Aufbau-Verlag, 1974), 58–64. Now also reprinted in Wolfgang Mieder, *Deutsche Sprichwörter und Redensarten* (Stuttgart: Reclam, 1979), 134–40 (here p. 139).

51. Quoted from *Hitlers Zweites Buch. Ein Dokument aus dem Jahr 1928,*

ed. Gerhard L. Weinberg (Stuttgart: Deutsche Verlags-Anstalt, 1961), 137; the English translations of the German proverbs are my own. This manuscript is not as rich in proverbial language as *Mein Kampf.* This is probably due to the fact that this second "book" is less aggressively propagandistic and more theoretical in nature. For other proverbs in this posthumous publication, see 137, 138, 140, 141, 162, 170, 171, 172, 174, 189, 205. Hitler had already used the proverb "Kleider machen Leute" (Clothes make the man) in *Mein Kampf* in order to scold the German youth for its modern clothes: "It is truly miserable to behold how our youth even now is subjected to a fashion madness which helps to reverse the sense of the old saying: 'Clothes make the man' into something truly catastrophic" (412).

52. *Hitlers Zweites Buch,* 141. Hitler uses this proverb of the third party also on the previous page (140). It should be noted that the German proverb "Wenn zwei sich streiten, freut sich der Dritte" has an older English equivalent that is not in current use any longer: "Two dogs strive for a bone, and the third runs away with it."

53. Ibid., 162.

54. Hitler also used this proverbial expression in his two speeches of 12 September 1938 and 19 September 1939; see Domarus, *Hitler,* vol. 1, p. 899; and vol. 2, p. 1358.

55. See also Hitler's additional use of this quotation in his speech on 6 April 1938: "I see in Mr. Schuschnigg one of those forces which wants to create evil but which in the execution of providence always brings about good in the end"; ibid., vol. 1, p. 846. Of general interest is also *Beschädigtes Erbe. Beiträge zur Klassikerrezeption in finsterer Zeit,* ed. Horst Claussen and Norbert Oellers (Bonn: Bouvier, 1984).

56. See Ruth Römer, *Sprachwissenschaft und Rassenideologie in Deutschland* (München: Fink, 1985).

57. See also the anti-Semitic proverb collection by Ernst Hiemer, *Der Jude im Sprichwort der Völker* (Nürnberg: Der Stürmer, 1942). Hiemer includes an entire chapter (41–47) entitled "Meister der Lüge" (Master in Lying) in which he attempts to show by means of proverbs and proverbial expressions that Jews are by nature liars. For additional comments on anti-Semitic proverb studies see Mieder, *Proverbs Are Never Out of Season,* esp. 238–48.

58. See Manfred Pechau, "Nationalsozialismus und deutsche Sprache" (diss., University of Greifswald, 1934; Greifswald: Hans Adler, 1935), 65–73. See, however, now also the critical studies by Dolf Sternberger, Gerhard Storz, and W. E. Süskind, *Aus dem Wörterbuch des Unmenschen* (Hamburg: Claassen, 1957); Joseph Wulf, *Aus dem Lexikon der Mörder. "Sonderbehandlung" und verwandte Worte in nationalsozialistichen Dokumenten* (Gütersloh: Sigbert Mohn, 1963); and Hans Winterfeldt, "Elemente der Brutalität im nationalsozialistischen Sprachgebrauch," *Muttersprache* 75 (1965): 231–36.

59. See Karl Müller, *Unseres Führers Sprachkunst auf Grund seines Werkes "Mein Kampf"* (Dresden: M. D. Groh, 1935).

60. See Karl Friedrich Wilhelm Wander, *Deutsches Sprichwörter-Lexikon*

(Leipzig: F. A. Brockhaus, 1867–80; rpt., Darmstadt: Wissenschaftliche Buchgesellschaft, 1964), vol. 3 (1873), col. 1517 (Recht), no. 9.

61. See also Hitler's use of this proverbial expression in his speech of 30 September 1942, in Domarus, *Hitler,* vol. 2, p. 1922.

62. See L. A. Morozova, "Upotreblenie V. I. Leninym poslovits," *Russkaia Rech'* no vol., no. 2 (1979): 10–14; and Edd Miller and Jesse J. Villarreal, "The Use of Clichés by Four Contemporary Speakers [Winston Churchill, Anthony Eden, Franklin D. Roosevelt, and Henry Wallace]," *Quarterly Journal of Speech* 31 (1945): 151–55. The use of proverbs by Willy Brandt and Ronald Reagan rests on my own observations.

63. See Domarus, *Hitler,* vol. 1, p. 607.

64. Klemperer, *LTI,* 236. See also his other reference to this proverb: *"Vox populi*—again and again the question of the contemporary person asking which of the many voices will be the decisive one" (248). For this classical proverb in general see G. Boas, *Vox Populi: Essays in the History of an Idea* (Baltimore: Johns Hopkins University Press, 1969), esp. 3–38.

65. For this see Friedrich Seiler, *Deutsche Sprichwörterkunde* (München: C. H. Beck, 1922; rpt., 1967), 3; and Lutz Röhrich and Wolfgang Mieder, *Sprichwort* (Stuttgart: Metzler, 1977), 2, 81.

66. See Wander, *Deutsches Sprichwörter-Lexikon,* vol. 3 (1873), col. 624 (Mensch), no. 771.

67. See ibid., vol. 4 (1876), col. 1465 (Unmöglich), no. 1; and vol. 5 (1880), col. 1313 (Gehen), no. 493.

68. See also Hitler's statement in his speech of 1 March 1935: "Faith can remove mountains, faith can also liberate peoples. Faith can strengthen nations and make them rise again no matter how humiliated they might have been"; quoted from Domarus, *Hitler,* vol. 1, p. 487.

69. See Wander, *Deutsches Sprichwörter-Lexikon,* vol. 1 (1867), col. 278 (Baum), no. 112.

70. Ibid., vol. 4 (1876), col. 1176 (Thun), no. 233.

71. Ibid., vol. 3 (1873), cols. 1528–29 (Recht), no. 203.

72. Ibid., vol. 3 (1873), col. 306 (Macht), no. 18.

73. For this see Wolfgang Mieder, *Das Sprichwort in unserer Zeit* (Frauenfeld: Huber, 1975), 82–84.

74. Hitler also liked the literary quotation "Der Mohr hat seine Schuldigkeit getan, der Mohr kann gehen" (The Moor has worked off his debt, the Moor can go) out of Friedrich Schiller's play *Die Verschwörung des Fiesco zu Genua.* For references see *Mein Kampf* (294) and the two speeches of 30 January 1941 and May 4, 1941, in Domarus, *Hitler,* vol. 2, 1659 and p. 1707.

75. See Burke, "Rhetoric of Hitler's 'Battle,'" 180.

76. Quoted from Domarus, *Hitler,* vol. 1, p. 609. This statement in German "Aus dem Volke bin ich gewachsen, im Volk bin ich geblieben, zum Volk kehre ich zurück!" is also included as a Hitler quotation in Büchmann, *Geflügelte Worte,* 645.

77. Schiller actually writes "Wir sind ein Volk und einig wollen wir handeln"

(We are one people and united we want to act). For the more modern use of this quotation turned proverb see Ulla Fix, "Der Wandel der Muster—Der Wandel im Umgang mit den Mustern. Kommunikationskultur im institutionellen Sprachgebrauch der DDR am Beispiel von Losungen," *Deutsche Sprache* no vol., no. 4 (1990): 332–47; and Hans-Manfred Militz, "Das Antisprichwort als semantische Variante eines sprichwörtlichen Textes," *Proverbium* 8 (1991): 107–11.

78. For a discussion of ship-of-state proverbs and proverbial expressions see Irene Meichsner, *Die Logik von Gemeinplätzen. Vorgeführt an Steuermannstopos und Schiffsmetapher* (Bonn: Bouvier, 1983); and Wolfgang Mieder, "'Wir sitzen alle in einem Boot': Herkunft, Geschichte und Verwendung einer neueren deutschen Redensart," *Muttersprache* 100 (1990): 18–37.

79. Hitler speaks in this quotation of the politics of Austria and could, of course, not surmise that he himself would become the most terrible incarnation of the "Pied Piper of Hamelin" motif. See also the numerous interpretations of Hitler as a Pied Piper in modern literature and caricatures in Wolfgang Mieder, "'The Pied Piper of Hamelin': Origin, History, and Survival of the Legend," in W. Mieder, *Tradition and Innovation in Folk Literature* (Hanover, N.H.: University Press of New England, 1987), 45–83, 236–43 (notes).

Chapter 2. "Make Hell While the Sun Shines"

An earlier version of this chapter was published in *Folklore* 106 (1995): 57–69.

1. See Wolfgang Mieder, *Proverbs in Literature: An International Bibliography* (Bern: Peter Lang, 1978); and W. Mieder, *International Proverb Scholarship: An Annotated Bibliography,* 3 vols. (New York: Garland Publishing, 1982, 1990, and 1993).

2. See Werner Koller, *Redensarten: Linguistische Aspekte, Vorkommensanalysen, Sprachspiel* (Tübingen: Max Niemeyer, 1977), esp. 122–74; Theres Gautschi, *Bildhafte Phraseologismen in der Nationalratswahlpropaganda* (Bern: Peter Lang, 1982); Edmund Kammerer, "Sprichwort und Politik: Sprachliche Schematismen in Politikerreden, politischem Journalismus und Graffiti" (M.A. thesis, University of Freiburg, 1983); Shirley L. Arora, "On the Importance of Rotting Fish: A Proverb and Its Audience [during the Michael Dukakis presidential campaign]," *Western Folklore* 48 (1989): 271–88; and Karen E. Richman, "'With Many Hands, the Burden Isn't Heavy': Creole Proverbs and Political Rhetoric in Haiti's Presidential Elections," *Folklore Forum* 23 (1990): 115–23.

3. See Démétrios Loukatos, "Proverbes et commentaires politiques: Le public devant les télé-communications actuelles," *Proverbium* 1 (1984): 119–26; and Peter Kühn, "Routine-Joker in politischen Fernsehdiskussionen. Plädoyer für eine textsortenabhängige Beschreibung von Phraseologismen," *Beiträge zur Phraseologie des Ungarischen und des Deutschen,* ed. Regina Hessky (Budapest: Loránd-Eötvös-Universität, 1988), 155–76.

4. See R. D. Hogg, "Proverbs," *Secretariat News* 14 (1960): 5–7; and Victor S. M. de Guinzbourg, *Wit and Wisdom of the United Nations: Proverbs and Apothegms on Diplomacy* (New York: privately printed, 1961; supplement 1965).

5. See Lutz Röhrich, "Die Bildwelt von Sprichwort und Redensart in der

Sprache der politischen Karikatur," *Kontakte und Grenzen: Probleme der Volks-, Kultur- und Sozialforschung. Festschrift für Gerhard Heilfurth,* ed. Hans Friedrich Foltin (Göttingen: Otto Schwartz, 1969), 175–207; Wolfgang Mieder, "'It's Five Minutes to Twelve': Folklore and Saving Life on Earth," *International Folklore Review* 7 (1989): 10–21; and Fionnuala Williams, "'To Kill Two Birds with One Stone': Variants in a War of Words," *Proverbium* 8 (1991): 199–201.

6. Published in *Western Folklore* 15 (1956): 153–58; and reprinted in *The Wisdom of Many: Essays on the Proverb,* ed. Wolfgang Mieder and Alan Dundes (New York: Garland Publishing, 1981), 300–308.

7. See Hugo Blümmer, *Der bildliche Ausdruck in den Reden des Fürsten Bismarck* (Leipzig: S. Hirzel, 1891), esp. 182–86; and H. Blümmer, "Der bildliche Ausdruck in den Briefen des Fürsten Bismarck," *Euphorion* 1 (1894): 590–603 and 771–87.

8. See Günter Wein, "Die Rolle der Sprichwörter und Redensarten in der Agitation und Propaganda," *Sprachpflege* 12 (1963): 51–52; Aleksandr M. Zhigulev, "Poslovitsy i pogovorki v bol'shevitskikh listovkakh," *Sovetskaia Etnografia* 5 (1970): 124–31; L. A. Morozova, "Upotreblenie V. I. Leninym poslovits," *Russkaia Rech'* no vol., no. 2 (1979): 10–14; N. A. Meshcherskii, "Traditsionno-knizhnye vyrazheniia v sovremennom russkom literaturnom iazyke (na materiale proizvedenii V. I. Lenina)," *Voprosy frazeologii* 9 (1975): 110–21; and Jean Breuillard, "Proverbes et pouvoir politique: Le cas de l'U.R.S.S.," *Richesse du proverbe,* ed. François Suard and Claude Buridant (Lille: Université de Lille, 1984), vol. 2, pp. 155–66.

9. See "Proverbs in Nazi Germany: The Promulgation of Anti-Semitism and Stereotypes Through Folklore," in Wolfgang Mieder, *Proverbs Are Never Out of Season: Popular Wisdom in the Modern Age* (New York: Oxford University Press, 1993), 225–55; a previous version of chap. 1 of this book was published as "'. . . As If I Were the Master of the Situation': Proverbial Manipulation in Adolf Hitler's *Mein Kampf,*" *International Folklore Review* 10 (1995): 35–53.

10. Manfred Weidhorn, "'Always the Same Set of Songs': Topoi," in M. Weidhorn, *Sir Winston Churchill* (Boston: Twayne Publishers, 1979), 34–45.

11. Ibid., 162.

12. See for example Robert Rhodes James, *Churchill: A Study in Failure, 1900–1939* (New York: The World Publishing Company, 1970); and Maurice Ashley, *Churchill as Historian* (New York: Charles Scribner's Sons, 1968).

13. Quoted from Reed Whittemore, "Churchill and the Limitation of Myth," *Yale Review* 44 (1954–55): 248 (entire article on 248–62); rpt. as "Churchill as a Mythmaker" in *Language and Politics,* ed. Thomas P. Brockway (Boston: D.C. Heath, 1965), 56 (entire article on 56–68). See also Keith Alldritt, *Churchill the Writer: His Life as a Man of Letters* (London: Hutchinson, 1992).

14. A. G. Gardiner, "Genius Without Judgment: Churchill at Fifty," in A. G. Gardiner, *Portraits and Portents* (New York: Harper and Row, 1926), 63 (entire article on 58–64); rpt. in *Churchill: A Profile,* ed. Peter Stansky (New York: Hill and Wang, 1973), 52 (entire article on 48–53).

15. Gardiner, 58 (rpt., 48–49).

16. James, *Churchill: Failure*, 29.

17. David Cannadine, ed., *Blood, Toil, Tears and Sweat: The Speeches of Winston Churchill* (Boston: Houghton Mifflin Company, 1989), 1.

18. Regarding these six volumes as "history" see Ashley, *Churchill as Historian*, 159–209; Keith Niles Hull, "The Literary Art of Winston Churchill's 'The Second World War'" (diss., University of Washington, 1969); and Manfred Weidhorn, *Sword and Pen: A Survey of the Writings of Sir Winston Churchill* (Albuquerque: University of New Mexico Press, 1974), 139–77.

19. Joseph W. Miller, "Winston Churchill, Spokesman for Democracy," *Quarterly Journal of Speech* 28 (1942): 137 (entire essay on 131–38).

20. Weidhorn, "'Always the Same,'" 133 (entire chapter on 130–50). On Churchill's use of imagery see also Joaquim Paço d'Arcos, *Churchill: The Statesman and Writer* (London: The Caravel Press, 1957), 25.

21. Weidhorn, "'Always the Same,'" 134. See also Gwendoline Lilian Reid, "Winston S. Churchill's Theory of Public Speaking as Compared to His Practice" (diss., University of Minnesota, 1987), 149–63.

22. Weidhorn, "'Always the Same,'" 136, 137. On Churchill's frequent use of colloquialisms see also Manfred Weidhorn, *Churchill's Rhetoric and Political Discourse* (Lanham, Md.: University Press of America, 1987), 31–32. See also the comment that Churchill "often rounded off [a discussion] by a sudden colloquialism that from most other people would be an anticlimax" by Collin Brooks, "Churchill the Conversationalist," in *Churchill by His Contemporaries*, ed. Charles Eade (London: The Reprint Society, 1953), 248 (entire essay on 240–48).

23. Cited from Randolph S. Churchill, *Winston S. Churchill*, companion vol. 1, pt. 2, 1896–1900 (Boston: Houghton Mifflin Company, 1967), 819–20 (entire essay on 816–21).

24. See the lack of comments on Churchill's use of proverbs in the following three essays included in Charles Eade, ed., *Churchill by His Contemporaries* (London: The Reprint Society, 1953): Colin Coote, "Churchill the Journalist," 114–21; Norman Birkett, "Churchill the Orator," 223–33; and Ivor Brown, "Churchill the Master of Words," 312–17. The following two studies are also void of any comments regarding his use of proverbs: Herbert Leslie Stewart, *Sir Winston Churchill as Writer and Speaker* (London: Sidgwick and Jackson, 1954); and Charles W. Lomas, "Winston Churchill: Orator-Historian," *Quarterly Journal of Speech* 44 (1958): 153–60. A special disappointment in this regard is the study by Edd Miller and Jesse J. Villarreal, "The Use of Clichés by Four Contemporary Speakers [Winston Churchill, Anthony Eden, Franklin D. Roosevelt, and Henry Wallace]," *Quarterly Journal of Speech* 31 (1945): 151–55.

25. See Wolfgang Mieder and George B. Bryan, *The Proverbial Winston S. Churchill: An Index to Proverbs in the Works of Sir Winston Churchill* (Westport, Conn.: Greenwood Press, 1995).

26. For bibliographical references concerning these nine citations see ibid. For the Maori proverb cited by Churchill see Raymond Firth, "Proverbs in Native Life, with Special Reference to Those of the Maori," *Folk-Lore* (London) 38 (1927): 153.

27. Herbert Howarth, "Behind Winston Churchill's Grand Style," *Commentary* 11 (1951): 551 (entire article on 549–57).

28. It should be noted that the following "popular" collections of Churchill's wit and wisdom do not contain any scholarly annotations and are, of course, limited to Churchill's own quotable statements (often in the form of entire paragraphs): Colin Coote, ed., *Maxims and Reflections of the Rt. Hon. Winston S. Churchill* (Boston: Houghton Mifflin Company, 1947); Bill Adler, *The Churchill Wit* (New York: Coward McCann, 1965); Adam Sykes and Iain Sproat, *The Wit of Sir Winston* (London: Leslie Frewin, 1965); Jack House, *Winston Churchill: His Wit and Wisdom* (London: Hyperion Books, n.d.); and James C. Humes, *The Wit and Wisdom of Winston Churchill* (New York: HarperCollins, 1994). See also James C. Humes's earlier collection of "Wit and Wisdom" in his book *Churchill: Speaker of the Century* (New York: Stein and Day, 1980), 261–79, with the following comment: "The titanic output of his work is staggering to those editors and anthologists who try to select for readers the choicest of his wit and wisdom. Among writers in the English language, perhaps only Shakespeare offers more quotable lines. . . . There are more gems to be gleaned in the writings and speeches of Churchill than in the sayings of Mao or the observations of Machiavelli" (263).

29. See chap. 1 of this book.

30. All quotations are from the following standard edition: Winston S. Churchill, *The Second World War* (London: Cassell and Company, 1948–54).

31. For a short study of this proverbial expression see Wolfgang Mieder and David Pilachowski, "Die 'Nacht der langen Messer,'" *Der Sprachdienst* 19 (1975): 149–52.

32. For proverbs expressing a fatalistic worldview see Matti Kuusi, "Fatalistic Traits in Finnish Proverbs," in *Fatalistic Beliefs in Religion, Folklore and Literature,* ed. Helmer Ringgren (Stockholm: Almqvist and Wiksell, 1967), 89–96; rpt. in Mieder and Dundes, *Wisdom of Many,* 275–83.

33. See Mieder and Bryan, *Proverbial Winston S. Churchill,* for precise references.

34. For two representative collections see Robert Hendrickson, *Salty Words* (New York: Hearst Marine Books, 1984); and Wolfgang Mieder, *Salty Wisdom: Proverbs of the Sea* (Shelburne, Vt.: New England Press, 1990).

35. For a history of this proverbial phrase see Dietmar Peil, "'Im selben Boot': Variationen über ein metaphorisches Argument," *Archiv für Kulturgeschichte* 68 (1986): 269–93; and Wolfgang Mieder, "'Wir sitzen alle in einem Boot': Herkunft, Geschichte und Verwendung einer neueren deutschen Redensart," *Muttersprache* 100 (1990): 18–37. See also the more general study by Irene Meichsner, *Die Logik von Gemeinplätzen. Vorgeführt an Steuermannstopos und Schiffsmetapher* (Bonn: Bouvier, 1983).

36. See Brown, "Churchill the Master of Words," 312.

37. Winston S. Churchill, *My Early Life: A Roving Commission* (1st ed., 1930; New York: Charles Scribner's Sons, 1958), 23.

38. Ibid., 116. See also Darrell Holley, *Churchill's Literary Allusions: An*

Index to the Education of a Soldier, Statesman and Litterateur (Jefferson, N.C.: McFarland and Company, 1987); Reid, "Winston S. Churchill's Theory of Public Speaking," 284–90; and more generally Paul F. Boller, *Quotesmanship: The Use and Abuse of Quotations for Polemical and Other Purposes* (Dallas, Tex.: Southern Methodist University Press, 1967).

39. See Victor L. Albjerg, *Winston Churchill* (New York: Twayne Publishers, 1973), 46. See also Ashley, *Churchill as Historian*, 23; and Weidhorn, "Always the Same," 30.

40. For a history of this Latin proverb see Anette Erler, "Zur Geschichte des Spruches 'Bis dat, qui cito dat' [He gives twice who gives quickly]," *Philologus* 13 (1986): 210–20.

41. Karl Friedrich Wilhelm Wander, *Deutsches Sprichwörter-Lexikon*, 5 vols. (Leipzig: F. A. Brockhaus, 1867–80; rpt. Darmstadt: Wissenschaftliche Buchgesellschaft, 1964), vol. 1 (1867), col. 278 (no. 112).

42. Ibid., vol. 2 (1870), col. 45 (no. 1024).

43. See Mieder and Bryan, *Proverbial Winston S. Churchill*, for precise references.

44. Quoted from Robert Rhodes James, ed., *Winston S. Churchill: His Complete Speeches, 1897–1963* (London: Chelsea House Publishers, 1974), vol. 8, p. 8507.

45. See J. Alan Pfeffer, *The Proverb in Goethe* (New York: King's Crown Press, 1948), p. 24 (no. 56).

46. The only reference work in which it is registered with a reference to Goethe is Lilian Dalbiac, *Dictionary of Quotations (German)* (1st ed., 1909; New York: Frederick Ungar, 1958), 155.

47. James, *Winston S. Churchill: Speeches*, vol. 6, p. 6220.

48. Winston S. Churchill, *The World Crisis* (New York: Charles Scribner's Sons, 1931 [1959]), vol. 6, p. 1. See Manfred Weidhorn, "Churchill the Phrase Forger," *Quarterly Journal of Speech* 58 (1972): 170 (entire essay on 161–74).

49. See John Bartlett, *Familiar Quotations*, ed. Justin Kaplan (16th ed.; Boston: Little, Brown and Company, 1992), p. 620, no. 5, n. 1.

50. For an intriguing article on possible classical origins of Churchill's phrase see Richard Henry Crum, "Blood, sweat and tears," *The Classical Journal* 42 (1947): 299–300.

51. Cited from James, *Winston S. Churchill: Speeches*, vol. 6, p. 6287.

52. Ibid., 6397–98.

53. Ibid., 6516.

54. Ibid., 6657.

55. Ibid., 6693.

56. For Churchill's six citations of this statement, see Mieder and Bryan, *Proverbial Winston S. Churchill*. Dr. Martin J. Routh, president of Magdalen College, seems to be the source of this sound scholarly advice, having made the statement in 1847: "You will find it a very good practice always to verify your quotations." Churchill's friend, Lord Rosebery, on 23 November 1897, altered it somewhat to "Always wind up your watch and verify your quotations." See Bur-

ton Stevenson, *The Home Book of Proverbs, Maxims, and Famous Phrases* (New York: Macmillan, 1948), p. 1929 (no. 3).

57. It is of interest to note that David Cannadine used the original quadratic form of the phrase for the title of his later edition of Churchill speeches: *Blood, Toil, Tears and Sweat: The Speeches of Winston Churchill* (Boston: Houghton Mifflin Company, 1989).

58. For analyses of this speech see W. R. Underhill, "Fulton's Finest Hour," *Quarterly Journal of Speech* 52 (1966): 155–63; Weidhorn, "Churchill the Phrase Forger," 162–63; Henry B. Ryan, "A New Look at Churchill's 'Iron Curtain' Speech," *The Historical Journal* 22 (1979): 895–920 (esp. 897–98); Fraser J. Harbutt, *The Iron Curtain: Churchill, America, and the Origins of the Cold War* (New York: Oxford University Press, 1986), 183–208; and John P. Rossi, "Winston Churchill's Iron Curtain Speech: Forty Years After," *Modern Age: A Quarterly Review* 30 (1986): 113–19.

59. Cited from James, *Winston S. Churchill: Speeches,* vol. 7, p. 7290.

60. Churchill delighted in using theatrical phrases. For some examples see Weidhorn, "Churchill the Phrase Forger," 162–63; Weidhorn, *Churchill's Rhetoric,* 70; and Mieder and Bryan, *Proverbial Winston S. Churchill,* 36–38.

61. For a detailed study of the origin and history of this phrase with many bibliographical references see Wolfgang Mieder, "Bibliographische Skizze zur Überlieferung des Ausdrucks 'Iron Curtain' / 'Eiserner Vorhang'," *Muttersprache* 91 (1981): 1–14.

62. For a complete list of references, see Mieder and Bryan, *Proverbial Winston S. Churchill.*

63. Cited from James, *Winston S. Churchill: Speeches,* vol. 7, p. 7509.

64. This inversion of the proverbial expression "to live from hand to mouth" refers to Churchill's literary activities during the years from 1931 to 1935 which he very much enjoyed: "I earned my livelihood by dictating articles which had a wide circulation not only in Great Britain and the United States, but also, before Hitler's shadow fell upon them, in the most famous newspapers of sixteen European countries. I lived in fact from mouth to hand" (vol. 1, p. 62).

65. This is a biblical proverb from *Proverbs* 16:32. Howarth, "Behind Winston Churchill's," 551, notes correctly that Churchill "likes to call on the Bible for prophetic metaphors." For many examples of this, see Mieder and Bryan, *Proverbial Winston S. Churchill,* 47–50.

66. For additional references see Mieder and Bryan, *Proverbial Winston S. Churchill.*

67. Churchill delighted in using this quotation as can be seen from ibid. It should be noted, however, that he sometimes cites its original source as the U.S. Constitution rather than the Declaration of Independence.

68. A page later Churchill returns again to this special relationship: "Thus began a friendship which across all the ups and downs of war I have preserved with deep satisfaction to this day" (vol. 4, p. 345).

69. Quoted from James, *Winston S. Churchill: Speeches,* vol. 6, p. 6266. See also Birkett, "Churchill the Orator," 226; Weidhorn, "Churchill the Phrase Forger," 168–69; and Bartlett, *Familiar Quotations,* p. 620, no. 10.

70. James, *Winston S. Churchill: Speeches,* vol. 7, p. 7158.

71. Ibid., vol. 8, p. 8243.

72. Ibid., vol. 6, p. 6238. See also Bartlett, *Familiar Quotations,* p. 620, no. 8, n. 50.

73. See Weidhorn, "Churchill the Phrase Forger," 174.

74. For this type of political use of proverbs see Charles H. Titus, "Political Maxims," *California Folklore Quarterly* 4 (1945): 377–89; Wolfgang Mieder, *Das Sprichwort in unserer Zeit* (Frauenfeld: Huber, 1975), 14–22; and W. Mieder, *Deutsche Sprichwörter in Literatur, Politik, Presse und Werbung* (Hamburg: Helmut Buske, 1983), 11–41.

75. Sources for these quotations are given in Mieder and Bryan, *Proverbial Winston S. Churchill.*

76. Albjerg, *Winston Churchill,* 51. Albjerg continues: "If he was not preparing a speech, organizing a report, planning a campaign, painting a mural, writing a book, building a wall, digging a ditch, he was off in the *Enchantress* inspecting dockyards or observing naval maneuvers. Each enterprise, whatever it was, constituted an entrancing experience which, in its performance, held him spellbound."

77. See also the interesting rephrasing of this proverb as "The iron stands hot for the striking" (vol. 6, p. 190), cited by Churchill from a communication to him by Sir A. Clark Kerr, British Ambassador in Moscow, concerning Churchill's upcoming trip to Russia to meet Stalin in October 1944.

78. A term of my own coining. See my collection of 4,500 German "antiproverbs" in *Antisprichwörter,* 3 vols. (Wiesbaden: Verlag für deutsche Sprache, 1982, 1985; Wiesbaden: Quelle and Meyer, 1989).

79. See Richard Jente, "Make Hay While the Sun Shines," *Southern Folklore Quarterly* 1 (1937): 63–68.

80. It might be of interest to note here that Churchill describes Stalin's pragmatism through a proverb as well, stating that "Marshall Stalin followed the Russian maxim, 'You may always walk with the Devil [in this case the Italian fascists] till you get to the end of the bridge'" (vol. 5, p. 167).

81. Churchill used this proverb five times; see Mieder and Bryan, *Proverbial Winston S. Churchill.*

82. Quoted in *The Churchill Years 1874–1965,* intro. Lord Butler of Saffron Walden (New York: The Viking Press, 1965), 231.

Chapter 3. "It Sure Is Hell to Be President"

1. *Public Papers of the Presidents of the United States: Harry S. Truman.* 1 January 1952 to 20 January 1953 (Washington, D.C.: U.S. Government Printing Office, 1966), 919. Hereafter cited as *PPP* with date of publication.

2. Harry S. Truman, *Off the Record: The Private Papers of Harry S. Truman,* ed. Robert H. Ferrell (New York: Harper and Row, 1980), 167.

3. Truman, *Off the Record,* 309.

4. For a complete list of proverbs and proverbial expressions used by Truman, see Wolfgang Mieder and George B. Bryan, *The Proverbial Harry S. Tru-*

man: An Index to Proverbs in the Works of Harry S. Truman (New York: Peter Lang, 1997).

5. Truman, *Off the Record,* 242. For a discussion of biblical proverbs, see Archer Taylor, *The Proverb* (Cambridge: Harvard University Press, 1931; rpt., Hatboro, Pennsylvania: Folklore Associates, 1962; rpt. again with an introduction and bibliography by Wolfgang Mieder, Bern: Peter Lang, 1985), 52–61. Useful collections are Burton Stevenson, *The Home Book of Bible Quotations* (New York: Harper and Brothers, 1949); and Wolfgang Mieder, *Not by Bread Alone: Proverbs of the Bible* (Shelburne, Vt.: New England Press, 1990).

6. For Truman's ethical appeal, see Edward Rogge, "The Speechmaking of Harry S. Truman" (diss., University of Missouri, 1958), 558–67. See also Andrew J. Dunar, *The Truman Scandals and the Politics of Morality* (Columbia: University of Missouri Press, 1984).

7. Harry S. Truman, *Letters from Father: The Truman Family's Personal Correspondence,* ed. Margaret Truman (New York: Arbor House, 1981), 74.

8. Ibid., 77.

9. Harry S. Truman, *Strictly Personal and Confidential: The Letters Harry Truman Never Mailed,* ed. Monte M. Poen (Boston: Little, Brown and Company, 1982), 45.

10. Harry S. Truman, *Mr. Citizen* (New York: Bernard Geis Associates, 1960), 261.

11. Harry S. Truman, *Dear Bess: The Letters from Harry to Bess Truman, 1910–1959,* ed. Robert H. Ferrell (New York: W. W. Norton and Company, 1983), 20.

12. See Victor R. West, "Folklore in the Works of Mark Twain," *University of Nebraska Studies in Language, Literature, and Criticism* 10 (1930): 1–87.

13. See Harry S. Truman, *Where the Buck Stops: The Personal and Private Writings,* ed. Margaret Truman (New York: Warner Books, 1989), 151–52.

14. Harry S. Truman, *Truman Speaks* (New York: Columbia University Press, 1960), 62.

15. Ibid., 128.

16. Truman, *Where the Buck Stops,* 234.

17. Truman, *Dear Bess,* 74.

18. Harry S. Truman, *Memoirs* (Garden City, N.Y.: Doubleday and Company, 1955), vol. 1, p. 161.

19. *PPP,* 1 January to 31 December 1946 (1962), 449.

20. *PPP,* 1 January to 31 December 1950 (1965), 451.

21. Truman, *Mr. Citizen,* 277. This may be an echo of Churchill's contention that "[b]roadly speaking, short words are best, and the old words, when short, are the best of all." John Bartlett, *Familiar Quotations,* ed. Justin Kaplan (16th ed., Boston: Little, Brown and Company, 1992), p. 622, no. 11.

22. Truman, *Dear Bess,* 141.

23. Ibid., 150.

24. Ibid., 263 (the letter is from 27 June 1918).

25. Ibid., 391.

26. Ibid., 395. For Bess Truman's biography, see Jhan Robbins, *Bess & Harry: An American Love Story* (New York: G. P. Putnam's Sons, 1980); Margaret Truman, *Bess W. Truman* (New York: Macmillan, 1986); and also, of course, Margaret Truman, *Harry S. Truman* (New York: William Morrow, 1973).

27. Truman, *Dear Bess,* 536.

28. Ibid., 118.

29. Ibid., 123.

30. Ibid., 105.

31. Quoted in Merle Miller, *Plain Speaking: An Oral Biography of Harry S. Truman* (New York: Berkley Publishing Corporation, 1974), 144.

32. Truman, *Where the Buck Stops,* 149.

33. Ibid., 316.

34. See Mieder and Bryan, *Proverbial Harry S. Truman.*

35. Harry S. Truman, *Letters Home,* ed. Monte M. Poen (New York: G. P. Putnam's Sons, 1984), 73.

36. Truman, *Dear Bess,* 548.

37. See R. Alton Lee, "The Turnip Session of the Do-Nothing Congress: Presidential Campaign Strategy," *Southwestern Social Science Quarterly* 43 (1963): 256–67.

38. *PPP,* 1 January 1952 to 20 January 1953 (1966), 1007.

39. Quoted in Miller, *Plain Speaking,* 257.

40. Truman, *Mr. Citizen,* 167.

41. Truman, *Dear Bess,* 20. For this proverb see Stewart A. Kingsbury, Mildred E. Kingsbury, and Wolfgang Mieder, *Weather Wisdom: Proverbs, Superstitions, and Signs* (New York: Peter Lang, 1996), p. 320, no. 3118. Our book does not register the turnip proverb. It does in fact appear to be restricted to the Missouri region, and we had not come across it during the preparation of our weather proverb dictionary.

42. See Wolfgang Mieder, Stewart A. Kingsbury, and Kelsie B. Harder, *A Dictionary of American Proverbs* (New York: Oxford University Press, 1992), 540.

43. Robert Underhill, *The Truman Persuasions* (Ames: Iowa State University Press, 1981), 327 (entire chapter on 309–39).

44. Ibid., 328.

45. See Robert H. Ferrell and Francis H. Heller, "Plain Faking? In the Classic 'Oral Biography' of Harry Truman, Many of the President's Most Trenchant Words May Simply Have Been Invented," *American Heritage* (May/June 1995): 14, 16.

46. See Robert Alan Aurthur, "The Wit and Sass of Harry S Truman," *Esquire* 75, no. 2 (August 1971): 62–67, 115.

47. Truman, *Letters Home,* 117. Contrariwise, the word may have been uttered and then expurgated.

48. Truman, *Off the Record,* 205.

49. Truman, *Strictly Personal and Confidential,* 177.

50. Truman, *Dear Bess,* 37.

51. Truman, *Letters Home*, 141.

52. Truman, *Off the Record*, 237.

53. Truman, *Strictly Personal and Confidential*, 64.

54. Truman, *Dear Bess*, xi.

55. Ibid., 39. Regarding the terms "nigger" and "Negro," it should be noted that Margaret Truman includes the following editorial note in her edition of her father's book *Where the Buck Stops:* "I've made a change here. My father used the word 'Negroes' throughout, but I've changed all references to 'blacks' because that's the word that African Americans now commonly employ. My father always had a desire to be modern and up-to-date, and I'm sure he would approve" (32). In any case, Merle Miller in his book *Plain Speaking* includes a footnote as well, claiming: "Privately Mr. Truman always said 'nigger'; at least he always did when I talked to him. That's what people in Independence said when he was growing up. Of course, Independence was a Southern town, a border town, one of whose more prominent organizations has been the United Daughters of the Confederacy" (183).

56. See Abraham A. Roback, *A Dictionary of International Slurs* (Cambridge Mass.: Sci-Art Publishers, 1944; rpt. Waukesha, Wis.: Maledicta Press, 1979). An earlier European collection is Otto von Reinsberg-Düringsfeld, *Internationale Titulaturen*, 2 vols. (Leipzig: Hermann Fries, 1863; rpt. with an introduction by Wolfgang Mieder, Hildesheim: Georg Olms, 1992). See also Alan Dundes, "Slurs International: Folk Comparisons of Ethnicity and National Character," *Southern Folklore Quarterly* 39 (1975): 15–38; rpt. in Wolfgang Mieder, ed., *Wise Words: Essays on the Proverb* (New York: Garland Publishing, 1994), 183–209.

57. Truman, *Dear Bess*, 41.

58. Ibid., 366. For Truman's relationship to Jewish concerns, see Zvi Ganin, *Truman, American Jewry, and Israel, 1945–1948* (New York: Kolmes and Meier, 1979); and Michael Joseph Cohen, *Truman and Isreal* (Berkeley: University of California Press, 1990).

59. Truman, *Dear Bess*, 385.

60. Ibid., 446.

61. Ibid., 459.

62. Harry S. Truman, *Freedom and Equality: Addresses*, ed. David S. Horton (Columbia: University of Missouri Press, 1960), 3. For Truman's civil rights record, see William C. Berman, *The Politics of Civil Rights in the Truman Administration* (Columbus: Ohio State University Press, 1970); and Donald R. McCoy, *Quest and Response: Minority Rights and the Truman Administration* (Lawrence: University Press of Kansas, 1973).

63. Quoted in Francis H. Heller, ed., *The Truman White House: The Administration of the Presidency 1945–1953* (Lawrence: The Regents Press of Kansas, 1980), 151.

64. W. R. Underhill, "The Bully Pulpit Under Truman," in William F. Levantrosser, ed., *Harry S. Truman: The Man from Independence* (Westport, Conn.: Greenwood Press, 1986), 197 (the entire article on 197–204). While scholars do

not tire of mentioning Truman's use of metaphorical folk speech, they never refer specifically to his frequent employment of proverbs and proverbial phrases. I assume, however, that Underhill has proverbs in mind when he speaks of "simple wisdoms."

65. Thomas Joseph Heed, "Prelude to Whistlestop: Harry S. Truman the Apprentice Campaigner" (diss., Columbia University, 1975), 242.

66. Eugene E. White and Clair R. Henderlider, "What Harry S. Truman Told Us About His Speaking," *Quarterly Journal of Speech* 40 (1954): 39 (entire article on 37–42).

67. Quoted in Heed, "Prelude to Whistlestop," 86–87.

68. Regarding Truman's Senate career, see Eugene Schmidtlein, "Truman the Senator" (diss., University of Missouri, 1962); David L. Jones, "Senator Harry S. Truman, the First Term" (diss., University of Kansas, 1964); and Donald H. Riddle, *The Truman Committee: A Study in Congressional Responsibility* (New Brunswick, N. J.: Rutgers University Press, 1964).

69. White and Henderlider, "What Harry S. Truman Told Us," 39.

70. Harry S. Truman, "Speech Before a Joint Session of the Missouri Legislature, March 21, 1939." *Congressional Record,* 76th Congress, 1st session, 1939, vol. 84, pt. 11, p. 1106.

71. Harry S. Truman, "Speech Before the Mississippi Valley Flood Control Association, New Orleans, Louisiana, December 19, 1942." *Congressional Record,* 78th Congress, 1st session, 1943, vol. 89, p. 9, p. A29.

72. Harry S. Truman, "Speech Before the Chamber of Commerce, Cleveland, Ohio, April 6, 1943." *Congressional Record,* 78th Congress, 1st session, 1943, vol. 89, pt. 10, p. A1673.

73. See Mieder, Kingsbury, and Harder, *Dictionary of American Proverbs,* 534.

74. Harry S. Truman, "Speech Before Women's National Democratic Club, March 6, 1944." *Congressional Record,* 78th Congress, 2d session, 1944, vol. 90, pt. 8, p. A1156.

75. For a discussion of this phenomenon in the modern use of fairy tales, legends, nursery rhymes, and proverbs, see Wolfgang Mieder, *Tradition and Innovation in Folk Literature* (Hanover, N.H.: University Press of New England, 1987).

76. Truman, *Dear Bess,* 151.

77. Truman, *Mr. Citizen,* 64.

78. *PPP,* 1 January to 31 December 1950 (1965), 187.

79. *PPP,* 1 January 1952 to 20 January 1953 (1966), 631–32.

80. *PPP,* 1 January to 31 December 1948 (1964), 742.

81. Truman, *Truman Speaks,* 17.

82. Truman, *Off the Record,* 182.

83. Ibid., 294.

84. *PPP,* 12 April to 31 December 1945 (1961), 23.

85. I am borrowing this term from the title of Manfred Weidhorn's essay "Churchill the Phrase Forger," *Quarterly Journal of Speech* 58 (1972): 161–74, where he discusses Winston S. Churchill's use of formulaic language.

86. As mentioned in n. 78 to chap. 2, I coined this term in *Antisprich-wörter,* 3 vols. (Wiesbaden: Verlag für deutsche Sprache, 1982, 1985; Wiesbaden: Quelle and Meyer, 1989).

87. See Mieder, Kingsbury, and Harder, *Dictionary of American Proverbs,* 510.

88. Truman, *Memoirs,* vol. 2, p. 211.

89. For a discussion of Truman's "off-the-cuff speaking style," see John E. Hopkins, "An Investigation of the Speech and Statement Preparation Process During the Presidential Administration of Harry S. Truman, 1945–1953" (diss., Ohio State University, 1970), 127–29.

90. Jennings Randolph, "The 1948 Presidential Campaign Speakers," *Quarterly Journal of Speech* 34 (1948): 300 (entire article on 300–326). See also J. Randolph, "Truman—A Winning Speaker," *Quarterly Journal of Speech* 34 (1948): 421–24.

91. See Cole S. Brembeck, "Harry Truman at the Whistle Stops," *Quarterly Journal of Speech* 38 (1952): 44–45 (entire article on 42–50).

92. See Rogge, "Speechmaking of Harry S. Truman," 367–70.

93. Quoted in Miller, *Plain Speaking,* 255. Another similar explanation by Truman can be found in his speech of 29 September 1952, in *PPP,* 1 January 1952 to 20 January 1953 (1966), 598.

94. *PPP,* 1 January to 31 December 1948 (1964), 539.

95. Ibid., 579. The proverb was recorded the first time in 1605 and is thus much older than Benjamin Franklin's use of it in 1777. See Bartlett Jere Whiting, *Early American Proverbs and Proverbial Phrases* (Cambridge: Harvard University Press, 1977), 217.

96. *PPP,* 1 January to 31 December 1948 (1964), 704.

97. Ibid., 720.

98. Ibid., 843.

99. Ibid., 893.

100. Ibid., 931.

101. See Mieder and Bryan, *Proverbial Harry S. Truman.*

102. *PPP,* 1 January to 31 December 1948 (1964), 862.

103. See Irwin Ross, *The Loneliest Campaign: The Truman Victory of 1948* (New York: New American Library, 1968).

104. "Truman Sets Up a Speech Factory . . . Charles S. Murphy Directs Assembly Line . . . Skilled Staff Polishes, Softens," *U.S. News and World Report* (10 November 1950): 28–29.

105. See Robert Underhill's summary report "Speeches and Speech Writing" in Richard S. Kirkendall, ed., *The Harry S. Truman Encyclopedia* (Boston: G. K. Hall and Company, 1989), 335–38. See also Hopkins, *"An Investigation of the Speech and Statement Preparation Process,"* 53–104, 112–18.

106. "Wife Is Truman Editor; Makes Speeches 'Homey,'" *New York Times,* 27 November 1949, p. 61.

107. Charles G. Ross, "How Truman Did It," *Collier's* 122 (25 December 1948): 13, 87–88.

108. Truman, *Where the Buck Stops,* 148.

109. Truman, *Memoirs,* vol. 1, p. 36.

110. See Mieder and Bryan, *Proverbial Harry S. Truman.*

111. See the chapter on "The No-Comment Comment" in Herbert Lee Williams, *The Newspaperman's President Harry S. Truman* (Chicago: Nelson-Hall, 1984), 52–61 (esp. 54). Other revealing studies are by Elmer E. Cornwell, "The Presidential Press Conference: A Study of Institutionalization," *Midwest Journal of Political Science* 4 (1960): 370–89 (esp. 376–81); and A. L. Lorenz, "Truman and the Press Conference," *Journalism Quarterly* 43 (1966): 671–79, 708.

112. *PPP,* 1 January to 31 December 1948 (1964), 433.

113. Ibid., 461.

114. See Truman's explanation of this policy in his *Memoirs,* vol. 1, p. 47.

115. *PPP,* 1 January 1952 to 20 January 1953 (1966), 166.

116. Ibid., 768.

117. Ibid., 806.

118. Ibid., 842.

119. Ibid., 898.

120. Ibid., 1039.

121. Truman, *Off the Record,* 16.

122. Truman, *Dear Bess,* 520.

123. Ibid., 549.

124. Truman, *Letters Home,* 189.

125. Truman, *Dear Bess,* 552. See Joyce O. Hertzler, "On Golden Rules," *International Journal of Ethics* 44 (1933–34): 418–36.

126. For a discussion of Churchill's use of proverbs in this book and its five companion volumes, see chap. 2 of this volume. See also Wolfgang Mieder and George B. Bryan, *The Proverbial Winston S. Churchill: An Index to Proverbs in the Works of Sir Winston Churchill* (Westport, Conn.: Greenwood Press, 1995). About proverbs and politics in general, see Joseph Raymond, "Tensions in Proverbs: More Light on International Understanding," *Western Folklore* 15 (1956): 153–58; rpt. in Wolfgang Mieder and Alan Dundes, eds., *The Wisdom of Many: Essays on the Proverb* (New York: Garland Publishing, 1981), 300–308.

127. Truman, *Letters from Father,* 110.

128. *PPP,* 1 January 1952 to 20 January 1953 (1966), 16.

129. See Herbert Druks, *Harry S. Truman and the Russians, 1945–1953* (New York: R. Speller, 1966); Richard J. Walton, *Henry Wallace, Harry Truman, and the Cold War* (New York: Viking Press, 1976), Robert L. Messer, *The End of an Alliance: James F. Byrnes, Roosevelt, Truman, and the Origins of the Cold War* (Chapel Hill: University of North Carolina Press, 1982); Robert James Maddox, *From War to Cold War: The Education of Harry S. Truman* (Boulder, Colo.: Westview Press, 1988); and William E. Pemberton, *Harry S. Truman: Fair Dealer and Cold Warrior* (Boston: Twayne, 1989).

130. Truman, *Off the Record,* 370.

131. Ibid., 378–79.

132. Ibid., 384.

133. Ibid., 189.

134. Ibid., 217.

135. Truman, *Dear Bess,* 530.

136. See Bartlett Jere Whiting, "The Devil and Hell in Current English Literary Idiom," *Harvard Studies and Notes in Philology and Literature* 20 (1938): 207–47.

137. See also the section title "Giving 'em Hell" in John Hollister Hedley, *Harry S. Truman: The 'Little' Man from Missouri* (Woodbury, N.Y.: Barron's, 1979), 178–83. Hedley notes, "Firmly believing that his was a crusade for the common man, Truman chose his homespun, hard-hitting rhetoric [during the campaign of 1948] accordingly" (179).

138. See Mieder and Bryan, *Proverbial Harry S. Truman.*

139. Truman, *Mr. Citizen,* 149. See the similar explanation in Miller, *Plain Speaking,* 260.

140. For examples see James N. Giglio and Greg G. Thielen, *Truman in Cartoon and Caricature* (Ames: Iowa State University, 1984), 54, 161.

141. See Eldorous L. Dayton, *Give 'em Hell [sic] Harry: An Informal Biography of The Terrible Tempered Mr. T.* (New York: The Devin-Adair Company, 1956) that includes a rather ridiculous cartoon with Truman biting a dog and the caption "Give 'em Hell Harry gets his teeth into a *real* S.O.B." The record *Give 'em hell, Harry* was released 1975 by United Artists Records (UA-LA540-H2).

142. *PPP,* 1 January 1952 to 20 January 1953 (1966), 702.

143. Ibid., 712.

144. Ibid., 820.

145. Truman, *Off the Record,* 403.

146. David McCullough, *Truman* (New York: Simon and Schuster, 1992), 584 (entire chapter on 584–652). See also his remark that Truman picked up most of his colloquial speech during his boyhood at home (54–55).

147. *PPP,* 1 January 1952 to 20 January 1953 (1966), 1085–6.

148. Truman, *Mr. Citizen,* 229.

149. See John A. Simpson, *The Concise Oxford Dictionary of Proverbs* (Oxford: Oxford University Press, 1982), 110. According to a *Time* magazine article of 28 April 1952 (p. 19), "President [Truman] gave a . . . down-to-earth reason for his retirement, quoting a favorite expression of his military jester, Major General Harry Vaughan: 'If you don't like the heat, get out of the kitchen.'" This was probably just a joking attribution of the proverb to Vaughan, for, after all, Truman had known it from the first quarter of the twentieth century. See also Nigel Rees, *Sayings of the Century* (London: George Allen and Unwin, 1984), 70; and Bartlett, *Familiar Quotations,* 655, no. 10.

150. For two general collections, see Caroline T. Harnsberger, ed., *Treasury of Presidential Quotations* (Chicago: Follett Publishing, 1964); and Elizabeth Frost, ed., *The Bully Pulpit: Quotations from America's Presidents* (New York: Facts on File Publications, 1988). For collections that deal specifically with Tru-

man, see George S. Caldwell, ed., *Good Old Harry: The Wit and Wisdom of Harry S Truman* (New York: Hawthorn Books, 1966); Alex J. Goldman, ed., *The Truman Wit* (New York: Citadel Press, 1966); T. S. Settel, ed., *The Quotable Harry S. Truman* (New York: Berkley Medallion Books, 1967); Robert J. Donovan, ed., *The Words of Harry S Truman* (New York: Newmarket Press, 1984); and Ralph Keyes, ed., *The Wit & Wisdom of Harry Truman* (New York: Harper-Collins, 1995).

151. Underhill, *Truman Persuasions,* 9.

152. Quoted in White and Henderlider, "What Harry S. Truman Told Us," 40.

153. See Rees, *Sayings of the Century,* 70; and Bartlett, *Familiar Quotations,* 655, no. 20.

154. Examples from the mass media proverb archive I have collected include *The New Yorker* (3 August 1981): 91; (20 March 1989): 39; and (26 June 1989): 91. Another cartoon was included in the *Burlington* (Vermont) *Free Press,* 12 April 1990, p. 10A; and yet another caricature with reference to Truman appeared in *Hemispheres* (June 1994): 107.

155. See, for example, the chapters in Cabell Phillips, *The Truman Presidency: The History of a Triumphant Succession* (New York: Macmillan Company, 1966), 329–50; and McCullough, *Truman,* 467–524.

156. See Harold Wentworth and Stuart Berg Flexner, eds., *Dictionary of American Slang* (2d ed.; New York: Thomas Y. Crowell, 1975), 67.

157. Quoted in J. E. Lighter, ed., *Random House Historical Dictionary of American Slang* (New York: Random House, 1994), vol. 1, p. 282, with many more references.

158. *PPP,* 1 January to 31 December 1951 (1965), 132.

159. *PPP,* 1 January 1952 to 20 January 1953 (1966), 1094–95.

160. Truman, *Dear Bess,* 275.

161. *PPP,* 1 January to 31 December 1948 (1964), 788.

162. *PPP,* 1 January 1952 to 20 January 1953 (1966), 1197.

163. Robert H. Ferrell, *Harry S. Truman and the Modern American Presidency* (Boston: Little, Brown and Company, 1983), 87–107. See also a chapter with the same title in Phillips, *Truman Presidency,* 144–59; and Underhill's comment on this proverbial statement in his *Truman Persuasions,* 210.

164. See Bert Cochran, *Harry Truman and the Crisis Presidency* (New York: Funk and Wagnalls, 1973); Robert J. Donovan, *Conflict and Crisis: The Presidency of Harry S. Truman, 1945–1948* (New York: Norton, 1977); Harold F. Gosnell, *Truman's Crises: A Political Biography of Harry S. Truman* (Westport, Conn.: Greenwood Press, 1980); and Robert J. Donovan, *Tumultuous Years: The Presidency of Harry S. Truman, 1949–1953* (New York: Norton, 1982).

Chapter 4. "Raising the Iron Curtain"

1. Winston S. Churchill, *The Second World War,* 6 vols. (London: Cassell and Co., 1948–54), vol. 6 (1954), pp. 498–99.

2. See Harry and Bonaro Overstreet, *The Iron Curtain: Where Freedom's Offensive Begins* (New York: W. W. Norton and Company, 1963).

3. William Safire, *Safire's Political Dictionary* (3rd ed.; New York: Random House, 1978), 127. See also 128–29 for more comments by Swope, Baruch, and Lippmann concerning the origin of this phrase.

4. For other studies that appeared during the Cold War, see above all Hugh Ross, ed., *The Cold War: Containment and Its Critics* (Chicago: Rand McNally, 1963); Norman A. Graebner, ed., *The Cold War: A Conflict of Ideology and Power* (2d ed.; Lexington, Mass.: D. C. Heath and Company, 1976); Bernard A. Weisberger, *Cold War, Cold Peace: The United States and Russia since 1945* (New York: American Heritage, 1984); Richard Crockett and Steve Smith, eds., *The Cold War Past and Present* (London: Allen and Unwin, 1987); and Peter Savigear, *Cold War or Détente in the 1980s: The International Politics of American-Soviet Relations* (New York: St. Martin's Press, 1987).

5. For other undeclared "wars," see the intriguing early study by Fritz Grob, *The Relativity of War and Peace: A Study in Law, History, and Politics* (New Haven: Yale University Press, 1949). Permit me to mention here that Prof. Grob was my invaluable mentor at Olivet College, Michigan, from 1962 to 1966, introducing me both to the world of German literature and political science. Words cannot express the profound influence that this scholar had on my own intellectual development.

6. For the rich scholarship on Gorbachev, see Ronald D. Liebowitz, ed., *Gorbachev's New Thinking: Prospects for Joint Ventures* (Cambridge, Mass.: Ballinger, 1988); Walter Joyce, Hillel Ticktin, and Stephen White, eds., *Gorbachev and Gorbachevism* (Totowa, N. J.: F. Cass, 1989); Isaac J. Tarasul, ed., *Gorbachev and Glasnost: Viewpoints from the Soviet Press* (Wilmington, Del.: SR Books, 1989); Stephen White, *Gorbachev and After* (New York: Cambridge University Press, 1991); and Joseph L. Wieczynski, ed., *The Gorbachev Encyclopedia: Gorbachev, the Man and His Times, Mikhail Gorbachev, March 11, 1985–December 25, 1991* (Los Angeles: C. Schlacks, 1993).

7. Ronald Reagan, "Remarks on East-West Relations at the Brandenburg Gate in West Berlin, June 12, 1987," *Public Papers of the Presidents of the United States: Ronald Reagan,* 1 January to 3 July 1987 (Washington, D.C.: U.S. Government Printing Office, 1989), 635 (the entire speech on 634–38).

8. From the flood of books presenting surveys of the entire Cold War, see also Charles S. Maier, ed., *The Cold War in Europe* (New York: Markus Wiener, 1991); Thomas H. Naylor, *The Cold War Legacy* (Lexington, Mass.: D. C. Heath and Company, 1991); Otto Pick, ed., *The Cold War Legacy in Europe* (New York: St. Martin's Press, 1992); Cori Elizabeth Dauber, *Cold War Analytical Structures and the Post-War World: A Critique of Deterrence Theory* (Westport, Conn.: Praeger, 1993); and Martin Walker, *The Cold War: A History* (New York: Henry Holt and Company, 1994).

9. Lynn Boyd Hinds and Theodore Otto Windt, *The Cold War as Rhetoric: The Beginnings, 1945–1950* (New York: Praeger, 1991), 1–2.

10. See for example Theodore O. Windt, "The Rhetoric of Peaceful Coexistence: A Criticism of Nikita Khrushchev's American Speeches" (diss., Ohio State University, 1965); Wayne E. Brockriede and Robert L. Scott, *Moments in the Rhet-*

oric of the Cold War (New York: Random House, 1970); and John F. Cragan, "The Origins and Nature of the Cold War Rhetorical Vision," in *Applied Communication: A Dramatic Perspective,* ed. J. F. Cragan and Donald Shields (Prospect Heights, Ill.: Waveland, 1981), 47–66.

11. See Hildegard Kornhardt, "'Summum ius'," *Hermes* 81 (1953): 77–85; and Karl Büchner, "'Summum ius summa iniuria'," in K. Büchner, *Humanitas Romana: Studien über Werke und Wesen der Römer* (Heidelberg: Carl Winter, 1957), 80–105.

12. See Wolfgang Mieder, "'Wir sitzen alle in einem Boot': Herkunft, Geschichte und Verwendung einer neueren deutschen Redensart," *Muttersprache* 100 (1990): 18–37.

13. See Hugo Blümmer, *Der bildliche Ausdruck in den Reden des Fürsten Bismarck* (Leipzig: S. Hirzel, 1891), 182–84; and "Der bildliche Ausdruck in den Briefen des Fürsten Bismarck," *Euphorion* 1 (1894): 590–603 and 771–87.

14. See N. A. Meshcherskii, "Traditsionno-knizhnye vyrazheniia v sovremennom russkom literaturnom iazyke (na materiale proizvedenii V. I. Lenina)," *Voprosy frazeologii* 9 (1975): 110–21; and L. A. Morozova, "Upotreblenie V. I. Leninym poslovits," *Russkaia Rech'* no vol., no. 2 (1979): 10–14.

15. See Wolfgang Mieder, "Proverbs in Nazi Germany: The Promulgation of Anti-Semitism and Stereotypes through Folklore," in W. Mieder, *Proverbs Are Never Out of Season: Popular Wisdom in the Modern Age* (New York: Oxford University Press, 1993), 225–55; and "Proverbs in Adolf Hitler's *Mein Kampf,*" *Proverbium* 11 (1994): 159–74.

16. See Wolfgang Mieder and George B. Bryan, *The Proverbial Winston S. Churchill: An Index to Proverbs in the Works of Sir Winston S. Churchill* (Westport, Conn.: Greenwood Press, 1995).

17. Due to space limitations, only a few English language publications can be listed here: Edd Miller and Jesse J. Villarreal, "The Use of Clichés by Four Contemporary Speakers [Winston Churchill, Anthony Eden, Franklin D. Roosevelt, and Henry Wallace]," *Quarterly Journal of Speech* 31 (1945): 151–55; Charles H. Titus, "Political Maxims," *California Folklore Quarterly* 4 (1945): 377–89; Shirley L. Arora, "On the Importance of Rotting Fish: A Proverb and Its Audience [referring to Michael S. Dukakis's presidential campaign in 1988]," *Western Folklore* 48 (1989): 271–88; Galit Hasan-Rokem, "The Aesthetics of the Proverb: Dialogue of Discourses from Genesis to Glasnost," *Proverbium* 7 (1990): 105–16; Karen E. Richman, "'With Many Hands, the Burden Isn't Heavy': Creole Proverbs and Political Rhetoric in Haiti's Presidential Elections," *Folklore Forum* 23 (1990): 115–23; and Fionnuala Williams, "'To Kill Two Birds with One Stone': Variants in a War of Words," *Proverbium* 8 (1991): 199–201. For additional references from other languages see Wolfgang Mieder, *International Proverb Scholarship: An Annotated Bibliography,* 3 vols. (New York: Garland Publishing, 1982, 1990, and 1993).

18. See also Guinzbourg's *Supplement: Wit and Wisdom of the United Nations or The Modern Machiavelli* (New York: privately printed, 1965). Guinzbourg published yet another large proverb collection based on his work as a lin-

guist at the United Nations with the title *The Eternal Machiavelli in the United Nations World* (New York: privately printed, 1969).

19. R. D. Hogg, "Proverbs," *Secretariat News* 14 (1960): 6 (entire article on 5–7).

20. The article appeared in sec. IV, p. 8, col. 5. See also the anonymous editorial entitled "Premier Shows Proverbial Wit: Khrushchev Strews Salty Quips and Old Russian Proverbs About Nation," *New York Times* (24 September 1959), p. 23, col. 8; and Günter Wein, "Die Rolle der Sprichwörter und Redensarten in der Agitation und Propaganda," *Sprachpflege* 12 (1963): 51–52.

21. The article appeared in sec. VI, p. 14, cols. 1–4.

22. The article appeared on p. E19, cols. 1–5.

23. The article appeared on p. 1, col. 6.

24. For a more recent scholarly book see Jay M. Shafritz, *Words on War: Military Quotations from Ancient Times to the Present* (New York: Prentice Hall, 1990). This book does, however, deal primarily with quotations and not proverbs.

25. Hinds and Windt, *The Cold War,* 11.

26. For two detailed chapters discussing the origin, history, and meaning of these proverbs, see Wolfgang Mieder, *Tradition and Innovation in Folk Literature* (Hanover, N.H.: University Press of New England, 1987), 157–77 and 178–228. See also A. W. Smith, "On the Ambiguity of the Three Wise Monkeys," *Folklore* 104 (1993): 144–50.

27. For many examples of how proverbs are used in modern American society, see Wolfgang Mieder, *American Proverbs: A Study of Texts and Contexts* (Bern: Peter Lang, 1989). For a similar treatment of German proverbs in the modern age, see W. Mieder, *Deutsche Sprichwörter in Literatur, Politik, Presse und Werbung* (Hamburg: Helmut Buske, 1983).

28. Hinds and Windt, *The Cold War,* 6. The authors are not referring to proverbs here or in any other part of their important study.

29. See Ronald Steel's introduction to the new edition of Walter Lippmann's *The Cold War: A Study in U.S. Foreign Policy* (New York: Harper Torchbooks, 1972), x; and above all the very useful chronological study starting with 1917 by John W. Young, *The Longman Companion to Cold War and Détente, 1941–91* (New York: Longman, 1993).

30. See Aleksandr M. Zhigulev, "Poslovitsy i pogovorki v bol'shevitskikh listovkakh," *Sovetskaia Etnografia* 5 (1970): 124–31; and Jean Breuillard, "Proverbes et pouvoir politique: Le cas de l'U.R.S.S.," in *Richesse du proverbe*, ed. François Suard and Claude Buridant, 2 vols. (Lille: Université de Lille, 1984), vol. 2, pp. 155–66.

31. *Simplicissimus* 44, no. 40 (8 October 1939): 477.

32. *Simplicissimus* 45, no. 35 (1 September 1940): 409. For this motif in literature and the mass media see Wolfgang Mieder, "'Sein oder Nichtsein'—und kein Ende: Zum Weiterleben des Hamlet-Zitats in unserer Zeit," in W. Mieder, *Sprichwort, Redensart, Zitat: Tradierte Formelsprache in der Moderne* (Bern: Peter Lang, 1985), 125–30.

33. *Simplicissimus* 45, no. 43 (23 October 1940): 507. For a detailed histori-

cal study of this proverb and its variants see Archer Taylor, "The Road to 'An Englishman's House . . .,'" *Romance Philology* 19 (1965–66): 279–85.

34. A reproduction of this poster was purchased in July 1990 at the Imperial War Museum in London.

35. *Kladderadatsch,* no. 16 (20 April 1941): 6.

36. *Fliegende Blätter* 194, no. 40 (2 October 1941): 218.

37. *Kladderadatsch,* no. 52 (28 December 1941): 6.

38. *Fortune* (September 1942): 115.

39. *Fortune* (November 1942): 141.

40. *Fortune* (May 1943): 35.

41. *Time* (21 June 1943), front cover.

42. A postcard reproduction of this poster was purchased at a World War II exhibition at the Vermont Historical Society Museum in June 1992.

43. *Time* (12 July 1943): 41.

44. For a historical study of this proverb, see W. A. Heidel, "'Charity that Begins at Home,'" *American Journal of Philology* 30 (1909): 196–98.

45. See the discussion by Wolfgang Mieder, "'It's Five Minutes to Twelve': Folklore and Saving Life on Earth," *International Folklore Review* 8 (1990): 10–21.

46. Cited from D. R. Fitzpatrick, *Cartoons. St. Louis Post-Dispatch* (St. Louis: Pulitzer Publishing Company, 1947), 212.

47. Cited from *Saturday Review* (11 December 1948): 17. The cartoon first appeared in the *Minneapolis Star-Journal.*

48. Cited from *The Progressive* (January 1959): 23. The cartoon appeared first in *The St. Louis Post-Dispatch.*

49. Cited from *Saturday Review* (25 February 1950): 10. The cartoon appeared first in *The Philadelphia Evening Bulletin.*

50. Cited from *Saturday Review* (19 January 1952): 43. The cartoon appeared first in *The Minneapolis Star.*

51. Hans Bohrmann, ed., *Politische Plakate* (Dortmund: Die bibliophilen Taschenbücher, 1984), 465 (no. 364). The poster was used during the German elections of 1953.

52. Cited from *Saturday Review* (8 August 1953): 15. The cartoon appeared first in the *Chicago Sun-Times.*

53. *U.S. News & World Report* (10 June 1985): 13.

54. *Billings [Montana] Gazette,* 27 June 1983, no pp.

55. *Pravda,* 12 December 1957, no pp. I owe this reference to my friend and colleague Prof. Kevin McKenna.

56. *Simplicissimus,* no. 36 (2 September 1961): 561. See also Richard J. Walton, *Cold War and Counterrevolution: The Foreign Policy of John F. Kennedy* (New York: Viking Press, 1972). For an intriguing study of German proverbial cartoons and caricatures see Lutz Röhrich, "Die Bildwelt von Sprichwort und Redensart in der Sprache der politischen Karikatur," in Hans Friedrich Foltin, ed., *Kontakte und Grenzen: Probleme der Volks-, Kultur- und Sozialforschung. Festschrift für Herhard Heilfurth* (Göttingen: Otto Schwartz, 1969), 175–207.

57. *Punch* (1 November 1961): 631. For Marie Antoinette's use of the proverbial imperative "Let them eat cake," see Archer Taylor, "And Marie Antoinette Said . . .," *Revista de Etnografia* 11 (1968): 245–60; also in A. Taylor, *Comparative Studies in Folklore: Asia—Europe—America* (Taipei: Orient Cultural Service, 1972), 249–65.

58. See John Bartlett, *Familiar Quotations,* ed. Justin Kaplan (16th ed.; Boston: Little, Brown and Company, 1992), p. 742, no. 4.

59. *Pravda* (13 December 1974), no pp. I owe this reference to Prof. Kevin McKenna.

60. Cited from Gerhard Langemeyer, et al., *Bild als Waffe: Mittel und Motive der Karikatur in fünf Jahrhunderten* (München: Prestel, 1984), 402 (illus. 2).

61. *Playboy* (June 1978): 95.

62. *Stuttgarter Zeitung* (1 December 1979): 1.

63. *Time* (28 January 1980): 15.

64. *The New Yorker* (14 April 1980): 52.

65. For a discussion of the origin and history of this proverb, see Wolfgang Mieder, "'A Picture Is Worth a Thousand Words': From Advertising Slogan to American Proverb," in *Proverbs Are Never Out of Season: Popular Wisdom in the Modern Age* (New York: Oxford University Press, 1993), 135–51.

66. For a collection of 4,500 German anti-proverbs, see Wolfgang Mieder, *Antisprichwörter,* 3 vols. (Wiesbaden: Verlag für deutsche Sprache, 1982; Wiesbaden: Gesellschaft für deutsche Sprache, 1985; Wiesbaden: Quelle and Meyer, 1989).

67. Horst Haitzinger, *Politische Karikaturen* (Rorschach: Nebelspalter-Verlag, 1981), no pp. The cartoon was drawn in February 1981.

68. Cited from Bartlett, *Familiar Quotations,* p. 773, no. 10, n. 1.

69. *Die Weltwoche,* no. 16 (15 April 1981): 1. I owe all references from this newspaper to my friend and colleague, Prof. Beatrice Wood.

70. *Der Spiegel,* no. 20 (11 May 1981): 21.

71. See Rudolf Bülck, "'Lewer duad üs Slaw': Geschichte eines politischen Schlagwortes," *Jahrbuch des Vereins für niederdeutsche Sprachforschung* 74 (1951): 99–126; Mac E. Barrick, "'Better Red than Dead,'" *American Notes & Queries* 17, no. 9 (May 1979): 143–44; and Nigel Rees, *Sayings of the Century* (London: George Allen and Unwin, 1984), 214–15.

72. Joseph Raymond, "Tensions in Proverbs: More Light on International Understanding," *Western Folklore* 15 (1956): 154 (entire essay on 153–58); rpt. in Wolfgang Mieder and Alan Dundes, eds., *The Wisdom of Many: Essays on the Proverb* (New York: Garland Publishing, 1981), 301 (entire essay on 300–308).

73. Raymond, "Tensions in Proverbs," 158; rpt., 305.

74. *Deutsches Allgemeines Sonntagsblatt,* no. 23 (7 June 1981): 3.

75. *Die Weltwoche,* no. 31 (19 August 1981): 1.

76. Horst Haitzinger, *Denkzettel* (München: Heyne, 1981), no pp.

77. *Der Spiegel,* no. 23 (7 June 1982): 17.

78. *Die Weltwoche,* no. 23 (7 June 1982): 17.

79. Raymond, "Tensions in Proverbs," 158; rpt., 305.

80. *Salzburger Nachrichten* (21 September 1982): 2. I owe this reference to my friend and colleague Prof. David Scrase.

81. Cited from *Buch der Zeit*, no. 10 (1983): 12. The book advertised on the bottom half of the page is *Die Taubenfeder: Schriftsteller der Welt für den Frieden der Welt* (Halle: Mitteldeutscher Verlag, 1983).

82. Cited from *Weekly Compilation of Presidential Documents*, ed. Office of the Federal Register, National Archives and Records Service, General Services Administration, Washington, D.C., 18, no. 45 (15 November 1982), 1459. See also *New York Times*, 24 November 1982, p. A19.

83. For the origin and history of this proverb, see Wolfgang Mieder and George B. Bryan, "'Zum Tango gehören zwei,'" in W. Mieder, *Sprichwort, Redensart, Zitat: Tradierte Formelsprache in der Moderne* (Bern: Peter Lang, 1985), 151–54.

84. *Nebelspalter*, no. 49 (7 December 1982): 22.

85. *Die Weltwoche*, no. 52 (29 December 1982): 1.

86. *Nebelspalter*, no. 28 (12 July 1983): 7.

87. *Der Spiegel*, no. 39 (26 September 1983): 191.

88. See Louisa S. Hulett, *From Cold Wars to Star Wars: Debates Over Defense and Détente* (Lanham, Md.: University Press of America, 1988).

89. The cartoon first appeared in the *Frankfurter Rundschau*, 5 April 1984. It is cited from Langemeyer et al., *Bild als Waffe* , 414 (illus. 28).

90. *Burlington Free Press*, 1 July 1985, p. 14A.

91. This card, produced by Ken Brown Cards, was purchased in October 1986 in Burlington, Vermont.

92. Harold Wentworth and Stuart Berg Flexner, *Dictionary of American Slang* (2d ed.; New York: Thomas Y. Crowell, 1975), 211.

93. *Detroit Free Press*, 1 May 1986, p. 12A. I owe this reference to my friend Prof. Donald Haase.

94. *Burlington Free Press*, 10 June 1985, p. 12A.

95. *The New Yorker* (22 September 1986): 75.

96. *Bunte*, no. 50 (3 December 1987): 15.

97. Cited from Bartlett, *Familiar Quotations*, p. 762, no. 13.

98. *Los Angeles Times*, 13 December 1987, p. 32. I owe this reference to Prof. Shirley Arora.

99. See Barbara and Wolfgang Mieder, "Tradition and Innovation: Proverbs in Advertising," *Journal of Popular Culture* 11 (1977): 308–19; rpt. in Mieder and Dundes, *The Wisdom of Many*, 309–22.

100. *Quick*, no. 40 (28 September 1989): 5.

101. See for example Allen Walker Read, *Classic American Graffiti* (Paris: privately printed, 1935; rpt., Waukesha, Wis.: Maledicta Press, 1977); Robert Reisner, *Graffiti: Two Thousand Years of Wall Writing* (New York: Cowles Book Company, 1971); Jess Nierenberg, "Proverbs in Graffiti: Taunting Traditional Wisdom," *Maledicta* 7 (1983): 41–58; rpt. in Wolfgang Mieder, ed., *Wise Words: Essays on the Proverb* (New York: Garland Publishing, 1994), 543–61; Reinhard Roche, "Demosprüche und Wandgesprühtes: Versuch einer linguistischen Beschrei-

bung und didaktischen Auswertung," *Muttersprache* 93 (1983): 181–96; Renate Neumann, *Das wilde Schreiben: Graffiti, Sprüche und Zeichen am Rand der Straßen* (Essen: Die Blaue Blume, 1986); and Beat Suter, *Graffiti: Rebellion der Zeichen* (Frankfurt am Main: Rita G. Fischer, 1988).

102. Quoted from Terry Tillmann, *The Writings on the Wall: Peace at the Berlin Wall* (Santa Monica, Cal.: 22/7 Publishing Company, 1990), 27.

103. Quoted from Klaus D. Appuhn, *Graffiti: Kunst an Mauern* (Dortmund: Die bibliophilen Taschenbücher, 1982), 149.

104. Photographed in the summer of 1988 at the Berlin Wall by my friend Prof. Mary Beth Stein.

105. See Wolfgang Mieder, "'The Grass Is Always Greener on the Other Side of the Fence': An American Proverb of Discontent," *Proverbium* 10 (1993): 151–84; rpt. in Mieder, *Wise Words*, 515–42.

106. Quoted from Tillmann, *Writings on the Wall*, 27.

107. Ibid., 31. For a discussion of the underlying proverb, see Jakob F. Franck, "'Blut ist dicker als Wasser,'" *Preußische Jahrbücher* 85 (1896): 584–94.

108. Thomas H. Naylor, *The Cold War Legacy* (Lexington, Mass.: D. C. Heath and Company, 1991), 37 (entire chapter on 13–37).

109. Wolfgang Mieder, Stewart A. Kingsbury, and Kelsie B. Harder, eds., *A Dictionary of American Proverbs* (New York: Oxford University Press, 1992), 639.

Chapter 5. "The Only Good Indian Is a Dead Indian"

An earlier version of this chapter was first published in *Journal of American Folklore* 106 (1993): 38–60. Copyright © 1993 American Folklore Society. Reprinted by permission from the *Journal of American Folklore,* volume 106, number 419.

1. See Otto von Reinsberg-Düringsfeld, *Internationale Titulaturen,* 2 vols. (Leipzig: Hermann Fries, 1863; rpt. with an introduction by Wolfgang Mieder, Hildesheim: Georg Olms, 1992); Henri Gaidoz and Paul Sébillot, *Blason populaire de la France* (Paris: Léopold Cerf, 1884); and Abraham A. Roback, *A Dictionary of International Slurs* (Cambridge, Mass.: Sci-Art Publishers, 1944; rpt. Waukesha, Wis.: Maledicta Press, 1979).

2. See William Hugh Jansen, "A Culture's Stereotypes and Their Expression in Folk Clichés," *Southwestern Journal of Anthropology* 13 (1957): 184–200; Américo Paredes, "Proverbs and Ethnic Stereotyping," *Proverbium,* no. 15 (1970): 511–13; Mariana D. Birnbaum, "On the Language of Prejudice," *Western Folklore* 30 (1971): 247–68; Alan Dundes, "Slurs International: Folk Comparisons of Ethnicity and National Character," *Southern Folklore Quarterly* 39 (1975): 15–38; Uta Quasthoff, "The Uses of Stereotype in Everyday Argument," *Journal of Pragmatics* 2 (1978): 1–48; and Wolfgang Mieder, "Proverbs in Nazi Germany: The Promulgation of Anti-Semitism and Stereotypes through Folklore," *Journal of American Folklore* 95 (1982): 435–64.

3. See for example J. C. H. Duijker and N. H. Fridja, *National Character and National Stereotypes* (Amsterdam: North-Holland Publishing Company,

1960); Bruno Bettelheim and Morris Janowitz, *Social Change and Prejudice, Including the Dynamics of Prejudice* (Glencoe, Ill.: Free Press, 1964); George E. Simpson and J. Milton Yinger, *Racial and Cultural Minorities: An Analysis of Prejudice and Discrimination* (New York: Harper and Row, 1965); and Sander L. Gilman, *Jewish Self-Hatred: Anti-Semitism and the Hidden Language of the Jews* (Baltimore: Johns Hopkins University Press, 1986).

4. See Elizabeth Arthur, "The Concept of the Good Indian: An Albany River 19th Century Managerial Perspective," *Canadian Journal of Native Studies* 5 (1985): 61–74; and Albert K. Weinberg, *Manifest Destiny: A Study of Nationalist Expansionism in American History* (Baltimore: Johns Hopkins [University] Press, 1935).

5. Quoted from Roy Harvey Pearce, *Savagism and Civilization: A Study of the Indian and the American Mind* (Baltimore: Johns Hopkins University Press, 1967), 55. The banquet where the toast was given is reported in the journal of Major James Norris, in Frederick Cook, ed., *Journals of the Military Expedition of Major General John Sullivan* (Auburn, N.Y.: Knapp, Peck and Thomson, 1887), 225–26.

6. See Priscilla Shames, "The Long Hope: A Study of American Indian Stereotypes in American Popular Fiction, 1890–1950" (diss., University of California at Los Angeles, 1969).

7. Dee Brown, *Bury My Heart at Wounded Knee. An Indian History of the American West* (1st ed., 1970; New York: Henry Holt and Company, 1990), 147–74.

8. Waubageshig, ed., *The Only Good Indian: Essays by Canadian Indians* (Toronto: New Press, 1970), vi.

9. Ralph E. and Natasha A. Friar, *The Only Good Indian . . . The Hollywood Gospel* (New York: Drama Book Specialists, 1972), 264.

10. See Rayna Green, "The Only Good Indian: The Image of the Indian in American Vernacular Culture" (diss., Indiana University, 1973), 56–65. A mere short paragraph (56–57) is dedicated to a general remark concerning the proverb "The only good Indian is a dead Indian."

11. For references see Roback, *Dictionary of International Slurs*, 181; Burton Stevenson, *The Home Book of Proverbs, Maxims, and Famous Phrases* (New York: Macmillan, 1948), 1236; Mitford Mathews, *A Dictionary of Americanisms on Historical Principles* (Chicago: University of Chicago Press, 1951), 866–76; Archer Taylor and Bartlett Jere Whiting, *A Dictionary of American Proverbs and Proverbial Phrases, 1820–1880* (Cambridge: Harvard University Press, 1958), 199; William and Mary Morris, *Dictionary of Word and Phrase Origins* (New York: Harper and Row, 1962), 189–90; Ramon F. Adams, *Western Words: A Dictionary of the American West* (Norman: University of Oklahoma Press, 1968), 159–61; Eric Partridge, *A Dictionary of Catch Phrases* (New York: Stein and Day, 1977), 88; Bartlett Jere Whiting, *Early American Proverbs and Proverbial Phrases* (Cambridge: Harvard University Press, 1977), 233; Neil Ewart, *Everyday Phrases: Their Origins and Meanings* (Poole, Dorset: Blandford Press, 1983), 77; James Rogers, *The Dictionary of Clichés* (New York: Facts on File Publications, 1985), 141; Laurence Urdang, Walter Hunsinger, and Nancy LaRoche, *Picturesque Ex-*

pressions: A Thematic Dictionary (Detroit: Gale Research Company, 1985), 82, 560, and 709; Bartlett Jere Whiting, *Modern Proverbs and Proverbial Sayings* (Cambridge: Harvard University Press, 1989), 337; and Doris Cray, *Catch Phrases, Clichés and Idioms* (Jefferson, N.C.: McFarland, 1990), 114–15.

12. Green, "Only Good Indian," 57.

13. Whiting, *Early American Proverbs*, 233.

14. Stevenson, *Home Book of Proverbs*, 2507; Taylor and Whiting, *Dictionary of American Proverbs*, 199; and Wolfgang Mieder, Stewart A. Kingsbury, and Kelsie Harder, *A Dictionary of American Proverbs* (New York: Oxford University Press, 1992), 329.

15. Mieder, Kingsbury, and Harder, *Dictionary of American Proverbs*, 329.

16. Ibid.

17. Hon. Alfred Benjamin Meacham, *Wigwam and War-Path; Or the Royal Chief in Chains* (Boston: John P. Dale, 1875), 515. I owe the following three important references from Meacham to Jan Harold Brunvand, *A Dictionary of Proverbs and Proverbial Phrases from Books Published by Indiana Authors before 1890* (Bloomington: Indiana University Press, 1961), 75.

18. Meacham, *Wigwam and War-Path*, 198.

19. Hon. Alfred Benjamin Meacham, *Wi-ne-ma (The Woman-Chief) and Her People* (Hartford, Conn.: American Publishing Company, 1876), 35.

20. Quoted from *The Congressional Globe: Containing the Debates and Proceedings of the Second Session [of the] Fortieth Congress* (City of Washington: Office of the Congressional Globe, 1868), 2638. I owe the reference to this significant quotation to Stevenson, *Home Book of Proverbs*, 1236. See also Mieder, Kingsbury, and Harder, *Dictionary of American Proverbs*, 329.

21. Major William Shepherd, *Prairie Experiences in Handling Cattle and Sheep* (London: Chapman and Hall, 1884), 61–63.

22. Alfred Gurney, *A Ramble through the United States. A Lecture Delivered (in part) in S. Barnabas' School, February 3, 1886* (London: William Clowes, 1886), 28–29.

23. See Archer Taylor, *The Proverb* (Cambridge: Harvard University Press, 1931; rpt., Hatboro, Penn.: Folklore Associates, 1962; rpt. again with an introduction and bibliography by Wolfgang Mieder, Bern: Peter Lang, 1985), 38.

24. Edward S. Ellis, *The History of Our Country: From the Discovery of America to the Present Time* (1st ed., 1895; Cincinnati, Ohio: Jones Brothers, 1900), 1483.

25. See Paul Andrew Hutton, *Phil Sheridan and His Army* (Lincoln: University of Nebraska Press, 1985), 180–200 (esp. 180).

26. Stephen E. Ambrose, *Crazy Horse and Custer: The Parallel Lives of Two American Warriors* (New York: Doubleday and Company, 1975), 310. I owe this reference to my colleague Prof. James Lubker.

27. Brig.-Gen. Michael V. Sheridan, *Personal Memoirs of Philip Henry Sheridan. With an Account of His Life from 1871 to His Death, in 1888* (new and enlarged ed., New York: D. Appleton, 1904), vol. 2, pp. 464–65.

28. Carl Coke Rister, *Border Command: General Phil Sheridan in the West*

(Norman: University of Oklahoma Press, 1944; rpt., Westport, Conn.: Greenwood Press, 1974), VII–VIII.

29. Ibid., 127.

30. I have not been able to locate the entire speech in any of the many volumes on Theodore Roosevelt that I have checked. The passage is quoted from Hermann Hagedorn, *Roosevelt in the Bad Lands* (Boston: Houghton Mifflin, 1921), 355. Parts of this passage (always citing Hagedorn) are also cited in Albert B. Hart and Herbert R. Ferleger, eds., *Theodore Roosevelt Cyclopedia* (New York: Roosevelt Memorial Association, 1941), 251; Richard Hofstadter, *The American Political Tradition and the Men Who Made It* (New York: Alfred A. Knopf, 1968), 209; Shames, "The Long Hope," 32; and Thomas G. Dyer, *Theodore Roosevelt and the Idea of Race* (Baton Rouge: Louisiana State University Press, 1980), 86. The latter book includes an important chapter on Roosevelt's prejudicial views of the "Indians" (69–88). It might be of interest that this statement did not make it into W. M. Handy's *Maxims of Theodore Roosevelt* (Chicago: Madison Book, 1903; rpt., Upper Saddle River, N. J.: Literature House, 1970), but the compiler does cite Roosevelt's slogan "A good American is a good American" (81).

31. See W. Gurney Benham, *Complete Book of Quotations* (New York: G. P. Putnam's Sons, 1926), 459b.

32. See H. L. Mencken, *A New Dictionary of Quotations on Historical Principles* (New York: Alfred A. Knopf, 1960), 585; and Bergen Evans, *Dictionary of Quotations* (New York: Avenel Books, 1968), 345.

33. See Gorton Carruth and Eugene Ehrlich, *The Harper Book of American Quotations* (New York: Harper and Row, 1988), 55; and John Daintith et al., *Who Said What When: A Chronological Dictionary of Quotations* (London: Bloomsbury, 1988; rpt., New York: Hippocrene Books, 1991), 167.

34. See Burton Stevenson, *The Home Book of Quotations* (1st ed., 1934; 5th ed., New York: Dodd, Mead and Company, 1947), 976.

35. See *The Oxford Dictionary of Quotations* (London: Oxford University Press, 1941), 400a; (2d ed., London: Oxford University Press, 1953), 499; (3d ed., London: Oxford University Press, 1979), 505. See now also Paul F. Boller and John George, *They Never Said It: A Book of Fake Quotes, Misquotes, and Misleading Attributions* (New York: Oxford University Press, 1989), 118.

36. See Christopher Morley, ed., *Familiar Quotations* (11th ed., Boston: Little, Brown and Company, 1941), 594; (12th ed., 1949), 594; (13th ed., 1955), 653b; Emily Morison Beck, ed., *Familiar Quotations* (14th ed., Boston: Little, Brown and Company, 1968), 742a; (15th ed., 1980), 610.

37. See Henry Davidoff, *The Pocket Book of Quotations* (New York: Pocket Books, 1942), 153; and J. M. and M. J. Cohen, *The Penguin Dictionary of Quotations* (Middlesex, England: Penguin Books, 1960), 364.

38. Vincent Stuckey Lean, *Lean's Collectanea* (Bristol: J. W. Arrowsmith, 1902; rpt., Detroit: Gale Research Company, 1969), vol. 1, p. 282.

39. Taylor, *Proverb*, 9–10.

40. Roback, *Dictionary of International Slurs*, 181.

41. Samuel Eliot Morison, *Builders of the Bay Colony* (Boston: Houghton Mifflin Company, 1930), 295–96.

42. Leroy V. Eid, "Liberty: The Indian Contribution to the American Revolution," *The Midwest Quarterly: A Journal of Contemporary Thought* 22 (1981): 290–91 (entire essay on 279–98). I owe this reference to my colleague Prof. Dennis Mahoney.

43. See *Congressional Globe,* 2638.

44. See Stevenson, *Home Book of Proverbs,* 1236 (with six references from 1868–1943); Mathews, *Dictionary of Americanisms,* 715 (with four references from 1868–1948); Adams, *Western Words,* 128 (with one reference, but no date); John A. Simpson, *The Concise Oxford Dictionary of Proverbs* (Oxford: Oxford University Press, 1982), 98 (with eight references from 1868–1980); Whiting, *Modern Proverbs,* 337 (with twenty-four references from 1908–1970); and Mieder, Kingsbury, and Harder, *Dictionary of American Proverbs,* 329 (with references to Simpson and Whiting).

45. Helen Pearce, "Folk Sayings in a Pioneer Family of Western Oregon," *California Folklore Quarterly* 5 (1946): 236–37 (entire article on 229–42).

46. See Mac E. Barrick, "Proverbs and Sayings from Cumberland County [Pennsylvania]," *Keystone Folklore Quarterly* 8 (1963): 170 (entire article on 139–203); and Frances M. Barbour, *Proverbs and Proverbial Phrases of Illinois* (Carbondale: Southern Illinois University Press, 1965), 98. Stewart A. Kingsbury also includes the proverb as an example of "Names in Proverbs and Proverbial Sayings," *Festschrift in Honor of Allen Walker Read,* ed. Laurence E. Seits (DeKalb, Ill.: North Central Name Society, 1988), 130 (entire article on 116–32).

47. This text was collected by Candace Bettencourt from Patricia Davis on 6 March 1969, in Berkeley, California. The student has added a note with a reference to Stevenson, *Home Book of Proverbs,* who mentions that the proverb is usually attributed to General Philip Sheridan. I would like to thank Frances Fischer and Alan Dundes for making this and the following two texts available to me.

48. This text was recorded by Linda Armstrong from Donald Geddes on 19 November 1977 in Palo Alto, California.

49. This text was collected by Anne Artoux from Marge Donovan on 28 November 1986 in San Mateo, California.

50. See Mieder, Kingsbury, and Harder, *Dictionary of American Proverbs,* 329. It is interesting to note that David Kin's unscholarly *Dictionary of American Proverbs* (New York: Philosophical Library, 1955) does not include this proverb.

51. Mary Roberts Rinehart, *The Circular Staircase* (New York: Grosset and Dunlap, 1908), 354. I would like to thank Patricia Mardeusz, Barbara Lambert, and Ruth Nolan from the Reference Department of the Bailey/Howe Library at the University of Vermont for getting many of the novels cited below for me through interlibrary loan.

52. Edgar Rice Burroughs, *A Princess of Mars* (New York: Ballantine Books, 1987), 72. The book was originally published with the title *Under the Moon of Mars* by Norman Bean (pseudonym) in *All-Story Magazine* as a six-part serial, February through July, 1912.

53. Robert Graves, *Good-bye to All That* (1st ed., 1929; Garden City, N.Y.: Doubleday and Company, 1957), 184–85.

54. "Bombardier X" (pseudonym), *So This Was War! The Truth about the Western and Eastern Fronts Revealed,* ed. Shaw Desmond (London: Hutchinson, 1930), 11–12 (preface).

55. Quoted from Whiting, *Modern Proverbs,* 337. Whiting claims that this variant is cited in Siegfried Sassoon, *Memoirs of a Fox-Hunting Man* (London: Faber and Faber, 1930), 16, but I was not able to find it in that work.

56. Anthony Gilbert, *Missing from Her Home* (New York: Random House, 1969), 124.

57. Agatha Christie, *N or M?* (New York: Dell, 1941), 27.

58. Manning Coles, *Green Hazard* (London: Hodder and Stoughton, 1945), 237.

59. C. Day Lewis, *The Buried Day* (New York: Harper and Brothers, 1960), 86.

60. Richard Butler, *A Blood-Red Sun at Noon* (Sydney: William Collins, 1980), 207.

61. I owe this reference to my colleague Prof. Kevin McKenna who remembers it from his student years at Oklahoma.

62. L. Sprague and Catherine C. de Camp, *Ancient Ruins and Archeology* (New York: Ballantine Books, 1964), 270.

63. Vernon Loder, *Suspicion* (London: William Collins, 1933), 173.

64. Stephen Leacock, *My Remarkable Uncle and Other Sketches* (New York: Dodd, Mead and Company, 1942), 64.

65. Paul Gallico, *Thomasina* (London: Michael Joseph, 1957), 40.

66. Leonard Lee Rue, *The World of the Raccoon* (Philadelphia: J. B. Lippincott, 1964), 82.

67. I owe this text to my colleague Prof. Kevin McKenna, who remembers it from oral use as a student in Oklahoma.

68. Arthur H. Lewis, *Carnival* (New York: Trident Press, 1970), 101.

69. Tony Kenrick, *The Only Good Body's a Dead One* (New York: Simon and Schuster, 1970), book title.

70. Ernest Priestley, "The Only Good Grades Are Good Grades. A New Teacher Confronts the Grading System and Tells What He Finds," *Changing Education* 4, no. 4 (Spring 1970): 17 (title of magazine article).

71. Barry Wilson, "The Only Good Cow's a Dead Cow. Huge Profits from Subsidized Slaughter for EEC Farmers on the Fiddle," *New Statesman* (29 February 1980): 317 (title of magazine article).

72. Howard Chapnick, "Since the Only Good Photojournalist is a Live Photojournalist, Beirut Underlines the Difference Between Dedication and Damnfoolishness," *Popular Photography* 93 (January 1986): 18 (title of magazine article).

73. Jacques Pépin, "Bluefish Fans Know This: The Only Good Fish Is a Fresh Fish," *New York Times,* 17 October 1990, p. C10 (title of newspaper article).

74. Mark Richard Zubro, *The Only Good Priest* (New York: St. Martin's Press, 1991), book title.

75. Gallico, *Thomasina*, 40.

76. Joseph B. Carr, *The Man with Bated Breath* (New York: Grosset and Dunlap, 1934), 33.

77. Quoted from Bernard Shaw, *Plays Political* (London: Penguin Books, 1986), 144–46.

78. See Mieder, "Proverbs in Nazi Germany."

79. John Buchan, *Salute to Adventures* (New York: Thomas Nelson, 1915), 74–75.

80. Carolyn Wells, *The Wooden Indian* (New York: Blue Ribbon Books, 1935), 35.

81. Laura Ingalls Wilder, *Little House on the Prairie* (1st ed., 1935; New York: Harper and Brothers, 1953), 211. The reference is located in chap. 17: "Pa Goes to Town."

82. Maxwell Bodenheim, *My Life and Loves in Greenwich Village* (New York: Bridgehead Books, 1954), 130.

83. *The New Yorker* (19 January 1957): 38.

84. Mignon G. Eberhart, *El Rancho Rio* (Roslyn, N.Y.: Walter J. Black, 1970), 128.

85. Anthony Price, *The '44 Vintage* (Garden City, N.Y.: Doubleday, 1978), 118.

86. See Alan Dundes, "Auschwitz Jokes," *Western Folklore* 38 (1979): 145–57; rpt. with a postscript in A. Dundes, *Cracking Jokes: Studies of Sick Humor Cycles & Stereotypes* (Berkeley, Cal.: Ten Speed Press, 1987), 19–38.

87. Mack Reynolds, "Good Indian," in John W. Campbell, ed., *Analog II* (Garden City, N.Y.: Doubleday, 1964), 54 (entire short story on 46–54).

Chapter 6. "No Tickee, No Washee"

An earlier version of this chapter was first published in *Western Folklore* 55 (1996): 1–40. This study has benefited greatly from the kind and much appreciated help of a number of colleagues and friends. I would like to acknowledge the invaluable help of Professors Alan Dundes, George B. Bryan, and Shirley L. Arora, who provided me with numerous textual references and significant demoscopic materials. Rebecca Maksel and Maggie Pinelli of the Folklore Archive at Berkeley provided me with unique references, and Prof. Dundes's American Folklore students filled out an invaluable questionnaire. I could not possibly have written this investigation without the help of all of these kind people. Their work, knowledge, and insights are present on every page of this study.

1. Archer Taylor, *The Proverb* (Cambridge: Harvard University Press, 1931; rpt. ed. with an introduction and bibliography by Wolfgang Mieder, Bern: Peter Lang, 1985), 11.

2. Letter to the author from Shirley L. Arora, 30 November 1994.

3. For a review of the vast scholarship, see Nelson R. Cauthen, Ira E. Robinson, and Herbert H. Krauss, "Stereotypes: A Review of the Literature 1926–1968," *Journal of Social Psychology* 84 (1971): 103–25; and John C. Brigham, "Ethnic Stereotypes," *Psychological Bulletin* 76 (1971): 15–38.

4. See Erdman B. Palmore, "Ethnophaulism and Ethnocentrism," *Ameri-*

can Journal of Sociology 67 (1962): 442–45; John Algeo, "Xenophobic Ethnica," *Maledicta* 1 (1977): 133–40; and Uta Quasthoff, "The Uses of Stereotype in Everyday Argument," *Journal of Pragmatics* 2 (1978): 1–48.

5. See Otto von Reinsberg-Düringsfeld, *Internationale Titulaturen,* 2 vols. (Leipzig: Hermann Fries, 1863; rpt. with an introduction by Wolfgang Mieder, Hildesheim: Georg Olms, 1992); Henri Gaidoz and Paul Sébillot, *Blason populaire de la France* (Paris: Léopold Cerf, 1884); and Abraham A. Roback, *Dictionary of International Slurs (Ethnophaulisms)* (Cambridge, Mass.: Sci-Art Publishers, 1944; rpt., Waukesha, Wis.: Maledicta Press, 1979). For more references and a detailed discussion of international slurs, see Alan Dundes, "Slurs International: Folk Comparisons of Ethnicity and National Character," *Southern Folklore Quarterly* 39 (1975): 15–38; now also rpt. in Wolfgang Mieder, ed., *Wise Words: Essays on the Proverb* (New York: Garland Publishing, 1994), 183–209.

6. See Peter Tamony, "Chinaman's Chance," *Western Folklore* 24 (1965): 202–5. See also Mariana D. Birnbaum, "On the Language of Prejudice," *Western Folklore* 30 (1971): 257–58 (entire article on 247–68); and the chapter "Chinaman's Chance" in Cheng-Tsu Wu, ed., *"Chink!" A Documentary History of Anti-Chinese Prejudice in America* (New York: The World Publishing Company, 1972), 145–212 (also pp. 5 and 233).

7. Roback, *Dictionary of International Slurs,* 24–25, 38. For additional lists of slurs against the Chinese population, see George Monteiro, "Derisive Adjectives: Two Notes and a List," *Western Folklore* 34 (1975): 244–46; Laurence French, "Racial and Ethnic Slurs," *Maledicta* 4 (1980): 117–26; and Irving Lewis Allen, *The Language of Ethnic Conflict: Social Organization and Lexical Culture* (New York: Columbia University Press, 1983), 41 (Chinese women) and 53 (males).

8. Richard O'Connor, *Bret Harte: A Biography* (Boston: Little, Brown and Company, 1966), 120.

9. Bret Harte, *Complete Poetical Works* (New York: P. F. Collier, 1902), vol. 8, pp. 129–31. For interpretive comments regarding this poem see William Purviance Fenn, *Ah Sin and His Brethren in American Literature* (Peiping: College of Chinese Studies, 1932), 45–50; and William F. Wu, *The Yellow Peril: Chinese Americans in American Fiction 1850–1940* (Hamden, Conn.: Archon Books, 1982), 20–21. See also the special edition of this poem with stereotypical illustrations: Bret Harte, *The Heathen Chinee: Plain Language from Truthful James.* With an introduction by Ina Coolbrith, and a bibliography by Robert Ernest Cowan; illustrated by Phil Little (San Francisco: John Henry Nash, 1936).

10. See "Background of Myth of Chinese Heathen" in James Leroy Evans, "The Indian Savage, the Mexican Bandit, the Chinese Heathen—Three Popular Stereotypes" (diss., University of Texas at Austin, 1967), 136–46.

11. Willard B. Farwell, *The Chinese at Home and Abroad: The Report of the Special Committee of the Board of Supervisors of San Francisco on the Condition of the Chinese Quarter of that City* (San Francisco: A. L. Bancroft, 1885), pt. 2, pp. 38–39 (entire section on 37–43).

12. Ibid., pt. 1, p. 59. See also the many stereotypical statements in Charles

R. Shepherd, *The Ways of Ah Sin: A Composite Narrative of Things as They Are* (New York: Fleming H. Revell, 1923).

13. For this inhumane misuse of proverbs, see my "Proverbs in Nazi Germany: The Promulgation of Anti-Semitism and Stereotypes through Proverbs," in *Proverbs Are Never Out of Season: Popular Wisdom in the Modern Age* (New York: Oxford University Press, 1993), 225–55.

14. Quoted from *The Other Side of the Chinese Question: Testimony of California's Leading Citizens* (San Francisco: Woodward and Company, 1886; rpt. San Francisco: R. and E. Research Associates, 1971), 40.

15. The report is printed in *Reports of Committees of the Senate of the United States for the Second Session of the Forty-Fourth Congress 1876–'77* (Washington, D.C.: U.S. Government Printing Office, 1877), vol. 3 (report no. 689).

16. Cited in the *Debates and Proceedings of the Constitutional Convention of the State of California [1878]* and here quoted from Luther W. Spoehr, "Sambo and the Heathen Chinee: Californians' Racial Stereotypes in the Late 1870s," *Pacific Historical Review* 42 (1973): 196 (n. 32) (entire article on 185–204).

17. Robert F. Heizer and Alan F. Almquist, *The Other Californians: Prejudice and Discrimination Under Spain, Mexico, and the United States to 1920* (Berkeley: University of California Press, 1971), 157. For additional comments on Chinese stereotypes, see Francis L. K. Hsu, *The Challenge of the American Dream: The Chinese in the United States* (Belmont, Cal.: Wadsworth, 1971), 95–108; Alexander Saxton, *The Indispensable Enemy: Labor and the Anti-Chinese Movement in California* (Berkeley: University of California Press, 1971), 19–45; and Betty Lee Sung, *A Survey of Chinese-American Manpower and Employment* (New York: Praeger, 1976), 207–21.

18. Cited from Sue Fawn Chung, "From Fu Manchu, Evil Genius, to James Lee Wong, Popular Hero: A Study of the Chinese-American in Popular Periodical Fiction from 1920 to 1940," *Journal of Popular Culture* 10 (1977): 535 (entire article on 534–47).

19. Palmore, "Ethnophaulism," 443.

20. Harte, *Complete Poetical Works,* vol. 8, p. 143 (entire poem on 142–45). For a list of other typical Chinese names (esp. Hop Sing) in Harte's works, see Fenn, *Ah Sin and His Brethren,* xv–xvi.

21. For the communicative importance of Pidgin English see the chapter on "Pidgins and Creoles" in David Crystal, *The Cambridge Encyclopedia of Language* (New York: Cambridge University Press, 1987), 334–39. For a discussion of the Chinese Pidgin-English, see also the "Introduction" in Charles G. Leland, *Pidgin-English Sing-Song or Songs and Stories in the China-English Dialect. With a Vocabulary* (London: Trübner, 1876), 1–9.

22. The two stanzas are quoted from Fenn, *Ah Sin and His Brethren,* 99–100. See his chapter on the absurd literary texts depicting the Pidgin English of the Chinese (92–100).

23. See Stuart W. Hyde, "The Chinese Stereotype in American Melodrama," *California Historical Society Quarterly* 34 (1955): 365 (entire article with many examples of this stereotypical language use on 357–67). See also Shirley Geok-lin

Lim and Amy Ling, *Reading the Literatures of Asian America* (Philadelphia: Temple University Press, 1992), 350–51.

24. Quoted from Isaac Goldberg and Hubert C. Heffner, eds., *Davy Crockett & Other Plays by Leonard Grover, Frank Murdock, Lester Wallack, G. H. Jessop, and J. J. McCloskey* (Princeton: Princeton University Press, 1940), 110 (entire play on 65–114).

25. See Joaquin Miller, *First Fam'lies in the Sierras* (London: George Routledge, 1875), 21–35. For a detailed discussion of this figure, see Wu, *Yellow Peril*, 23–25. Wu also refers to the children's book *Little Sky-High or the Surprising Doings of Washee-Washee Wang* (1901) by Hezekiah Butterworth, showing how the word "washee" had become synonymous with Chinese laundrymen. See Wu, *Yellow Peril*, 111–12.

26. Quoted from *Joaquin Miller's Poems* (San Francisco: Whitaker and Ray, 1910), vol. 6 *(Poetic Plays)*, p. 2. For a short discussion of the novel and the play, see John Burt Foster, "China and the Chinese in American Literature, 1850–1950" (diss., University of Illinois, 1952), 38–39.

27. Bartley Campbell, *The White Slave & Other Plays* (Princeton: Princeton University Press, 1941), 97.

28. The person with whom Hop Sing is discussing this matter is calling him John, which is the shortened form of the generic stereotype "John Chinaman." See, for example, the first stanza of the song "John Chinaman" (1871) in Wu, *Yellow Peril*, 27:

> John Chinaman, my woe, John,
> It costs you but a cent
> To live from morn till even,
> In one perpetual Lent.
> But though your skin is swart, John,
> You "washee" white as snow;
> And you are always up to snuff,
> John Chinaman, my woe.

29. Harte, *Complete Poetical Works,* vol. 12, pp. 367–68.

30. Alfred Trumble, *The Heathen Chinee at Home and Abroad* (New York: Fox, 1882), 50.

31. Quoted from Paul C. P. Siu, *The Chinese Laundryman: A Study of Social Isolation* (New York: New York University Press, 1987), 16 (the ellipses are in the cited text). Originally a 1953 dissertation from the University of Chicago. See also Leong Gor Yun, "The Laundry Alliance" in L. Yun, *Chinatown Inside Out* (New York: Barrows Mussey, 1936), 85–106; and Fred DeArmond, *The Laundry Industry* (New York: Harper and Brothers, 1950).

32. Siu, *Chinese Laundryman,* 16–17.

33. Ibid., 22. The entire chapter on "The Chinese Laundryman in the Eyes of the American Public" (8–22) presents such racial stereotypes. See also Paul Man Ong, "The Chinese and the Laundry Laws: The Use and Control of Urban Space" (M.A. thesis, University of Washington, 1977), 25–31, 71–80.

34. See Betty Lee Sung, *Mountain of Gold: The Story of the Chinese in America* (New York: Macmillan, 1967), 188. See also Chalsa M. Loo, *Chinatown: Most Time, Hard Time* (New York: Praeger, 1991), 45–46.

35. Sung, *Mountain of Gold*, 187 (entire chapter on 187–201).

36. Sung, *Chinese-American Manpower and Employment*, 209.

37. See Jack Chen, *The Chinese of America* (New York: Harper and Row, 1980), 58.

38. Renqiu Yu, *To Save China, To Save Ourselves: The Hand Laundry Alliance of New York* (Philadelphia: Temple University Press, 1992), 25 (the ellipses are part of the original).

39. See Paul C. P. Siu, "The Isolation of the Chinese Laundryman," in Ernest W. Burgess and Donald J. Bogue, *Contributions to Urban Sociology* (Chicago: University of Chicago Press, 1964), 429–42.

40. For this language barrier, see Siu, *Chinese Laundryman*, 138; and Yu, *To Save China*, 24–25.

41. Mark Twain, *Roughing It* (Hartford, Conn.: American Publishing Company, 1872), 392 (entire chapter on 391–97).

42. Siu, *Chinese Laundryman*, 63–64 (with an illustration of a laundry ticket from the early 1950s).

43. Quoted from the conveniently alphabetized collection by W. Carew Hazlitt, *English Proverbs and Proverbial Phrases* (London: Reeves and Turner, 1907; rpt. Detroit, Mich.: Gale Research Company, 1969), 331–36 (with many examples).

44. Burton Stevenson, *The Book of Proverbs, Maxims, and Famous Phrases* (New York: Macmillan, 1948), 1611–12 (no. 7).

45. See, for, example Owen S. Adams, "Traditional Proverbs and Sayings from California," *Western Folklore* 6 (1947): 59–64; Owen S. Adams, "More California Proverbs," *Western Folklore* 7 (1948): 136–44; Archer Taylor and C. Grant Loomis, "California Proverbs and Sententious Sayings," *Western Folklore* 10 (1951): 248–49; C. Grant Loomis, "Proverbs in Business," *Western Folklore* 23 (1964): 91–94; and Mary Turner, *Pioneer Proverbs: Wit and Wisdom from Early America* (High Point, N. C.: Hutcraft, 1971).

46. For bibliographical references, see my *Proverbs in Literature: An International Bibliography* (Bern: Peter Lang, 1978); and *American Proverbs: A Study of Texts and Contexts* (Bern: Peter Lang, 1989).

47. Eric Partridge, *A Dictionary of Catch Phrases* (New York: Stein and Day, 1977), 157.

48. Robert Hendrickson, *The Facts on File Encyclopedia of Word and Phrase Origins* (New York: Facts on File Publications, 1987), 381–82.

49. Bartlett Jere Whiting, *Modern Proverbs and Proverbial Sayings* (Cambridge: Harvard University Press, 1989), 625 (T113).

50. Wolfgang Mieder, Stewart A. Kingsbury, and Kelsie B. Harder, *A Dictionary of American Proverbs* (New York: Oxford University Press, 1992), 595.

51. P. R. Wilkinson, *Thesaurus of Traditional English Metaphors* (London: Routledge, 1993), 378.

52. An exception today is Nigel Rees in London who has edited the intrigu-

ing *"Quote . . . Unquote" Newsletter* since 1992. See foremost his *Sayings of the Century* (London: George Allen and Unwin, 1984). Alas, this invaluable book does not include the proverb "No tickee, no washee."

53. Robert Kimball, ed., *The Complete Lyrics of Ira Gershwin* (New York: Alfred A. Knopf, 1993), 204. The song and its proverb are also mentioned in a newspaper report from 1987 that announces the new staging of this Gershwin musical; see Lon Tuck, "The Gershwin Gold," *Washington Post,* 16 May 1987, p. G1.

54. Richard Shattuck (pseud. Dora [Richards] Shattuck), *The Snark Was a Boojum* (New York: William Morrow, 1941), 170. I owe this reference to Stevenson, *Book of Proverbs,* 1611–12 (no. 7).

55. Richard Burke, *Here Lies the Body* (New York: Popular Library, 1942), 86.

56. Eleazar Lipsky, *Murder One* (Garden City, N.Y.: Doubleday and Company, 1948), 106.

57. George Baxt, *Swing Low, Sweet Harriet* (New York: Simon and Schuster, 1967), 58. My colleague Prof. George B. Bryan informs me that Charlie Chan, fictional detective sergeant of the Honolulu Police, in Earl Derr Biggers's *Charlie Chan: Five Complete Novels* (New York: Avenel Books, 1981), does not speak Pidgin English. In fact, Biggers has Chan state: "All my life I study to speak fine English words" (184). These detective novels contain much proverbial language and plenty of Pidgin English, but not the proverb under discussion here.

58. The cover title of the private recording is "And Then There Were None." The Walt Whitman School Dance Band of South Huntington, New York, was under the music directorship of Clement De Rosa.

59. *Ethel Smith's Cha-Cha-Cha Album* (New York: Decca, 1955).

60. Piri Thomas, *Down These Mean Streets* (New York: Vintage Books, 1967), 116. I owe this reference to my wife Barbara Mieder.

61. Maxine Hong Kingston, *The Woman Warrior: Memoirs of a Girlhood Among Ghosts* (New York: Vintage Books, 1976), 123. For interpretive comments regarding this particular scene, see Elaine H. Kim, *Asian American Literature: An Introduction to the Writings and Their Social Context* (Philadelphia: Temple University Press, 1982), 203–5. This proverbial statement was also cited by Walter Clemons in his review of Kingston's book in *Newsweek* (11 October 1976): 109.

62. Denis Collins and Ina Lee Selden, "3 Va. Localities Not Enforcing Pupil Shot Rule," *Washington Post,* 5 September 1979, p. B1.

63. Unsigned editorial "The Years with White" in *Nation* (12 October 1985): 329.

64. Barbara Carton, "Telling It to the Judge in Fairfax County Traffic Court's Fast Lane," *Washington Post,* 16 January 1986, p. C1.

65. Bernie Lincicome, "Ski Racing Calls for Deep Thinking," *Chicago Tribune,* 6 February 1989, p. C1.

66. Stephen Guy and Peter Beal, "I Want to Be a Dad, Dodd Tells Tax Fraud Trial," *Press Association Newsfile,* 10 July 1989, no pp. given.

67. Frank Keating, "No, Not Everyone Jumps Into the Pool," *Newsday,* 31 December 1989, p. 36.

68. Eve Zibart, "Openings," *Washington Post,* 1 June 1990, p. N43.

69. David Klinghoffer, "Message to Moose: Keep Coming Back," *Washington Times,* 1 June 1990, p. E3.

70. A program on "New Asian Movies May Signify Trend in Hollywood" broadcast on "All Things Considered," *National Public Radio,* 6 June 1993. The text is cited precisely as it appears in the LEXIS/NEXIS database, only the [*sic*] having been added.

71. William Zimmer, "The Asian-American Artist Clad in the Cloak of Invisibility," *New York Times,* 27 March 1994, sec. 13WC, p. 18.

72. For a discussion of the multifunctionality, multisemanticity, and multi-situationality of proverbs, see my "'The Wit of One, and the Wisdom of Many': General Thoughts on the Nature of the Proverb" in *Proverbs Are Never Out of Season,* 3–17.

73. Bob Levey, "Bob Levey's Washington," *Washington Post,* 5 July 1982, p. D12.

74. Ibid.

75. James Lardner, "Thick & Think Tank: David Abshire's CSIS Ponder Policy With Kissinger & Fred Flintstone," *Washington Post,* 21 September 1982, p. B1.

76. Muriel Broadman, "Dance Directions: Old Forms and New Influences," *Back Stage* (26 April 1985): 1A.

77. Kenneth Reich, "Secrets of the Organizing Committee: Going for Gold Takes New Trust," *Los Angeles Times,* 31 July 1985, part 3, p. 1.

78. Robert A. Mamis, "A Deal for all Seasons," *Inc. Publishing Company* (January 1986): 105.

79. Claudia M. Christie, "The Customer Is Always Wrong," *New England Business,* 16 June 1986, p. 59.

80. Kenneth Mason, "Four Ways to Overpay Yourself Enough," *Harvard Business Review* (July/August 1988): 69.

81. Brian Farkas, "Secretary Salaries Must Come from Savings," *United Press International,* 27 January 1989, regional news broadcast.

82. David Evans, "Costly 'Sniper' Missile Stirs Many Doubts," *Chicago Tribune,* 8 February 1989, p. 1C.

83. Thomas Ferraro, "Bennett Seeks Governors' Help," *United Press International,* 27 February 1989, news broadcast.

84. "Copping out on the Contras," *National Review* (16 June 1989): 10.

85. Jim Thomas, "Illini, Sneaky in 1988, Expect More in 1989," *St. Louis Post-Dispatch,* 30 July 1989, p. 3F.

86. Elaine Hiruo, "Civilian Waste Program Right Now Taking Back Seat," *Nuclear Fuel* (16 October 1989): 7.

87. Curry Kirkparrick, "So Whay's [*sic*] the Story?: The Nation's Media Made Their Annual Assault Upon the Super Bowl in a Desperate Search for News of Import," *Sports Illustrated* (5 February 1990): 28.

88. Charlotte Hays, "Bookshelf," *Washington Times,* 2 May 1990, p. E1.

89. Furman Bisher, "Trying to Watch Nuggets Play Will Keep Your Head Swiveling," *Atlanta Journal and Constitution,* 7 March 1991, p. 3E.

90. Jerry Crowe and Thomas Bonk, "U.S. Olympic Festival," *Los Angeles Times*, 18 July 1991, p. C1.

91. Michael Madden, "They'll Sell You Shirts off Their Backs: The Winter Olympics '92," *Boston Globe*, 21 February 1992, p. 51.

92. "No Tickee, No Gretzky," *Financial Post*, 22 April 1992, p. 40.

93. Karen Branch and Patty Shillington, "Judge in Lotto Case: 'No Tickee, No Pay,'" *Miami Herald*, 9 May 1992, p. 1A.

94. Marla Hart, "Redeker's on the Sidelines, But Still in the Game," *Chicago Tribune*, 29 April 1993, p. 5.

95. Stuart Wavell, "Good and Great Compete in Foot-in-Mouth Game," *Sunday Times*, 4 July 1993, Home News sec., no pp. given.

96. Tom Gavin, "One More Shot," *Denver Post*, 15 July 1994, p. B7.

97. For this term and numerous examples, see the chapter on "Proverb Parodies" in Mieder, *American Proverbs*, 239–75.

98. "Great American Ins. Co. v. Katani Shipping Co." Case no. 24138, United States Court of Appeals for the Ninth Circuit, 428 F. 2d 612 (7 July 1970).

99. "William John Pacheco v. The State of Texas." Case no. 776-84, Court of Criminal Appeals of Texas, 692 S.W.2d 59 (20 March 1985).

100. Hazlitt, *English Proverbs*, 332.

101. Letter to the author from Shirley L. Arora, 30 January 1995.

102. Letter to the author from Shirley L. Arora, 18 November 1994.

103. Shirley L. Arora, "'No Tickee, No Shirtee': Proverbial Speech and Leadership in Academe," in Michael Owen Jones, Michael Dane Moore, and Richard Christopher Snyder, eds., *Inside Organizations: Understanding the Human Dimension* (Newbury Park, Cal.: Sage Publisher, 1988), 182–83 (entire article on 179–89).

104. Letter to the author from Shirley L. Arora, 18 November 1994.

105. Ibid., 8 February 1995.

106. Collected by an unnamed folklore student from Genevieve Palabay ca. 1981 in San Francisco, California.

107. Collected by Dan Siegel from his mother Jerrell Siegel on 31 October 1987 in Menlo Park, California.

108. Personal recollection and thoughts of David Wingate, recorded on 10 August 1981 in Piedmont, California.

109. Collected by Paul Makaue from Leticia Miranda on 2 November 1982 at Berkeley, California.

110. For some comments on such racial rhymes, see Kenneth Porter, "Racism in Children's Rhymes and Sayings, Central Kansas, 1910–1918," *Western Folklore* 24 (1965): 191–96; and Carol Parker, "'White is the Color,'" *Western Folklore* 34 (1975): 153–54.

111. See the chapter on "'Proverbs Everyone Ought to Know': Paremiological Minimum and Cultural Literacy," in my *Proverbs Are Never Out of Season*, 41–57 (with secondary literature dealing with the question of proverb knowledge).

112. See Shay Totten, "Asian Immigrants Work to Build Lives in Vermont," *Burlington Free Press*, 20 February 1995, pp. 3A-5A.

113. See the enlightening comments by Américo Paredes in his short discussion of "Proverbs and Ethnic Stereotypes," *Proverbium* 15 (1970): 511–13. Paredes refers especially to "the conservative nature of the proverb" which causes "proverbs expressing ethnic stereotypes [to] remain current in oral tradition long after the stereotypes have lost their original meaning" (513).

114. I owe this reference to John Mason (18 November 1994).

115. Cited from Mieder, Kingsbury, and Harder, *Dictionary of American Proverbs*, 595. This text immediately precedes the proverb "No tickee, no washee" in our *Dictionary of American Proverbs*.

Bibliography

This bibliography contains only those publications which deal with proverbial matters. The endnotes to the individual chapters register numerous additional references concerning politics and stereotypes in general. For easy reference the present bibliography is divided into four parts: bibliographies, proverb journals, collections of proverbs and quotations, and scholarly studies on the proverb.

Bibliographies

Bonser, Wilfrid. *Proverb Literature: A Bibliography of Works Relating to Proverbs.* London: William Glaisher, 1930. Reprint. Nendeln, Liechtenstein: Kraus Reprint, 1967.

de Caro, Francis (Frank) A., and William K. McNeil. *American Proverb Literature: A Bibliography.* Bloomington: Folklore Forum, Indiana University, 1971.

Mieder, Wolfgang. *International Bibliography of Explanatory Essays on Individual Proverbs and Proverbial Expressions.* Bern: Peter Lang, 1977.

Mieder, Wolfgang. *Proverbs in Literature: An International Bibliography.* Bern: Peter Lang, 1978.

Mieder, Wolfgang. *International Proverb Scholarship: An Annotated Bibliography.* 3 vols. New York: Garland Publishing, 1982, 1990, and 1993.

Mieder, Wolfgang. "International Bibliography of New and Reprinted Proverb Collections." Annual bibliography in *Proverbium: Yearbook of International Proverb Scholarship,* 1984ff.

Mieder, Wolfgang. "International Proverb Scholarship: An Updated Bibliography." Annual bibliography in *Proverbium: Yearbook of International Proverb Scholarship,* 1984ff.

Mieder, Wolfgang. *Investigations of Proverbs, Proverbial Expressions, Quotations and Clichés: A Bibliography of Explanatory Essays which Appeared in "Notes and Queries" (1849–1983).* Bern: Peter Lang, 1984.

Moll, Otto. *Sprichwörterbibliographie.* Frankfurt am Main: Vittorio Klostermann, 1958.

Urdang, Laurence, and Frank R. Abate. *Idioms and Phrases Index.* 3 vols. Detroit: Gale Research Co., 1983.

Proverb Journals

De Proverbio: An Electronic Journal of International Proverb Studies, 1995ff. [http://
info.utas.edu.au/docs/flonta/]. Ed. Teodor Flonta et al. (Tasmania, Australia).

Paremia: Boletín de Investigaciones Paremiológicas, 1993ff. Ed. Julia Sevilla
Muñoz et al. (Madrid).

Proverbium: Bulletin d'information sur les recherches parémiologiques, 1–25
(1965–75), 1–1008. Ed. Matti Kuusi et al. (Helsinki). Reprint (2 vols.). Ed.
Wolfgang Mieder. Bern: Peter Lang, 1987.

Proverbium Paratum: Bulletin d'information sur les recherches parémiologiques,
1–4 (1980–89), 1–460. Ed. Vilmos Voigt et al. (Budapest).

Proverbium: Yearbook of International Proverb Scholarship, 1984ff. Ed. Wolfgang Mieder et al. (Burlington, Vermont).

Collections of Proverbs and Quotations

Adams, Owen S. "Traditional Proverbs and Sayings from California." *Western
Folklore* 6 (1947): 59–64; and 7 (1948): 136–44.

Adams, Ramon F. *Western Words: A Dictionary of the American West.* Norman:
University of Oklahoma Press, 1968.

Apperson, G. L. *English Proverbs and Proverbial Phrases: A Historical Dictionary.* London: J. M. Dent, 1929. Reprint. Detroit: Gale Research Co., 1969.

Appuhn, Klaus D. *Graffiti: Kunst an Mauern.* Dortmund: Die bibliophilen Taschenbücher, 1982.

Barbour, Frances M. *Proverbs and Proverbial Phrases of Illinois.* Carbondale:
Southern Illinois University Press, 1965.

Barrick, Mac E. "Proverbs and Sayings from Cumberland County [Pennsylva-
nia]." *Keystone Folklore Quarterly* 8 (1963): 139–203.

Bartlett, John. *Familiar Quotations.* 16th ed., ed. Justin Kaplan. Boston: Little,
Brown and Company, 1992 (1st ed. 1855).

Benham, William Gurney. *Putnam's Complete Book of Quotations, Proverbs and
Household Words.* New York: G. P. Putnam's Sons, 1926.

Boller, Paul F., and John George. *They Never Said It: A Book of Fake Quotes, Misquotes, and Misleading Attributions.* New York: Oxford University Press, 1989.

Brewer, Ebenezer Cobham. *Dictionary of Phrase and Fable.* New York: Harper
and Row, 1970. Centenary ed., revised by Ivor H. Evans. New York: Harper
and Row, 1970.

Brunvand, Jan Harold. *A Dictionary of Proverbs and Proverbial Phrases from
Books Published by Indiana Authors before 1890.* Bloomington: Indiana University Press, 1961.

Büchmann, Georg. *Geflügelte Worte.* 33d ed., ed. Winfried Hofmann. Berlin: Ull-
stein, 1986 (1st ed. 1864).

Carruth, Gorton, and Eugene Ehrlich. *The Harper Book of American Quotations.* New York: Harper and Row, 1988.

Champion, Selwyn Gurney. *Racial Proverbs: A Selection of the World's Proverbs
Arranged Linguistically with Authoritative Introductions to the Proverbs of*

27 Countries and Races. London: George Routledge, 1938. Reprint. London: Routledge and Kegan, 1963.

Christy, Robert. *Proverbs, Maxims and Phrases of All Ages.* New York: G. P. Putnam's Sons, 1887. Reprint. Norwood, Pennsylvania: Norwood Editions, 1977.

Cohen, M. J. *The Penguin Dictionary of Quotations.* Middlesex, England: Penguin Books, 1960.

Cray, Doris. *Catch Phrases, Clichés and Idioms.* Jefferson, N.C.: McFarland, 1990.

Daintith, John, et al. *The Macmillan Dictionary of Quotations.* New York: Macmillan, 1987.

Daintith, John, et al. *Who Said What When: A Chronological Dictionary of Quotations.* London: Bloomsbury, 1988. Reprint. New York: Hippocrene Books, 1991.

Dalbiac, Lilian. *Dictionary of Quotations (German).* New York: Frederick Ungar, 1958 (1st ed. 1909).

Darwin, Bernard. *The Oxford Dictionary of Quotations.* Oxford: Oxford University Press, 1953 (3d ed. 1979).

Davidoff, Henry. *The Pocket Book of Quotations.* New York: Pocket Books, 1942.

Dent, Robert W. *Shakespeare's Proverbial Language: An Index.* Los Angeles: University of California Press, 1981.

Dent, Robert W. *Proverbial Language in English Drama Exclusive of Shakespeare, 1495–1616.* Los Angeles: University of California Press, 1984.

Evans, Bergen. *Dictionary of Quotations.* New York: Avenel Books, 1968 (2d ed. 1978).

Ewart, Neil. *Everyday Phrases. Their Origins and Meanings.* Poole, Dorset: Blandford Press, 1983.

Fergusson, Rosalind. *Dictionary of Proverbs.* New York: Facts on File Publications, 1983.

Frost, Elizabeth, ed. *The Bully Pulpit: Quotations from America's Presidents.* New York: Facts on File Publications, 1988.

Gaidoz, Henri, and Paul Sébillot. *Blason populaire de la France.* Paris: Léopold Cerf, 1884.

Guinzbourg, Lt. Colonel Victor S. M. de. *Wit and Wisdom of the United Nations: Proverbs and Apothegms on Diplomacy.* New York: Privately printed, 1961.

Guinzbourg, Lt. Colonel Victor S. M. de. *Supplement: Wit and Wisdom of the United Nations or The Modern Machiavelli.* New York: Privately printed, 1965.

Guinzbourg, Lt. Colonel Victor S. M. de. *The Eternal Machiavelli in the United Nations World.* New York: Privately printed, 1969.

Harnsberger, Caroline T., ed. *Treasury of Presidential Quotations.* Chicago: Follett Publishing, 1964.

Hazlitt, W. Carew. *English Proverbs and Proverbial Phrases.* London: Reeves and Turner, 1869. Reprint. Detroit: Gale Research Company, 1969.

Hendrickson, Robert. *Salty Words.* New York: Hearst Marine Books, 1984.

Hendrickson, Robert. *The Facts on File Encyclopedia of Word and Phrase Origins.* New York: Facts on File Publications, 1987.

Hiemer, Ernst. *Der Jude im Sprichwort.* Nürnberg: Der Stürmer, 1942.

Hirsch, E. D., Joseph Kett, and James Trefil. *The Dictionary of Cultural Literacy: What Every American Needs to Know.* Boston: Houghton Mifflin Company, 1988 ("Proverbs" on 46–57).

Kin, David. *Dictionary of American Proverbs.* New York: Philosophical Library, 1955.

Kingsbury, Stewart A., Mildred E. Kingsbury, and Wolfgang Mieder. *Weather Wisdom: Proverbs, Superstitions, and Signs.* New York: Peter Lang, 1996.

Lean, Vincent Stuckey. *Lean's Collectanea: Collections of Proverbs (English and Foreign), Folklore, and Superstitions, also Compilations Towards Dictionaries of Proverbial Phrases and Words, Old and Disused.* Ed. T. W. Williams. 4 vols. Bristol, England: J. W. Arrowsmith, 1902–1904. Reprint. Detroit: Gale Research Company, 1969.

Lighter, J. E., ed. *Random House Historical Dictionary of American Slang.* New York: Random House, 1994.

Loomis, C. Grant. "Proverbs in Business." *Western Folklore* 23 (1964): 91–94.

Mathews, Mitford. *A Dictionary of Americanisms on Historical Principles.* Chicago: University of Chicago Press, 1951.

Mencken, H. L. *A New Dictionary of Quotations on Historical Principles from Ancient and Modern Sources.* New York: Alfred A. Knopf, 1942 (2d ed. 1960).

Mieder, Wolfgang. *Antisprichwörter.* 3 vols. Wiesbaden: Verlag für deutsche Sprache, 1982. Wiesbaden: Gesellschaft für deutsche Sprache, 1985. Wiesbaden: Quelle and Meyer, 1989.

Mieder, Wolfgang. *The Prentice-Hall Encyclopedia of World Proverbs.* Englewood Cliffs, N.J.: Prentice-Hall, 1986.

Mieder, Wolfgang. *Yankee Wisdom: New England Proverbs.* Shelburne, Vt.: New England Press, 1989.

Mieder, Wolfgang. *Not By Bread Alone: Proverbs of the Bible.* Shelburne, Vt.: New England Press, 1990.

Mieder, Wolfgang. *Salty Wisdom: Proverbs of the Sea.* Shelburne, Vt.: New England Press, 1990.

Mieder, Wolfgang, Stewart A. Kingsbury, and Kelsie B. Harder, eds. *A Dictionary of American Proverbs.* New York: Oxford University Press, 1992.

Morris, William and Mary. *Dictionary of Word and Phrase Origins.* New York: Harper and Row, 1962.

Partington, Angela, ed. *The Oxford Dictionary of Quotations.* 4th ed. Oxford: Oxford University Press, 1992 (1st ed. 1941, 2d ed. 1953, 3d ed. 1979).

Partridge, Eric. *A Dictionary of Slang and Unconventional English.* New York: Macmillan, 1937 (7th ed. 1970).

Partridge, Eric. *A Dictionary of Catch Phrases.* New York: Stein and Day, 1977.

Pearce, Helen. "Folk Sayings in a Pioneer Family of Western Oregon." *California Folklore Quarterly* 5 (1946): 229–42.

Read, Allen Walker. *Classic American Graffiti.* Paris: Privately printed, 1935. Reprint. Waukesha, Wis.: Maledicta Press, 1977.

Rees, Nigel. *Sayings of the Century: The Stories Behind the Twentieth Century's Quotable Sayings.* London: George Allen and Unwin, 1984.

Rees, Nigel. *Dictionary of Popular Phrases*. London: Bloomsbury, 1990.

Reinsberg-Düringsfeld, Otto von. *Internationale Titulaturen*. 2 vols. Leipzig: Hermann Fries, 1863. Reprint, ed. by Wolfgang Mieder. Hildesheim: Georg Olms, 1992.

Reisner, Robert. *Graffiti: Two Thousand Years of Wall Writing*. New York: Cowles Book Company, 1971.

Roback, Abraham Aaron. *A Dictionary of International Slurs*. Cambridge, Mass.: Sci-Art Publishers, 1944. Reprint. Waukesha, Wis.: Maledicta Press, 1979.

Rogers, James. *The Dictionary of Clichés*. New York: Facts on File Publications, 1985.

Schulze, Carl. *Die biblischen Sprichwörter der deutschen Sprache*. Göttingen: Vandenhoeck and Ruprecht, 1860. Reprint, ed. by Wolfgang Mieder. Bern: Peter Lang, 1987.

Shafritz, Jay M. *Words on War: Military Quotations from Ancient Times to the Present*. New York: Prentice Hall, 1990.

Simpson, John A. *The Concise Oxford Dictionary of Proverbs*. Oxford: Oxford University Press, 1982 (2d ed. 1992).

Stevenson, Burton. *The Macmillan (Home) Book of Proverbs, Maxims and Familiar Phrases*. New York: Macmillan, 1948.

Stevenson, Burton. *The Home Book of Bible Quotations*. New York: Harper and Brothers, 1949.

Taylor, Archer, and C. Grant Loomis. "California Proverbs and Sententious Sayings." *Western Folklore* 10 (1951): 248–49.

Taylor, Archer, and Bartlett Jere Whiting. *A Dictionary of American Proverbs and Proverbial Phrases, 1820–1880*. Cambridge: Harvard University Press, 1958.

Tilley, Morris Palmer. *A Dictionary of the Proverbs in England in the Sixteenth and Seventeenth Centuries*. Ann Arbor: University of Michigan Press, 1950.

Turner, Mary. *Pioneer Proverbs: Wit and Wisdom from Early America*. High Point, N.C.: Hutcraft, 1971.

Urdang, Laurence, and Nancy LaRoche. *Picturesque Expressions: A Thematic Dictionary*. Detroit: Gale Research Company, 1980. Reprint, enlarged with the help of Walter W. Hunsinger. Detroit: Gale Research Company, 1985.

Urdang, Laurence, and Ceila Dame Robbins. *Slogans*. Detroit: Gale Research Company, 1984.

Wander, Karl Friedrich Wilhelm. *Deutsches Sprichwörter-Lexikon*. 5 vols. Leipzig: F. A. Brockhaus, 1867–80. Reprint. Darmstadt: Wissenschaftliche Buchgesellschaft, 1964.

Wentworth, Harold, and Stuart Berg Flexner, eds. *Dictionary of American Slang*. 2d ed. New York: Thomas Y. Crowell, 1975.

Whiting, Bartlett Jere. *Proverbs, Sentences, and Proverbial Phrases from English Writings Mainly Before 1500*. Cambridge, Mass.: Harvard University Press, 1968.

Whiting, Bartlett Jere. *Early American Proverbs and Proverbial Phrases*. Cambridge, Mass.: Harvard University Press, 1977.

Whiting, Bartlett Jere. *Modern Proverbs and Proverbial Sayings*. Cambridge, Mass.: Harvard University Press, 1989.

Wilkinson, P. R. *Thesaurus of Traditional English Metaphors*. London: Routledge, 1992.

Wilson, F. P. *The Oxford Dictionary of English Proverbs*. 3d ed. Oxford: Clarendon Press, 1970 (1st ed. 1935).

Studies on the Proverb

Albig, William. "Proverbs and Social Control." *Sociology and Social Research* 15 (1931): 527–35.

Allen, Irving Lewis. *The Language of Ethnic Conflict: Social Organization and Lexical Culture*. New York: Columbia University Press, 1983.

Arora, Shirley L. "'No Tickee, No Shirtee': Proverbial Speech and Leadership in Academe." In *Inside Organizations: Understanding the Human Dimension*, ed. Michael Owen Jones, Michael Dane Moore, and Richard Christopher Snyder, 179–89. Newbury Park, Cal.: Sage Publishers, 1988.

Arora, Shirley L. "On the Importance of Rotting Fish: A Proverb and Its Audience." *Western Folklore* 48 (1989): 271–88.

Bain, Read. "Verbal Stereotypes and Social Control." *Sociology and Social Research* 23 (1939): 431–46.

Barrick, Mac E. "'Better Red than Dead.'" *American Notes & Queries* 17, no. 9 (May 1979): 143–44.

Birnbaum, Mariana D. "On the Language of Prejudice." *Western Folklore* 30 (1971): 247–68.

Blümmer, Hugo. *Der bildliche Ausdruck in den Reden des Fürsten Bismarck*. Leipzig: S. Hirzel, 1891.

Blümmer, Hugo. "Der bildliche Ausdruck in den Briefen des Fürsten Bismarck." *Euphorion* 1 (1894): 590–603, 771–87.

Boas, George. *Vox Populi: Essays in the History of an Idea*. Baltimore: Johns Hopkins University Press, 1969.

Boller, Paul F. *Quotesmanship: The Use and Abuse of Quotations for Polemical and Other Purposes*. Dallas, Tex.: Southern Methodist University Press, 1967.

Breuillard, Jean. "Proverbes et pouvoir politique: Le cas de l'U.R.S.S." In *Richesse du proverbe*, ed. François Suard and Claude Buridant, vol. 2, pp. 155–66. Lille: Université de Lille, 1984.

Bryan, George B. *Black Sheep, Red Herrings, and Blue Murder: The Proverbial Agatha Christie*. Bern: Peter Lang, 1993.

Büchner, Karl. "'Summum ius summa iniuria.'" In K. Büchner, *Humanitas Romana: Studien über Werke und Wesen der Römer*, 80–105. Heidelberg: Carl Winter, 1957.

Bülck, Rudolf. "'Lewer duad üs Slaw': Geschichte eines politischen Schlagwortes." *Jahrbuch des Vereins für niederdeutsche Sprachforschung* 74 (1951): 99–126.

Cornette, James C. "Proverbs and Proverbial Expressions in the German Works of Luther." Diss., University of North Carolina, 1942.

Crum, Richard Henry. "'Blood, Sweat and Tears.'" *The Classical Journal* 42 (1947): 299–300.

Dundes, Alan. "Slurs International: Folk Comparisons of Ethnicity and National Character." *Southern Folklore Quarterly* 39 (1975): 15–38. Also in *Wise Words: Essays on the Proverb,* ed. Wolfgang Mieder, 183–209. New York: Garland Publishing, 1994.

Dundes, Alan. *Life is Like a Chicken Coop Ladder: A Portrait of German Culture Through Folklore.* New York: Columbia University Press, 1984.

Erler, Anette. "Zur Geschichte des Spruches 'Bis dat, qui cito dat' [He gives twice who gives quickly]." *Philologus* 13 (1986): 210–20.

Firth, Raymond. "Proverbs in Native Life, with Special Reference to Those of the Maori." *Folk-Lore* (London) 38 (1927): 134–53, 245–70.

Fix, Ulla. "Der Wandel der Muster—Der Wandel im Umgang mit den Mustern: Kommunikationskultur im institutionellen Sprachgebrauch der DDR am Beispiel von Losungen." *Deutsche Sprache* no vol., no. 4 (1990): 332–47.

Franck, Jakob F. "'Blut ist dicker als Wasser.'" *Preußische Jahrbücher* 85 (1896): 584–94.

French, Laurence. "Racial and Ethnic Slurs." *Maledicta* 4 (1980): 117–26.

Gautschie, Theres. *Bildhafte Phraseologismen in der Nationalratswahlpropaganda.* Bern: Peter Lang, 1982.

Green, Rayna. "The Only Good Indian: The Image of the Indian in American Vernacular Culture." Diss., Indiana University, 1973.

Hasan-Rokem, Galit. "The Aesthetics of the Proverb: Dialogue of Discourses from Genesis to Glasnost." *Proverbium: Yearbook of International Proverb Scholarship* 7 (1990): 105–16.

Heidel, W. A. "'Charity that Begins at Home.'" *American Journal of Philology* 30 (1909): 196–98.

Heuseler, J. A. *Luthers Sprichwörter aus seinen Schriften gesammelt.* Leipzig: Johann Barth, 1824. Reprint. Walluf: Sändig, 1973.

Hogg, R. D. "Proverbs." *Secretariat News* 14 (1960): 5–7.

Holley, Darrell. *Churchill's Literary Allusions: An Index to the Education of a Soldier, Statesman and Litterateur.* Jefferson, N.C.: McFarland and Company, 1987.

Hulme, F. Edward. *Proverb Lore; Being a Historical Study of the Similarities, Contrasts, Topics, Meanings, and Other Facets of Proverbs, Truisms, and Pithy Sayings, as Expressed by the Peoples of Many Lands and Times.* London: Elliot Stock, 1902. Reprint. Detroit: Gale Research Company, 1968.

Jansen, William Hugh. "A Culture's Stereotypes and Their Expression in Folk Clichés." *Southwestern Journal of Anthropology* 13 (1957): 184–200.

Jente, Richard. "The American Proverb." *American Speech* 7 (1931–32): 342–48.

Jente, Richard. "'Make Hay While the Sun Shines.'" *Southern Folklore Quarterly* 1 (1937): 63–68.

Kammerer, Edmund. "Sprichwort und Politik: Sprachliche Schematismen in Politikerreden, politischem Journalismus und Graffiti." M.A. thesis, University of Freiburg, 1983.

Kingsbury, Stewart A. "Names in Proverbs and Proverbial Sayings." In *Festschrift in Honor of Allen Walker Read*, ed. Laurence E. Seits, 116–32. DeKalb, Ill.: North Central Name Society, 1988.

Koller, Werner. *Redensarten: Linguistische Aspekte, Vorkommensanalysen, Sprachspiel.* Tübingen: Max Niemeyer, 1977.

Kornhardt, Hildegard. "'Summum ius.'" *Hermes* 81 (1953): 77–85.

Kühn, Peter. "Routine-Joker in politischen Fernsehdiskussionen: Plädoyer für eine textsortenabhängige Beschreibung von Phraseologismen." In *Beiträge zur Phraseologie des Ungarischen und des Deutschen*, ed. Regina Hessky, 155–76. Budapest: Loránd-Eötvös University, 1988.

Kuusi, Matti. "Fatalistic Traits in Finnish Proverbs." In *Fatalistic Beliefs in Religion, Folklore and Literature*, ed. Helmer Ringgren, 89–96. Stockholm: Almqvist and Wiksell, 1967. Also in *The Wisdom of Many: Essays on the Proverb*, ed. Wolfgang Mieder and Alan Dundes, 275–83. New York: Garland Publishing, 1981.

Loukatos, Démétrios. "Proverbes et commentaires politiques: Le Public devant les télé-communications actuelles." *Proverbium: Yearbook of International Proverb Scholarship* 1 (1984): 119–26.

Meichsner, Irene. *Die Logik von Gemeinplätzen: Vorgeführt an Steuermannstopos und Schiffsmetapher.* Bonn: Bouvier, 1983.

Meshcherskii, N. A. "Traditsionno-knizhnye vyrazheniia v sovremennom russkom literaturnom iazyke (na materiale proizvedenii V. I. Lenina)." *Voprosy frazeologii* 9 (1975): 110–21.

Mieder, Barbara and Wolfgang. "Tradition and Innovation: Proverbs in Advertising." *Journal of Popular Culture* 11 (1977): 308–19. Also in *The Wisdom of Many: Essays on the Proverb*, ed. W. Mieder and Alan Dundes, 309–22. New York: Garland Publishing, 1981.

Mieder, Wolfgang. *Das Sprichwort in unserer Zeit.* Frauenfeld: Huber, 1975.

Mieder, Wolfgang. *Deutsche Sprichwörter und Redensarten.* Stuttgart: Reclam, 1979.

Mieder, Wolfgang. "Karl Kraus und der sprichwörtliche Aphorismus." *Muttersprache* 89 (1979): 97–115. Also in W. Mieder, *Deutsche Sprichwörter in Literatur, Politik, Presse und Werbung*, 113–31. Hamburg: Helmut Buske, 1983.

Mieder, Wolfgang. "'Sein oder Nichtsein'—und kein Ende: Zum Weiterleben des Hamlet-Zitats in unserer Zeit." *Der Sprachdienst* 23 (1979): 81–85. Also in W. Mieder, *Sprichwort, Redensart, Zitat: Tradierte Formelsprache in der Moderne*, 125–30. Bern: Peter Lang, 1985.

Mieder, Wolfgang. "A Sampler of Anglo-American Proverb Poetry." *Folklore Forum* 13 (1980): 39–53.

Mieder, Wolfgang. "Bibliographische Skizze zur Überlieferung des Ausdrucks 'Iron Curtain'/'Eiserner Vorhang.'" *Muttersprache* 91 (1981): 1–14.

Mieder, Wolfgang. "Proverbs in Nazi Germany: The Promulgation of Anti-Semitism and Stereotypes Through Folklore." *Journal of American Folklore* 95 (1982): 435–64. Also in W. Mieder, *Proverbs Are Never Out of Season: Popular Wisdom in the Modern Age*, 225–55. New York: Oxford University Press, 1993.

Mieder, Wolfgang. *Deutsche Sprichwörter in Literatur, Politik, Presse und Werbung.* Hamburg: Helmut Buske, 1983.

Mieder, Wolfgang. *Sprichwort, Redensart, Zitat: Tradierte Formelsprache in der Moderne.* Bern: Peter Lang, 1985.

Mieder, Wolfgang. "History and Interpretation of a Proverb about Human Nature: 'Big Fish Eat Little Fish.'" In W. Mieder, *Tradition and Innovation in Folk Literature*, 178–228. Hanover, N.H.: University Press of New England, 1987.

Mieder, Wolfgang. "The Proverbial Three Wise Monkeys: 'Hear No Evil, See No Evil, Speak No Evil.'" In W. Mieder, *Tradition and Innovation in Folk Literature*, 157–77. Hanover, N.H.: University Press of New England, 1987.

Mieder, Wolfgang. *Tradition and Innovation in Folk Literature.* Hanover, N.H.: University Press of New England, 1987.

Mieder, Wolfgang. *American Proverbs: A Study of Texts and Contexts.* Bern: Peter Lang, 1989.

Mieder, Wolfgang. "'It's Five Minutes to Twelve': Folklore and Saving Life on Earth." *International Folklore Review* 7 (1989): 10–21.

Mieder, Wolfgang. "'A Picture Is Worth a Thousand Words': From Advertising Slogan to American Proverb." *Southern Folklore* 47 (1990): 207–25. Also in W. Mieder, *Proverbs Are Never Out of Season: Popular Wisdom in the Modern Age*, 135–51. New York: Oxford University Press, 1993.

Mieder, Wolfgang. "'Wir sitzen alle in einem Boot': Herkunft, Geschichte und Verwendung einer neueren deutschen Redensart." *Muttersprache* 100 (1990): 18–37. Also in W. Mieder, *Deutsche Redensarten, Sprichwörter und Zitate: Studien zu ihrer Herkunft, Überlieferung und Verwendung*, 140–59. Wien: Edition Praesens, 1995.

Mieder, Wolfgang. "General Thoughts on the Nature of the Proverb." *Revista de etnografie si folclor* 36 (1991): 151–64. Also in W. Mieder, *Proverbs Are Never Out of Season: Popular Wisdom in the Modern Age*, 3–17. New York: Oxford University Press, 1993.

Mieder, Wolfgang. *Proverbs Are Never Out of Season: Popular Wisdom in the Modern Age.* New York: Oxford University Press, 1993.

Mieder, Wolfgang. "'The Grass Is Always Greener on the Other Side of the Fence': An American Proverb of Discontent." *Proverbium: Yearbook of International Proverb Scholarship* 10 (1993): 151–84. Also in *Wise Words: Essays on the Proverb*, ed. W. Mieder, 515–42. New York: Garland Publishing, 1994.

Mieder, Wolfgang. "Proverbs in Adolf Hitler's *Mein Kampf.*" *Proverbium: Yearbook of International Proverb Scholarship* 11 (1994): 159–74 (shorter version of the chapter in this book).

Mieder, Wolfgang, ed. *Wise Words: Essays on the Proverb.* New York: Garland Publishing, 1994.

Mieder, Wolfgang. *Deutsche Redensarten, Sprichwörter und Zitate: Studien zu ihrer Herkunft, Überlieferung und Verwendung.* Wien: Edition Praesens, 1995.

Mieder, Wolfgang, and George B. Bryan. "'Zum Tango gehören zwei.'" *Der Sprachdienst* 27 (1983): 100–102. Also in W. Mieder, *Sprichwort, Redensart, Zitat: Tradierte Formelsprache in der Moderne*, 151–54. Bern: Peter Lang, 1985.

Mieder, Wolfgang, and George B. Bryan. *The Proverbial Winston S. Churchill: An Index to Proverbs in the Works of Sir Winston Churchill.* Westport, Conn.: Greenwood Press, 1995.

Mieder, Wolfgang, and George B. Bryan. *The Proverbial Harry S. Truman: An Index to Proverbs in the Works of Harry S. Truman.* New York: Peter Lang, 1997.

Mieder, Wolfgang, and Alan Dundes, eds. *The Wisdom of Many: Essays on the Proverb.* New York: Garland Publishing, 1981. Paperback ed., Madison: University of Wisconsin Press, 1994.

Mieder, Wolfgang, and David Pilachowski. "Die 'Nacht der langen Messer.'" *Der Sprachdienst* 19 (1975): 149–52.

Militz, Hans-Manfred. "Das Antisprichwort als semantische Variante eines sprichwörtlichen Textes." *Proverbium: Yearbook of International Proverb Scholarship* 8 (1991): 107–11.

Miller, Edd, and Jesse J. Villarreal. "The Use of Clichés by Four Contemporary Speakers [Winston Churchill, Anthony Eden, Franklin D. Roosevelt, and Henry Wallace]." *Quarterly Journal of Speech* 31 (1945): 151–55.

Monteiro, George. "Derisive Adjectives: Two Notes and a List." *Western Folklore* 34 (1975): 244–46.

Morozova, L. A. "Upotreblenie V. I. Leninym poslovits." *Russkaia Rech'* no. vol., no. 2 (1979): 10–14.

Moser, Dietz-Rüdiger. "'Die wellt wil meister klueglin bleiben . . . ': Martin Luther und das deutsche Sprichwort." *Muttersprache* 90 (1980): 151–66.

Neumann, Renate. *Das wilde Schreiben: Graffiti, Sprüche und Zeichen am Rand der Straßen.* Essen: Die Blaue Blume, 1986.

Nierenberg, Jess. "Proverbs in Graffiti: Taunting Traditional Wisdom." *Maledicta* 7 (1983): 41–58. Also in *Wise Words: Essays on the Proverb,* ed. Wolfgang Mieder, 543–61. New York: Garland Publishing, 1994.

Norrick, Neal R. *How Proverbs Mean: Semantic Studies in English Proverbs.* Amsterdam: Mouton, 1985.

Paredes, Américo. "Proverbs and Ethnic Stereotyping." *Proverbium* no. 15 (1970): 511–513. Also in *Proverbium,* ed. Wolfgang Mieder, vol. 1, pp. 511–13. Bern: Peter Lang, 1987.

Parker, Carol. "'White is the Color.'" *Western Folklore* 34 (1975): 153–54.

Peil, Dietmar. "'Im selben Boot': Variationen über ein metaphorisches Argument." *Archiv für Kulturgeschichte* 68 (1986): 269–93.

Pfeffer, J. Alan. *The Proverb in Goethe.* New York: King's Crown Press, 1948.

Porter, Kenneth. "Racism in Children's Rhymes and Sayings, Central Kansas, 1910–1918." *Western Folklore* 24 (1965): 191–96.

Quasthoff, Uta. "The Uses of Stereotype in Everyday Argument." *Journal of Pragmatics* 2 (1978): 1–48.

Raymond, Joseph B. "Tensions in Proverbs: More Light on International Understanding." *Western Folklore* 15 (1956): 153–58. Also in *The Wisdom of Many: Essays on the Proverb,* ed. Wolfgang Mieder and Alan Dundes, 300–308. New York: Garland Publishing, 1981.

Richman, Karen E. "'With Many Hands, the Burden Isn't Heavy': Creole Proverbs and Political Rhetoric in Haiti's Presidential Elections." *Folklore Forum*
  23 (1990): 115–23.
Roche, Reinhard. "Demosprüche und Wandgesprühtes: Versuch einer linguisti-
  schen Beschreibung und didaktischen Auswertung." *Muttersprache* 93 (1983):
  181–96.
Röhrich, Lutz. "Die Bildwelt von Sprichwort und Redensart in der Sprache der
  politischen Karikatur." In *Kontakte und Grenzen: Probleme der Volks-,
  Kultur- und Sozialforschung. Festschrift für Gerhard Heilfurth,* ed. Hans
  Friedrich Foltin, 175–207. Göttingen: Otto Schwarz, 1969.
Röhrich, Lutz, and Wolfgang Mieder. *Sprichwort.* Stuttgart: Metzler, 1977.
Seiler, Friedrich. *Deutsche Sprichwörterkunde.* München: C. H. Beck, 1922.
  Reprint, 1967.
Smith, A. W. "On the Ambiguity of the 'Three Wise Monkeys.'" *Folklore* 104
  (1993): 144–50.
Suard, François, and Claude Buridant, eds. *Richesse du proverbe.* Vol. 1: *Le prov-
  erbe au Moyen Age.* Vol. 2: *Typologie et fonctions.* Lille: Université de Lille,
  1984.
Suter, Beat. *Graffiti: Rebellion der Zeichen.* Frankfurt am Main: Rita G. Fischer,
  1988.
Tamony, Peter. "'Chinaman's Chance.'" *Western Folklore* 24 (1965): 202–5.
Taylor, Archer. *The Proverb.* Cambridge: Harvard University Press, 1931. Reprint. Hatboro, Penn.: Folklore Associates, 1962. Reprint, with an introduc-
  tion and bibliography by Wolfgang Mieder. Bern: Peter Lang, 1985.
Taylor, Archer. "The Road to 'An Englishman's House . . .'" *Romance Philology*
  19 (1965–66): 279–85.
Taylor, Archer. "And Marie Antoinette Said . . ." *Revista de Etnografia* 11 (1968):
  245–60. Also in A. Taylor, *Comparative Studies in Folklore: Asia—Europe—
  America,* 249–65. Taipei: The Orient Cultural Service, 1972.
Taylor, Archer. *Comparative Studies in Folklore: Asia—Europe—America.* Taipei:
  The Orient Cultural Service, 1972.
Taylor, Archer. *Selected Writings on Proverbs.* Ed. Wolfgang Mieder. Helsinki:
  Suomalainen Tiedeakatemia, 1975.
Tillmann, Terry. *The Writings on the Wall: Peace at the Berlin Wall.* Santa Mon-
  ica, Cal.: 22/7 Publishing Co., 1990.
Titus, Charles H. "Political Maxims." *California Folklore Quarterly* 4 (1945):
  377–89.
Weckmann, Berthold. "Sprichwort und Redensart in der Lutherbibel." *Archiv für
  das Studium der neueren Sprachen und Literaturen* 221 (1984): 19–42.
Weidhorn, Manfred. "Churchill the Phrase Forger." *Quarterly Journal of Speech*
  58 (1972): 161–74.
Wein, Günter. "Die Rolle der Sprichwörter und Redensarten in der Agitation und
  Propaganda." *Sprachpflege* 12 (1963): 51–52.
West, Victor R. "Folklore in the Works of Mark Twain." *University of Nebraska
  Studies in Language, Literature and Criticism* 10 (1930): 1–87.

Whiting, Bartlett Jere. "The Devil and Hell in Current English Literary Idiom." *Harvard Studies and Notes in Philology and Literature* 20 (1938): 207–47.

Whiting, Bartlett Jere. *"When Evensong and Morrowsong Accord": Three Essays on the Proverb*. Ed. Joseph Harris and Wolfgang Mieder. Cambridge: Department of English and American Literature and Language at Harvard University, 1994.

Williams, Fionnuala. "'To Kill Two Birds with One Stone': Variants in a War of Words." *Proverbium: Yearbook of International Proverb Scholarship* 8 (1991): 199–201.

Zhigulev, Aleksandr M. "Poslovitsy i pogovorki v bol'shevitskikh listovkakh." *Sovetskaia Etnografia* 5 (1970): 124–31.

Name Index

Albjerg, Victor, 62
Aldrich, Winthrop, 77
Ambrose, Stephen, 145
Andropov, Yuri V., 125, 127
Armstrong, Neil, 131
Arora, Shirley L., 161, 178–81
Aurthur, Robert Alan, 76
Auth, Tony, 128

Bailey, Pearl, 125
Baliles, Gerald, 176
Bartlett, John, 11, 50, 148
Baruch, Bernard, 99, 215*n3*
Beck, Emily Morison, 148
Benham, Gurney, 147
Bergen, Evans, 147
Berning, Cornelia, 10
Betz, Werner, 10
Bhatia, Gurdip Singh, 104
Birnbaum, Mariana, 138
Bismarck, Otto von, 4, 39, 102
Bloch, Ernst, 11
Blümmer, Hugo, 39
Bodenheim, Maxwell, 157
Bork, Siegfried, 10, 13
Brandt, Willy, 32, 40
Brecht, Bertolt, 11, 125
Brembeck, Cole S., 83
Brezhnev, Leonid I., 101, 116–19, 121, 125
Bridges, Edward, 63
Brown, Dee, 139, 158
Bryan, George B., 43, 44
Buchan, John, 156
Büchmann, Georg, 11, 14
Burke, Kenneth, 14

Burroughs, Edgar, 152
Bush, George, 133
Butler, Richard, 153
Byron, Lord George, 53

Caesar, Julius, 47, 48
Campbell, Bartley, 166
Cannadine, David, 205*n57*
Carr, Joseph, 155
Carter, Jimmy, 114, 116
Cavanaugh, James Michael, 142–43, 146, 149
Cervantes Saavedra, Miguel de, 3
Chamberlain, Austen, 61
Chamberlain, Neville, 46
Champion, Selwyn Gurney, 104
Chaucer, Geoffrey, 3, 39
Christie, Agatha, 3, 39, 153
Churchill, Clementine, 40
Churchill, Winston S., 4–6, 32, 39–66, 67, 88–91, 97, 99, 101, 102, 105, 106, 109, 202*n22*, 203*n28*, 204*n50*, 205*n60*, 205*n64*, 205*n65*, 205*n67*, 205*n68*, 207*n21*, 210*n85*
Cicero, Marcus Tullius, 4, 50, 53, 80, 102
Clifford, Clark, 85
Coles, Manning, 153
Columbus, Christopher, 139
Cromwell, Oliver, 155

Darwin, Charles, 27
Dayton, Eldorous L., 93
De Gaulle, Charles, 59
Desmond, Shaw, 152
Dewey, Thomas E., 74
Dickens, Charles, 39

248

Subject Index

Index of Key Words in Proverbs